Myriad Worlds

Buddhist Cosmology in Abhidharma, Kālacakra, and Dzog-chen

Myriad Worlds

Buddhist Cosmology in Abhidharma, Kālacakra, and Dzog-chen

Jamgön Kongtrul Lodrö Tayé

Translated and edited by
the International Translation Committee
founded by the V.V. Kalu Rinpoché

Snow Lion Publications
Ithaca, New York

Snow Lion Publications
P.O. Box 6483
Ithaca, New York 14851 USA
607-273-8519

Printed in the United States of America.

ISBN 1-55939-033-6

Photo on page 8 of V.V. Kalu Rinpoché by Don Farber.
Drawing on page 16 of Jamgön Kongtrul Lodrö Tayé by Robert Beer.

Library of Congress Cataloging-in-Publication Data

Koṅ-sprul Blo-gros-mtha'-yas, 1813-1899.
[Śes bya mtha' yas pa'i rgya mtsho. English. Selections]
Myriad worlds: Buddhist cosmology in Abhidharma, Kālacakra, and Dzog-chen / Kongtrul Lodrö Tayé; translated and edited by the International Translation Committee founded by Kalu Rinpoché.
p. cm.
Includes bibliographical references and index.
ISBN 1-55939-033-6
1. Koṅ-sprul Blo-gros-mtha'-yas, 1813-1899. Śes bya kun khyab. 2. Buddhism—China—Tibet—Doctrines. 3. Buddhist cosmology. I. Title. II. Title: Śes bya mtha' yas pa'i rgya mtsho.
BQ7632.K66213 1995
294.3'424—dc20

94-24741
CIP

Contents

Foreword

by His Holiness the Dalai Lama

Kongtrul Yönten Gyatso or Jamgön Kongtrul Lodrö Tayé was one of the leading scholars of the nineteenth century to break through sectarian constraints and achieve a deep understanding of the different philosophical approaches in Tibet. In his autobiography he tells how, at the age of thirty-six, he received the Kālacakra Tantra and many other teachings from Jamyang Kyentsé Wangpo. This was the turning point in his career.

Afterwards he said, "Nowadays, even well-known lamas and geshés have only a partial understanding of a few texts of their own system of tenets. Apart from that they have little insight, appreciation or comprehensive understanding of the variety of the Buddha's teachings. Most people have little familiarity with the teachings and often do not remain impartial. Those in positions of power, despite lacking the eye of Dharma, speak forcefully of the superiority or inferiority of a particular teaching. Not to speak of appreciating other systems, they are apprehensive even of their own system. They are as full of suspicion as a blind yak that runs from its own imagined fears.

"In my own case too, although I cherished the Dharma wholeheartedly, I was not mentally strong enough to make my own decisions. Consequently, I was unable to fulfill my aspirations. But from this time on, the lotus of unbiased devotion towards the wide variety of teachings and their teachers blossomed and my understanding gradually developed. Thus, my not having committed the heinous deed of discarding the Dharma is due only to the kindness of this precious lama."

It is worth noting here that to be "sectarian" in the sense of exclusively dedicating yourself to the study and practice of one particular school is not necessarily a negative thing. Most Tibetan lamas train in this way. This is positive sectarianism. Negative sectarianism is to follow one tradition exclusively, while looking down on other traditions.

I have no doubt that by studying Kongtrul's works readers will be inspired to emulate his great qualities of humility, dedication, patience and nonsectarianism. Therefore, I congratulate the International Buddhist Translation Committee at Samdrup Dargyé Chöling Monastery for preparing this English translation of the first four chapters of Kongtrul's *Sheja Kunkhyab.*

December 2, 1993

V.V. Kalu Rinpoché

Preface

Myriad Worlds is the first of ten books contained within the major treatise *The Infinite Ocean of Knowledge (Shes bya mtha' yas pa'i rgya mtsho)*, which itself is a commentary on the root verses *The Encompassment of All Knowledge (Shes bya kun khyab)*. The author of the work is Kongtrul Lodrö Tayé, an outstanding scholar of nineteenth-century Tibet. The English translation of this work has been conducted by an international group of translators inspired and organized by the Venerable Kalu Rinpoché, founder of the project and himself a recognized incarnation of Kongtrul Lodrö Tayé.

Kalu Rinpoché's life and work have given spiritual inspiration and insight to people throughout the world. Born in Tibet in 1905, he spent the early part of his life studying Buddhist philosophy and practicing meditation under the tutelage of the greatest teachers of his day. He mastered their teachings through many arduous years of intensive meditation in retreat; first the traditional three-year, three-month retreat, and then a solitary period of twelve years spent in remote caves in the Tibetan mountains. After leaving Tibet in the 1950s, Kalu Rinpoché worked tirelessly to provide spiritual guidance to others. He first taught in Bhutan and India, and later became instrumental in spreading the teachings of the Buddha to all corners of the world.

Although Kalu Rinpoché spoke only Tibetan, persons of all cultures were profoundly touched by his words. His compassionate concern for the welfare of people from all races and cultures was completely open and impartial. Though ordained as a monk in a religious tradition that was once dominated by men, he consistently treated men and women with equal respect. He shared the treasure trove of Buddhist meditation with everyone and encouraged all people to regard those precious teachings as their own. Although he spent his life practicing and teaching Buddhism, he always showed sincere respect for all religious traditions. Some people considered him to be a special, extraordinary individual, but it was his directness, simplicity, warmth, humor, and boundless concern for others that most deeply touched those who met him.

The translation of *The Infinite Ocean of Knowledge,* a text that touches on every topic within the range of Buddhist knowledge, is one of Kalu Rinpoché's most ambitious projects, for which he requested translators, scholars, and meditation masters of the various Tibetan traditions to work together. Kalu Rinpoché explained the importance of this work as follows:

> The world is currently experiencing unprecedented material development and the discovery of new scientific knowledge, creating good fortune and well-being for everyone. At such a time as this, the unsurpassable wisdom of Buddhism can bring immense happiness and benefit to humanity. This wisdom is contained in the great treatise *The Infinite Ocean of Knowledge,* written by Kongtrul Lodrö Tayé (1813-1899), the nonsectarian master of all Buddhist teachings whose life was prophesied by the Buddha. If this great work is translated into English, the nature of all existence and nirvana will appear as vividly as a reflection in a clear mirror in the minds of the most learned people in the world, as though the expanse of their understanding were illuminated with sunlight.

It was his wish that the completion of the English translation would lay the foundation for the translation of this text into many other languages. During the winters of 1988 and 1989, Rinpoché invited his students from many countries to gather at Bodhgaya, the site of the Buddha's enlightenment, for three-month sessions of translation. He then encouraged the participants to continue their work full-time at his main seat, Samdrup Dargyé Chöling Monastery, in Sonada, West Bengal.

Rinpoché passed away in May of 1989, dying exactly as he had lived, his mind perfectly calm and clear in the radiant peace of meditation. Shortly before his death, he expressed his deep hope that this project would be continued and completed. He entrusted this responsibility to his spiritual heir, the Venerable Bokar Rinpoché, and to his personal secretary and nephew, Lama Gyaltsen Ratak. Under their direction, a small committee of core translators has striven to complete this project as Rinpoché intended. These persons have been the joyful witnesses to the return to this world of the reincarnate Kalu Rinpoché, born as the son of Kalsang Drolkar and Lama Gyaltsen Ratak on September 17, 1990. He currently resides at his monastery in Sonada, where he occasionally appears at the translators' house, as though to check on the progress of the work.

About the Translation

Ven. Kalu Rinpoché originally suggested three principles to follow in the translation of this work: literal, accurate, and accessible. He felt that our efforts should be aimed at translating the actual text into English (*tshig bsgyur*—translating the words) rather than at interpreting the text in English (*don bsgyur*—translating the meaning). Secondly, he was more interested in an accurate translation than one that sacrificed accuracy for elegance. Finally, he encouraged us to use a vocabulary that would be accessible to the average educated reader rather than a highly technical vocabulary that depended on prior training in Buddhist or East Asian studies. Reasonable and sensible as these principles are, we found that they sometimes conflicted with each other. We found ourselves forced to make choices and compromises with these aims for reasons outlined below. The reader will ultimately decide the extent to which our endeavors have been successful.

The Infinite Ocean of Knowledge is a compilation that draws on a variety of texts—scriptures (sūtras and tantras), treatises (śāstras), and works by Tibetan scholars and masters. Not only do the styles of the source texts differ, but context and meaning vary so widely that a given Tibetan term cannot be translated by the same English word throughout. The aim of a strictly lexical or literal translation thus received its first blow. To follow that principle blindly would have meant significant sacrifices in both accuracy and accessibility. We have tried to maintain consistency wherever context and meaning were similar.

The glossary of technical terms at the end of this volume should help the interested reader to follow our translation choices.

A second blow to the aim of literal translation came when we realized that Kongtrul's overly condensed compilation was intended for the well-read and well-educated Tibetan reader. Kongtrul is concise to the point of being telegraphic. A literal rendering in English would have been virtually unreadable, let alone comprehensible. Thus, the translation had to be supplemented with additional words to meet the demands of reasonable syntax and grammar in English. Our aim here was to keep interpolated material to a minimum in order to preserve as much as possible the style in which Kongtrul writes.

An interpretive translation was also impractical. Several parts of the text are sufficiently complex that they exhausted both our knowledge and that of our consultants and resources. When we approached Kalu Rinpoche with these kinds of problems, he pragmatically replied, "An archer can shoot his arrow only to the limits of his physical strength, no further!" We have done our best to provide reasonable readings for such passages. The task of elucidating this text through commentary we have left to others.

With a few exceptions, we have rendered Sanskrit and Tibetan technical terms into English. The absence of foreign words in the translated text increases its accessibility to the reader. We also feel that important names and terms need to be expressed directly in English and not shielded by exotic and often difficult to comprehend expressions. Only in this way will these concepts and ideas truly come into our thinking and understanding. This approach led us to make significant decisions about the translation of some difficult terms. More conservative scholars and translators may well criticize these decisions but the discussion engendered by such criticism can only contribute to the further clarification of our understanding of Buddhism and how best to express it in English.

Where the subject matter is very technical, we have tried to be as precise as possible by employing terminology that in our estimation best conveys the intended meaning. We have also attempted to maintain internal consistency in the vocabulary. Less technical terms, while perhaps more accessible, would have diluted or distorted the meaning. We hope the reader will remember that philosophy is difficult in any language.

In order to capture as much of the meaning as possible and to convey it in clear English while retaining the flavor of the original, we had to refine and sharpen our own understanding of the concepts involved and the ideas expounded in the text. This refinement often led to our redoing sections of the text as we appreciated deeper levels of structure and meaning. We also had to keep an open mind and discover how to be truly sympathetic towards the author and how to appreciate his work even when the subject matter challenged our own views. This sympathy and appreciation steadily deepened in the course of the translation as we came to see more and more clearly what Kongtrul was setting out. When our own understanding failed, we relied on Tibetan commentaries and oral explanations from knowledgeable and respected scholars and lamas. These resources were indispensable in helping us to arrive at a proper understanding of this text. Some points of the text were given very different explanations by different scholars. In such cases we chose what, to us, made most sense in the context. We don't claim to have provided a definitive rendering free from errors and freely invite the reader to point out areas where he or she feels we may have been mistaken.

Translation always involves three steps: understanding, interpretation, and transmission. As we have just outlined, we took as much care and effort as possible in arriving at a sound understanding of the text. We then balanced our own understanding and interpretations with the text itself to provide the reader with as much material as possible for his or her own interpretations yet still be reasonably clear. And finally, we endeavored to express the meaning in clear, accessible English as faithful to the original words and style as possible.

The translation was undertaken by a group, rather than by an individual. There are many advantages and disadvantages in this approach. Given the scope of Kongtrul's scholarship, we feel that this collaborative effort was both essential and enriching. The range of viewpoints and skill present among the translators lead to a deep exchange of perspectives which certainly contributed to the quality of the final result.

Acknowledgments

At every stage of the translation of *Myriad Worlds,* the committee has sought the advice of Tibetan and Western scholars and meditation masters. Our sincere thanks go to Bokar Trulku Rinpoché and Kenpo Lodrö Dönyö, not only for their wisdom and patience in providing answers to our many questions but also for their continued encouragement and support; to Dodrup Chen Rinpoché, Dilgo Kyentsé Rinpoché, and Nyoshul Kenpo Rinpoché for their detailed clarification of the subject of primordial purity; to Sakya Kenpo Rinpoché, Gyaltsap Rinpoché, Zenkar Rinpoché, Tara Trulku, and Kenpo Tsultrim Gyatso for their invaluable assistance in explicating difficult points in the text; and to Pönlop Rinpoché and Karma Trinlé Rinpoché for their helpful suggestions regarding the translation.

The translation of *Myriad Worlds* was largely prepared by Elio Guarisco, Könchog Tenzin, Tenpa Kalsang, Peter Roberts, Sarah Harding, Ingrid McLeod, Anthony Chapman, Ngawang Zangpo and Yeshe Wangmo; research of the citations was conducted by Lydia and Olivier Brunet; and the Introduction was written by Elio Guarisco. Grateful acknowledgement is made to several other translators with whom we collaborated: Daniel Boschero, Ken McLeod, Eric Pema Kunzang, Dechen Cronin, Norbu Tsewang, Daniel Perdue, Surya Das, and Samten Zangmo. We wish to thank Susan Kyser of Snow Lion Publications, Shawn Woodyard, and Daniel Reid for their careful revision of the final English manuscript, Kristine Paknys and David Patt for their correction of the Sanskrit, Roar Vestre for his technical assistance, and the many other persons who helped in countless ways.

The committee is indebted to Lama Gyaltsen Ratak for providing us with the facilities necessary for our work over the course of several years and to the many people whose kind patronage enabled us to accomplish our task.

Above all, we are grateful to our spiritual mentor, His Eminence Kalu Rinpoché, for his original vision and continual guidance and for providing us with the opportunity to study this exceptional work.

Translators' Introduction

Kongtrul Lodrö Tayé

Kongtrul Lodrö Tayé (Kong-sprul Blo-gros-mtha'-yas) (1813-1899) was born on the second of December, 1813, at Rong-gyab (Rong-rgyab), near Pema Lhatsé (Padma-lha-rtse), in Drida Zalmogang (Bri-zla Zal-mo-sgang), eastern Tibet. Rong-gyab is a small hidden valley that is considered to be one of the twenty-five sacred places of eastern Tibet, a place where the enlightened activity of the Buddha family manifests. Kongtrul's adoptive father was Sönam Pel (bSod-nams 'Phel), a lay tantric practitioner of the Bön religion, and his mother was Trashi Tso (bKras-shis 'Tsho). In his autobiography,[1] Kongtrul says that his natural father was Yungdrung Tendzin (gYung-drung bsTan-'dzin), an illustrious lama of the Kyungpo, or Garuda, clan whose lineage was on the verge of becoming extinct; the continuity of such a precious lineage was ensured by the union of his mother with Yungdrung Tendzin. Kongtrul provides a lengthy account of the divine origin of the ancestors of the Kyungpo clan, whose descendants include some of the most outstanding figures of both the Buddhist and the Bönpo traditions, such as Milarepa,[2] Kyungpo Neljor,[3] and the first Karmapa, Dusum Kyenpa[4] among the Buddhists, and the *tertön*[5] Loden Nyingpo (Blo-ldan sNying-po) and Trashi Gyaltsen (bKra-shis rGyal-mtshan) among the Bönpos.

Kongtrul's mother had many auspicious dreams while carrying him in her womb. One night, for example, she dreamed that a raven[6] coming from the northwest landed on the altar of her home. Other portents also indicated the greatness of the

Jamgön Kongtrul Lodrö Tayé

child who was about to take birth: although the harvests in the years prior to Kongtrul's birth were poor, the crops were exceptionally abundant the year he was born.

At the age of four, Kongtrul found a meditative text on White Mañjuśrī. He imitated the monks who chanted the text and in that way was able to recite it himself while pointing at the words. His playtime pantomimes included giving empowerments, building temples, making sacrificial cakes and offering them to the guardians, and so on. Kongtrul learned the letters of the Tibetan alphabet as soon as they were shown to him.

While he was still a child, he had numerous visionary experiences. Once, while lying in his mother's lap, he had a vision of an ascetic holding a standard and three blazing spheres. On another occasion, he dreamed of a soothsayer who made a cryptic prophecy about him; the soothsayer's words seemed to indicate the direction of Shechen (Zhe-chen) and Pelpung (dPal-spungs), the monasteries that Kongtrul would enter years later. Kongtrul mentions in his autobiography that as soon as he could think, he had great faith in Guru Rinpoché, the great master from Oddiyana who dispelled obstacles that had blocked the spread of Buddhism in Tibet. With pride, he would proclaim to the other children that he was the emanation of Guru Rinpoché. He was overjoyed when he heard that a practitioner in the area had gained recognition of the nature of the mind, and he yearned to find somebody who could teach him how to bring about this experience. He had an intense desire to recognize the dream state, and by means of the force of his desire, he actually acquired the ability to do so. In short, his childhood games, dreams, and thoughts reflected a deep propensity for the spiritual life and an innate high regard for all people.

In 1815, Sönam Lodrö (bSod-nams Blo-gros), the twenty-second abbot of Menri (sMan-ri) Monastery,[7] visited Kongtrul's village; he cut a tuft of his hair and named him Tendzin Yungdrung (bsTan-'dzin gYung-drung), a name that Kongtrul used until he became a monk. Kongtrul was trained in the Bön tradition by his adoptive father and by Yungdrung Puntsog (gYung-drung Phun-tshogs), the yogi and master of the Bön hermitage of Tardé (Thar-bde), close to his native area. By the age of eight, he knew all the divinities of the Bön pantheon and was proficient in the rites of Bön, but it was to the peaceful and wrathful forms of Guru Rinpoché that he was primarily attracted. Having received the appropriate instructions, he engaged in a retreat to practice the "transference of consciousness," and after three days, he developed the signs that indicate the accomplishment of that practice. Soon after, he dreamed of flying in the sky with crossed legs, a dream that was to repeat itself throughout his life. Furthermore, he showed interest and skill in religious dance and painting even from his childhood. By the time he was a teenager, he already had knowledge of the identification of herbs and minerals, which he learned from Karma Puntsog (Karma Phun-tshogs). He continued this training and later became one of the best physicians and alchemists in Tibet.

Around that time, a once wealthy and highly respected family living in his area fell into miserable conditions, losing its possessions and reaching the end of its line of descendants. This dramatic change of circumstances became the "teacher" that revealed to Kongtrul the impermanent nature of wealth and possessions, producing in him a genuine inclination to disengage from worldly affairs. Then, around 1827, his father Sönam Pel and other kinsmen were imprisoned by the Degé (sDe-dge)[8] authorities for alleged complicity in a political assassination. In the wake of this turmoil that reduced the area to poverty, his mother encouraged Kongtrul to enter the monastic life.

Shortly afterward, Kongtrul met Tsepel of the Kangsar family (Tshe-'phel Khang-sar-tshang), the governor of Chödé (Chos-sde) Fortress, who was impressed by the intellect and talents of Kongtrul and requested him to be his secretary. Once, while they were at the summer residence of the governor of Degé, Kongtrul was introduced by his patron to Jigmé Losel ('Jigs-med Blo-gsal), a teacher at Shechen (Nyingmapa) Monastery. During a conversation with the youth, the teacher was greatly impressed by Kongtrul's knowledge of the Bön doctrine and his ability to articulate it. The teacher advised Kongtrul's patron to send him to study at Shechen. The patron agreed and sent Kongtrul to study at Shechen with the outstanding master Gyurmé Tutob Namgyel ('Gyur-med mThu-stobs rNam-rgyal).

Although he had been trained exclusively in the Bön religion, Kongtrul did not experience any difficulty in the Buddhist environment. To test Kongtrul's intelligence, his teacher taught him the mother-son, enemy-friend relationships of Chinese astrology,[9] which he readily understood, demonstrating a remarkably brilliant intellect. Kongtrul was taught *The Mirror of Poetry*,[10] a famous textbook used to teach vocabulary and composition, and he continued to study various Tibetan and Sanskrit grammars, such as the *Cāndrapa*, *Kālapa*, and *Sarasvatī*.[11] He received the empowerment of White Mañjuśrī, the deity symbolizing wisdom, and the transmission of the *Mañjuśrī-namā-saṃgīti-tantra (Chanting the Names of Mañjuśrī Tantra)*,[12] which he recited daily for the rest of his life. In 1831, he started to receive the transmissions of the teachings and practices of the Nyingma school. In 1832, Kongtrul received full ordination as a Buddhist monk from Tutob Namgyel, according to the "Eastern Vinaya" (sMad-lugs), the tradition followed by both the Nyingma and the Gelug schools, whose lineage had been introduced by Śāntarakṣita and rekindled by Lachen Gongpa Rabsel (Bla-chen dGong-pa Rab-gsal) following the suppression of the Buddhist doctrine by Langdarma (Glang-dar-ma).

That same year, Kongtrul made a pilgrimage to the power place of Sengé Namdzong (Seng-ge rNam-rdzong) with the Nyingmapa master Lama Kunzang Sang Ngag (Kun-bzang gSang-sngags). The path to their destination was snow-bound, and they were unable to eat or rest all day. Finally, they stopped to rest against a large slab of rock. The teacher said to Kongtrul, "If one looks directly at the nature of the mind when overcome by fatigue and hunger, one will perceive nothing but the actual nature of the mind." They sat together in silence. Kongtrul then had a direct and indescribable experience of the nature of mind. "Even later in my life," he wrote, "there was nothing to add or develop with respect to the nature I have seen." Certainly, his enthusiasm for contemplation to keep alive the awareness of mind's nature continued unabated throughout his life.

Kongtrul spent his first years as a monk receiving instructions and transmissions of the *kama* and *terma*[13] and undertaking retreats. Countless signs in dreams and in the waking state indicated his close spiritual affinity with Guru Rinpoché. He studied liturgy and various scripts, old and new; never distracted by senseless activities, he enthusiastically pursued each field of study.

In 1833, Wöngen Trulku (dBon-rgan sPrul-sku) of Pelpung Monastery, the brother of Situ Rinpoché, requisitioned the services of Kongtrul as his secretary. Regretfully, Kongtrul left Shechen Monastery and moved to Pelpung. Just before Kongtrul left, his teacher advised him to maintain a gentle attitude, always to be mindful, and not to be sectarian or partial in any way. The move seemed to have no detrimental effect on him: he remarks that on his journey to Pelpung, snow fell and other auspicious signs appeared.

On the first day of the tenth lunar month of that year, Kongtrul met for the first time the ninth Situ, Pema Nyinjé (Si-tu Padma-nyin-byed) (1774-1853), who would be his principal Kagyu teacher. Wöngen Trulku insisted that Kongtrul retake ordination as a monk, probably because he did not like to acknowledge the validity of the lineage of the Vinaya vows that Kongtrul had received the previous year. The master who presided over the ceremony was Situ Pema Nyinjé, who on that occasion conferred on him the name Karma Ngawang Yönten Gyatso Trinlé Kunkyab Pelzangpo (Karma Ngag-dbang Yon-tan-rgya-mtsho 'Phrin-las Kun-khyab dPal-bzang-po). For this ordination, the lineage was that of the "Western Vinaya" (sTod-lugs), which had been introduced to Tibet in the early thirteenth century by the Kashmiri scholar Śākyaśrī,[14] had been developed by four monastic communities, and had been followed by the Sakya and Karma Kagyu schools. On the occasion of taking the full monk's ordination for the second time, Kongtrul felt that the residue of the vows he had previously taken was still present in his mind as he took his new vows, so that he did not have the proper sense of receiving the new ordination. Some people think that this episode of his life exposed him to the intolerance and sectarianism that were common factors in the spirituality of that time. It would seem to have been significant in directing Kongtrul's interest toward the ecumenical approach that came to characterize his life and his writings.

By the age of thirty, Kongtrul had received teachings and empowerments from more than sixty masters representing all the different schools and esoteric lineages in Tibet. In those times, brilliant monks, unless they were recognized as incarnate lamas, were taken from the monasteries to become secretaries to the local landlords and governors. When Kongtrul's reputation as a promising scholar started to spread, the Pelpung authorities wished to prevent the Degé government from removing Kongtrul in the same way that he had been taken from Shechen. This they managed to do by "recognizing" him as the incarnation of a learned monk, Bamten Trulku (Bam-steng sPrul-sku), who had acted as the servant to the previous Situ during the early part of his life. Because Bamten Trulku had been from the region of Kongpo,[15] the newly recognized lama came to be called Kongtrul ("the incarnation from Kong").

Although Kongtrul had acquired the title of incarnate lama in this way, it was not an undeserved title. In fact, Gyurmé Tutob Namgyel had proclaimed Kongtrul to be an emanation of Vairocana,[16] one of the greatest translators during the first propagation of the Buddha's doctrine in Tibet. Many scholars and masters, such as Jamyang Kyentsé Wangpo,[17] came to regard him as an incarnation of a number of previous masters, both Indian and Tibetan. Among these were Ānanda (Buddha's cousin), Āryadeva,[18] Kyungpo Neljor, Tāranātha,[19] Terdag Lingpa,[20] and others.[21] A verse from the *Laṇkāvatāra Sūtra* was taken as a prophecy referring to him.[22] Later in his life, finding himself in the unique position of being a great teacher and a high-level practitioner, Kongtrul wondered about his previous lives; his own investigation led him to the conclusion that he was an emanation of Vajrapāṇi, Vairocana, the discipline master Lumé Tsultrim Sherab,[23] and the renowned doctor Sumpa Kenpo Yeshé Peljor.[24] In any case, throughout his life Kongtrul showed himself to be an unequaled scholar and accomplished master.

At Pelpung, under the guidance of Situ Pema Nyinjé and other spiritual mentors, Kongtrul made rapid progress. By the time he was in his mid-twenties, he was already a teacher of note whose guidance on spiritual matters and instruction in Tibetan and Sanskrit grammar were sought by many people. It is noteworthy that this man who became one of the foremost authorities on all subjects of Buddhist study never entered a Buddhist college or scholastic institution.

From Situ, he received *The Collection of the One Hundred Empowerments of Tāranātha* and the transmission of the Tibetan canon; Chagmé Trulku (Chags-med sPrul-sku) gave him numerous empowerments and teachings of the higher tantras, such as Guhyasamāja and Hayagrīva; and Dzigar Chogtrul ('Dzi-sgar mChog-sprul) gave him the four tantras that form the basis for the study and practice of Tibetan medicine. He became the receptacle of countless teachings. Kongtrul engaged in the various practices he was taught, one after the other, unwaveringly pursuing inner realization and invariably experiencing wonderful portents. For example, when in 1836 he undertook a retreat on the Five-Deity Cakrasaṃvara practice, one night he dreamed that he was entering a magnificent house. Some persons arrived carrying religious books written in gold, wrapped in silk brocade, and emanating the scent of camphor. In the courtyard of the house, he saw Lūyipa, Kṛṣṇacārya, and Ghaṇṭapa, the three most important Indian mahāsiddhas with respect to the transmission of the Cakrasaṃvara Tantra. They appeared in the guise of children, dressed in a variety of costumes. After a time, the three siddhas disappeared, and Kongtrul remained in the natural state of the mind.

The most frequent recurrent dreams that Kongtrul had were those of Guru Rinpoché or of being Guru Rinpoché, dreams with prophetic implications that manifested during and after the spiritual practices in which he engaged. Kongtrul writes that in the latter part of his life, the visions and extraordinary experiences occurred less frequently because he used the facilities that the monastic community provided for him, and therefore his mind was darkened by the force of karmic debt.

A few years after he first entered Pelpung, the main seat of the Kagyu school in eastern Tibet, Kongtrul began to believe that he was a "Kagyupa"; he thus developed a sense of belonging to a particular school. Simultaneously, his attraction to the ancient tradition (Nyingma) diminished. Soon, however, he recognized that what was occurring in his mind was a karmic obstacle. He thereupon felt regret and confessed this shift of faith. Immediately afterward, his close affinity with the ancient tradition manifested once again in various dreams. Some of these dreams revealed to him the locations of hidden teachings. At times, he dreamed of ancient translators who showed him unknown tantras and gave him their transmissions. His dreams at that time also revealed to him that he was an emanation of various ancient masters. In other dreams, he met ancient Indian masters such as Atiśa,[25] Śāntideva,[26] and Candragomin,[27] and countless Tibetan masters of the past.

In 1839, Kongtrul offered all that he had been given as offerings while accompanying on tour the fourteenth Karmapa, Tegchog Dorjé (Theg-mchog rDo-rje) (1798-1868), to Situ Pema Nyinjé in order to receive the ceremony in which the awakening mind (bodhicitta) is engendered. On that occasion, Kongtrul received the name Jangchub Sempa Lodrö Tayé (Byang-chub Sems-dpa' Blo-gros-mtha'-yas), "The Bodhisattva of Infinite Intelligence." Kongtrul frequently performed the bodhicitta ceremony at the request of others; this fact indicates the importance that he attached to the bodhisattva ideal. During this same year, Kongtrul met for the first time Jamyang Kyentsé Wangpo, received teachings from him, and developed great faith in him.

When Kongtrul entered his first traditional three-year retreat, he was interrupted after a year and a half. The fourteenth Karmapa, Tegchog Dorjé, was visiting the monastery and had asked to be taught Sanskrit. Kongtrul was deemed proficient enough to act as his tutor. In 1842, when he was almost thirty, Kongtrul had managed to extricate himself from outside demands for his time and attention. After an initial refusal, Situ Pema Nyinjé finally granted him permission to reenter a three-year period of retreat. He constructed a small meditation hut, to which Situ gave the name Kunzang Dechen Ösel Ling (Kun-bzang bDe-chen 'Od-gsal-gling), which was an hour's walk from Pelpung Monastery in a power place named Tsadra Rinchen Drag (Tswa-'dra Rin-chen-brag). This time he managed to complete his retreat without interruption, and thereafter he continued to live in his hermitage. This remained his principal residence for the rest of his life and eventually became the site of a tiny three-year retreat center that he directed. It was here that Kongtrul composed his literary works, including *The Encompassment of All Knowledge* and its commentary, *The Infinite Ocean of Knowledge.*

Kongtrul's will to put into practice all the teachings he received from others or discovered himself, to realize them, and to have the necessary potential to transmit them to others never diminished. Consequently, he completed the preliminaries to the Mahāmudrā practice four times in a row. As a result, he acquired great mental clarity and experienced innumerable good omens and dreams. He lived at all times with an awareness of the certainty of death. Whenever his life was threatened by obstacles, Kongtrul overcame them by supplicating Guru Rinpoché and by engaging in various practices such as the life-extending practice of White Tārā, which had been transmitted in Tibet by the saintly Atiśa. For other types of obstacles, he practiced the rites of Vajrakīlaya.[28]

The night he received the Long Life Vajra Meteorite[29] empowerment from Wön Trulku, he dreamed of seeing the sun and moon shining together in the sky; his Direct Leap[30] visions expanded, and from that time forward he recited fewer daily prayers, but he continued to recite the Mahāmudrā preliminary, Cakrasaṃvara, and Vārāhī[31] liturgies. He began to spend considerable time composing his works. At the same time, he acquired stability in the generation stage of tantra. As a sign of this stability, in his dreams he conquered spirits and enemies by transforming himself into the wrathful form of Guru Rinpoché that holds a scorpion or the forms of other deities. Kongtrul said that throughout his life, he derived wonderful signs of attainment as a result of performing the practice called The Union of the Minds of the Masters,[32] perhaps because of a karmic link with this unequaled hidden teaching.

Often he had dreams of girls who showed him the locations of hidden treasures of teachings. In one dream, a well-dressed girl prophesied that his activity on behalf of the Buddhist doctrine and the welfare of others would be extremely significant, and that he would ultimately discover twenty-five hidden treasures of teachings.

Kongtrul spent the rest of his life writing, practicing, and teaching. He lived most of his time in retreat, but, realizing the role that he had to play in the maintenance and transmission of countless spiritual methods that were on the verge of extinction, Kongtrul demonstrated a perfect balance between a contemplative and an active life, between learning and practice. Poverty was one of his closest companions for many years, and unlike most teachers of his day, he chose to live without servants or attendants, like the great Indian sage Asaṅga, a pioneer of the Cittamātra philosophy, who only in his advanced old age chose to keep a novice monk as his helper. Only Kongtrul's mother and niece (after his mother's death) shared his residence and helped with the household chores. His circumstances were always modest: he complained that he almost abandoned his resolve to be compassionate to all beings because of the mice and rats in his home that ate his precious books.

Once he dreamed of ascending a celestial ladder to the sky, which was perhaps a sign of his having attained the bodhisattva levels of awakening. On one occasion, when performing a tantric feast of offering (*ganacakra*), he beheld in a waking vision the face of Guru Rinpoché, large as a mountain, after which he recognized the natural state of the mind, the ordinary mind without concepts, a state in which there is nothing to be confirmed or rejected, the experience of the unmodified state of being. That was also the first time that Kongtrul transcended the mental creations that limit the original spaciousness of the mind. Subsequently he dreamed of the eight medicine buddhas, who prophesied that in the future Kongtrul would be Buddha Well-Honored Universal Monarch (bDe-bzhin-gshegs-pa rDzogs-par 'khor-los-sgyur). His dreams also repeatedly indicated his previous affiliation with Terdag Lingpa and the Nyingma monastery of Mindroling. Once, he dreamed of the master Dzogchen Sönam Zangpo (rDzogs-chen bSod-rnams bZang-po), an embodiment of Dromtön ('Brom-ston),[33] who told him: "Your practice should be that of the Great Perfection and your meditational deity the Highly Compassionate One.[34] Other masters have given the same instructions!"

At the beginning of 1847, Kongtrul engaged in the retreat of the Highly Compassionate One, following a practice called Self-Liberation from the Lower Realms. The benefits of this practice were immense: during the night, his mind remained in a state of intermingled compassion and emptiness; in the daytime, he enhanced his understanding of the scriptures while experiencing a rain of inner blessings. At this time, he wrote a work of praise to the eight bodhisattvas, which he called *The Eight Great Clouds;* that marked the beginning of his literary output.

Kongtrul traveled widely in eastern Tibet, revitalizing the spirituality of the monasteries and retreat places, educating monks and laypersons by giving teachings, empowerments, and transmissions for a multitude of practices. He gave everything that was offered to him to Situ Pema Nyinjé.

The year 1849 was astrologically critical for Kongtrul. Consequently, he engaged in various spiritual practices to avert negative influences and obstacles. At that time, he dreamed of a green plateau, in the center of which was a throne made of white stone adorned with self-originated Chinese and Tibetan characters. On the throne was Padmasambhava, who told him: "From now on up to the age of forty-four, because of my blessing, there will be no obstacles to your life. Then, you will meet me in person." This dream foretold that Kongtrul would meet Chogyur Dechen Lingpa (Chogling) (mChog-'gyur bDe-chen Gling-pa) (1829-1879) and receive from him a particular practice to remove obstacles.

From Jamyang Kyentsé Wangpo, Kongtrul received, on numerous occasions, teachings and empowerments of all traditions of Tibetan Buddhism, at times without having requested them. In particular, he received the three series of the Dzogchen, the transmissions of the various Sakya lineages, and that of Marpa.[35] In turn, Kongtrul conferred the teachings, empowerments, longevity rites, and blessings that Kyentsé requested of him. Thus, each was both the student and the teacher of the other. It was Kyentsé, however, who was more the teacher; Kongtrul asked his advice on all matters, especially after the passing away of Situ Pema Nyinjé. The relationship of Kongtrul, Kyentsé, and Chogling played an important part in the nineteenth-century cultural renaissance in eastern Tibet. Other teachers, such as Mipam (Mi-pham)[36] (1846-1912), Kenpo Shenga (mKhen-po gZhan-dga'),[37] A-Dzom Drugpa (A-Dzom 'Brug-pa),[38] Peltrul Rinpoché,[39] and Shardza Trashi Gyaltsen (Shar-rdza bKra-shis rGyal-mtshan), a Bönpo, made important contributions as well, but undoubtedly the three mentioned above were the chief protagonists of the renaissance. Kyentsé was the inspiring force, realized in all aspects; Kongtrul was the saintly scholar who had the capacity to put everything in writing and the power of transmission; and Chogling was the unhindered mystic. That Kyentsé was the inspirational force behind the renaissance is evident in the words of Kongtrul himself; in his autobiography, Kongtrul writes that Kyentsé, by merely supplicating Guru Rinpoché, could encounter in visions and dreams the ancient masters and *tertön* and receive from them their teachings, some of which either no longer existed or belonged to transmission lineages that had been interrupted. He thus infused with vitality those teachings that had lost their freshness through a long lineage of transmission and perpetuated the transmission of others that would otherwise have been lost.

Although Buddhist scholars speak of a Rimé (*ris-med*), or nonsectarian, movement in connection with Kyentsé, Kongtrul, Chogling and other masters of eastern Tibet, it is unlikely that these masters intended to create a movement that encompassed the various Tibetan traditions. These masters were, however, unbiased in their approach to the teachings in that their interests were not directed exclusively toward the traditions to which they belonged. They collected, committed to writing, taught, and thereby preserved, revitalized, and propagated instruction lineages that encompassed every aspect of Buddhist teaching. Significantly, they did so at a time when, as a result of the policy of strict adherence to particular teachings that was followed by various schools and traditions, there was a real danger that many instruction lineages would disappear. Therefore, these masters had a tremendous impact on the Tibetan Buddhist tradition, and the results of their efforts to preserve the teachings are felt even now.

The renaissance to which these masters gave rise may have occurred in eastern rather than central Tibet because central Tibet was dominated by the new monastically oriented schools. The intellectual tendency of these schools to focus on philosophical subtleties certainly did not predispose them to favor an approach based on synthesis; such an approach requires a certain degree of simplification and the concomitant abandonment of petty theological disquisitions. Eastern Tibet, which was far from the theocratic government of Lhasa and was the home of schools that tended to be experientially—rather than intellectually—oriented, was the ideal environment in which a nonsectarian revival of the teachings could flourish.

The ancient Nyingma school had been severely suppressed since the second period of the propagation of the Buddhist doctrine in Tibet.[40] Therefore, the teachings of the Nyingma school—and particularly the Dzog-chen system—received the lion's share of the attention of the three masters. In fact, the longest of Kongtrul's many writings is *The Treasury of Precious Treasure Teachings (Rin chen gter mdzod)*, which contains more than sixty volumes of important cycles of the Nyingma treasure teachings. In *The Encompassment of All Knowledge (Shes bya kun khyab)*, the Dzog-chen system is identified as the highest of the nine vehicles that, collectively, constitute the paths taught in the sutras and tantras.

The all-embracing attitude of Kongtrul and his colleagues clearly was not intended to merge into a single system the various Tibetan Buddhist traditions, but it did have the effect of overcoming sectarianism, the sense of belonging to a school, the belief that only one tradition is valid. It is easy for a small intellect that knows only a single philosophical presentation, only one secret oral instruction, or only one system of practice, to fall prey to the idea that that is the only correct way. Being open to various traditions can free the mind from bias and partiality, bestowing the insight that perceives the interconnectedness of the various teachings and traditions, their scope, and their particular qualities: this benefit alone outweighs the danger of becoming confused when confronted by different and sometimes apparently divergent Buddhist teachings and traditions. In his different discourses, even the Buddha gave contradictory explanations. The context of the explanation and the audience for whom it was intended must be considered if one is to understand the explanation fully. Kongtrul, who had become a receptacle for innumerable teachings and secret instructions of all traditions, spoke critically of contemporary teachers:

> Nowadays, even famous masters and scholars have very little faith in and knowledge of the various Buddhist teachings in general; their education is restricted to their own tradition, based on the study of just a few scriptures. Most people, both the influential and the ordinary, are not learned and have little understanding of the meaning of the teaching.
>
> In particular, at the present time many persons who are partial and lack the eye of understanding the doctrine arrogantly proclaim which Buddhist tradition is good and which is bad, which teaching lineage is pure and which impure. Like the blind yak who flees imagined dangers, they are dubious and cautious of their own school, to say nothing of other traditions.

Kongtrul's extreme humility is obvious in his autobiography. Nevertheless, his exceptional qualities and activities shine through clearly; he acknowledges having faith in and respect for all teachings and the authentic masters who uphold them. His faith nurtured his broad-minded approach, and in no way did he ever reject any aspect of the Buddha's teaching. Thus, he was an example worthy of being followed by any Buddhist.

In 1855, Chogling recognized Kongtrul as a *tertön*, or treasure discoverer, and gave him the name Chimé Tennyi Yungdrung Lingpa ('Chi-med bsTan-gnyis gYung-drung Gling-pa). Kongtrul had great respect for Chogling, and on many occasions he was requested by Chogling to participate in or perform rites involving the discovery of hidden treasures. For example, when Chogling and Kyentsé recovered texts belonging to the three series of the Dzog-chen tradition from the Crystal Lotus Cave in Dzam Nang, Chogling gave Kongtrul a blazing statue of Mahākāla carved by Nāgārjuna out of a black rock from Cool Grove[41] that bore Nāgārjuna's handprint. In return,

Kongtrul gave Chogling an exceptional antique statue of Guru Rinpoché. In the second lunar month of 1867, Chogling and Kyentsé jointly enthroned Kongtrul, gave him the official title of treasure discoverer, and performed long-life rituals for him.

Kongtrul often traveled back and forth to the twenty-five power places of eastern Tibet that had been discovered by Chogling, performing endless tantric feasts of offering or performing the great rites that are associated with various deities and are popular in the ancient tradition. Often he combined the great rites with the preparation of the blessing-medicine (*sman-sgrub*), exercising his great interest and skill in the arts of healing and alchemy. His formula for detoxifying mercury became famous, and his books on medicine are highly valued even today by doctors of traditional Tibetan medicine.

Because Kyentsé and Chogling often requested Kongtrul's presence when extracting hidden treasures from mountains, rocks, and caves, and when performing the necessary rites and tantric feasts of offering preceding or following the extractions, Kongtrul became a receptacle for the hidden teachings. On a trip to central Tibet, he taught many such teachings to the fourteenth Karmapa, Tegchog Dorjé, and to Drugpa ('Brug-pa) Rinpoché,[42] who hesitated to receive empowerments from Kongtrul until in his own dreams he learned the precious nature of such transmissions and the need to receive them. The importance of the activities of Kongtrul in the preservation of many lineages of instruction can be discerned in the importance that Tibetan masters nowadays attach to the transmissions and empowerments contained in Kongtrul's compilation *The Treasury of Precious Treasure Teachings*. When Kongtrul decided to compile old and new hidden teachings, he sought the advice of Kyentsé, who told him to take as a basis four texts that he himself had composed by collecting scattered hidden teachings, and to write a complete work on the highest tantras and Dzog-chen. In order to be empowered to write such a text, Kongtrul engaged in several retreats, until in 1856 he had numerous auspicious dreams in which he found precious pills belonging to the Indian Dzog-chen master Vimalamitra and some belonging to Yeshé Tsogyel (Ye-shes mTsho-rgyal), the Tibetan consort of Guru Rinpoché. He also dreamed of being seated on a throne reading a scripture written in silver that contained exceptional teachings. He dreamed of the dawning of the sun and the moon and of receiving a blessing from a vase that Chogling Rinpoché had discovered. All these signs he took as indications that it was time to begin composing the work. After the completion of each part of the work, Kongtrul was requested by incarnate lamas and meditators to start to confer the empowerments and transmissions that were contained in it. Rapidly, these transmissions were propagated among the monasteries and communities of practitioners throughout eastern Tibet; as a result, they developed as had no other teachings.

Kongtrul's name is sometimes mentioned in connection with diplomacy. In 1857, he was sent to central Tibet to recover the incarnation of Situ Rinpoché, who had died in 1853. There, he had to exercise his diplomatic skill with Shedra (bShad-grwa),[43] the prime minister of the Tibetan government, in order to bring the young Situ, whose parents were subject to Trashi Lhunpo Monastery[44] authorities, to Pelpung. On another occasion, a demand had been made by some of the Gelug monasteries of eastern Tibet that the Kagyu monasteries in the area be destroyed; this was demanded of the army of central Tibet, which had come into the region to repel the invading Nyarong[45] army, headed by Gönpo Namgyel (mGon-po rNam-rgyal).[46] By exercising his skill as a doctor, Kongtrul was able to cure Dongkam Trulku (gDong-kam),[47] the leader of the Dragyab (Brag-gyab) Gelug monasteries, of a serious illness; as a result, Kongtrul succeeded in a covert diplomatic mission to save Pelpung and other Kagyu monasteries from being destroyed and their property from being confiscated. Kongtrul's services as mediator or peacemaker were requested in a number of situations: he accepted these requests, but he never became a politician. He remained a true spiritual seeker who simply played the political role that was part of his altruistic activity as a bodhisattva in the world.

Despite the importance that Kongtrul had in the Buddhist environment in eastern Tibet, at the age of sixty-one, after he had composed many of the works that cause him to be held in the highest esteem even today, a few degenerate monks from Pelpung Monastery initiated a dispute to discredit him and the lama Wön. They probably did so because they could not tolerate Kongtrul's broad vision and all-embracing attitude toward all teachings, especially toward those of the ancient tradition. Kyentsé told him that what was happening was a great obstacle to the doctrine. Finally, the senior manager of Degé, Tsering Döndrub (Tshe-ring Don-grub), was asked to investigate the matter. The allegations were found to be baseless. The dispute was subsequently dissolved, and the few monks responsible were arrested. It was decided that Wön Lama would take residence in Drentang (Dren-thang) and that Kongtrul would live at his own hermitage. The following year, Wön Lama died, Kongtrul wrote, as a direct result of the obstacle caused by his students' transgression of their relationship with their master. In a letter to Kongtrul, Kyentsé advised:

> In Pelpung Monastery, you increased the activities of teaching and empowerments. You taught the great rites of the ancient and new traditions, and when they were performed, you acted in them as the tantric master. You also taught the various sciences. At your hermitage you spent long periods in retreat. Now nothing worse can happen to you than what has just happened, other than your being killed. Therefore, follow the words of advice of Atiśa: Stay at least a hundred miles away from the place where there is a dispute.

Kongtrul said that he bore no grudge against the monks who reviled him but felt for them only compassion, recognizing that their minds had been under the influence of strong emotions and that they had broken the sacred bond with their teacher. At the same time, because they had repaid in a perverse way the kindness that Wön Lama (who was one of Kongtrul's masters) had shown them, Kongtrul admitted to feeling dislike for the monks and teachers who had caused the problem. From that time for about fourteen years, he did not enter Pelpung Monastery. By the end of his life, however, most of the greatest masters and incarnate teachers of the nineteenth century were among his disciples.

Kongtrul died in his eighty-seventh year, on Thursday, December 28, 1899; many auspicious signs appeared at that time.

Kongtrul was an extremely prolific writer who composed more than ninety volumes on theory and practice according to the Nyingma, Kadampa, Sakyapa, Kagyu, and Bönpo traditions. Although he cannot be considered an innovator, he had the great merit of collecting rare teachings and information on many subjects related to Buddhism, and giving them impetus to survive beyond the nineteenth century. At times, he rewrote teachings to make them more accessible to the minds of his contemporaries. He represents the best effort to synthesize all knowledge contained in Buddhist literature in the Tibetan language after the period of doctrinal systematization that occurred during the fourteenth and fifteenth centuries. These were the periods during which geniuses such as Tsongkapa (Tsong-kha-pa),[48] the founder of the Gelug school, and Longchenpa (Klong-chen-pa),[49] the greatest Nyingma mind, appeared. One characteristic of Kongtrul's scholastic works is his emphasis on original Indian treatises after a long period during which monastic institutions had developed indigenous works that specialized in subtly interpreting Indian treatises.

Kongtrul either wrote or compiled some ninety volumes on various subjects. His major works are traditionally known as the Five Great Treasuries (*mDzod chen lnga*), a name that Kyentsé gave them when Kongtrul showed him the first draft of the first of the five, *The Encompassment of All Knowledge*. The four others are *The Kagyu Treasury of Mantra, The Treasury of Key Instructions, The Treasury of Precious Treasure Teachings,* and *The Special Secret Treasury of Advice.*

The Kagyu Treasury of Mantra (*bKa' brgyud sngags mdzod*) contains the mandala practices of the thirteen tantric deities, as well as ancient and new tantras (some of which were transmitted by Marpa the Translator), accompanied by the teachings on the completion stage of the tantra, the rites of empowerment, and various authorizations. It consists of six volumes.

The Treasury of Precious Treasure Teachings (*Rin chen gter mdzod*) contains empowerments, teachings, rites, and instructions on how to apply them in retreat for all the cycles of *terma* that Kongtrul could find. The collections begin with the Earth Treasures[50] of treasure discoverers such as Nyangrel Nyimé Özer (Nyang-ral Nyi-ma'i 'od-zer),[51] Guru Chökyi Wangchug (Guru Chos-kyi-dbang-phyug), Longchenpa, Rigdzin Gödem (Rig-'dzin rGod-ldem),[52] Tangtong Gyelpo (Thang-stong rGyal-po) (1385-1509); the various *lingpa* (Gling-pa) such as Rinchen (Rin-chen) (1340-1396), Dorjé (rDo-rje) (1346-1405), Karma (Kar-ma), Pema (Pad-ma) (1450-?), Letro (Las-'phro) (1585-1656), and Chogling; and also Bönpo treasure discoverers. The second part of the work contains the cycles of teachings derived from the Mind Treasures and Pure Visions[53] of discoverers such as the fifth Dalai Lama, Dorjé Togmé Tsel (rDo-rje Thogs-med rTsal) (1617-1682), Namchö Migyur Dorjé (gNam-chos Mi-'gyur rDo-rje) (seventeenth century), and Jigmé Lingpa ('Jig-med Gling-pa). The last part of the work contains those treasure teachings whose transmissions had become rare; it contains a compilation of texts on minor *terma* with clarifications. It consists of sixty volumes.

The Treasury of Key Instructions (*gDams ngag mdzod*) contains empowerments and instructions related to the eight practice lineages of Tibet—Nyingma, Kadam, Sakya, Marpa Kagyu, Shangpa Kagyu, Pacification [of Suffering] (Zhi-byed), the Yoga of the Indestructible State (rDo-rje rnal-'byor), the Three Indestructible States, Familiarization and Attainment (rDo-rje gsum-gi-bsnyen-sgrub)—and a ninth section dealing with miscellaneous teachings of other lineages. It consists of twelve volumes.

Finally, *The Special Secret Treasury of Advice* (*Thun mong min gsang mdzod*), whose fifteen outlines were composed by Kyentsé to provide an auspicious beginning to the work, contains *The Union of the Minds of the Three Roots* and other teachings originating from the yellow scrolls (containing treasure teachings) and mind treasures discovered by Kongtrul himself. It consists of seven volumes.

In addition, Kongtrul wrote about rites, provided words of advice for students, wrote philosophical exegeses, and discussed Indian and Chinese astrology, medicine, grammar, and other subjects.

Kongtrul's huge literary output gives the impression that he must have spent most of his life writing. In fact, however, most of his time was dedicated to retreats and various practices, and he said that he often wrote his works "in the breaks between his meditations." It was because of his perspicacity in writing and his unequaled scholarship that Kongtrul came to be known as Jamgön ('Jam-mgon), "Gentle Protector," which is an epithet of Mañjuśrī, the bodhisattva who symbolizes superior wisdom.

The Encompassment of All Knowledge and the Commentary *The Infinite Ocean of Knowledge*

As Kongtrul was gaining his reputation as a brilliant teacher, the learned scholar Ngedön Tenpa Rabgyé (Nges-don bsTan-pa Rab-rgyas), the first Dazang (Zla-bzang) incarnation and the founder of Tilyag (Til-yag) Monastery in the Nangchen (Nang-chen) district, requested him to write a treatise on the three Buddhist disciplines— the vows of personal liberation, the precepts of awakening mind (bodhicitta), and the commitments of the mantra way. He promised that if Kongtrul wrote a root text, he would compose a commentary on it. Reflecting on the scholar's request, Kongtrul came to the conclusion that since treatises on the three disciplines were very common in Tibet, it would be more useful to write a book that contained a full presentation of the various Buddhist paths, in keeping with his nonsectarian attitude toward all teachings.

In fact, Sakya Paṇḍita, by writing his famous *Exposition on the Three Disciplines (Dom gsum rab dbye)*, had set the example for that kind of literature. Many tried to imitate him by writing commentaries on the same subject. It is probable that Kongtrul did not want to be redundant by writing yet another work of that nature. Consequently, he started to write a root text called *The Encompassment of All Knowledge (Shes bya kun khyab)* between meditation sessions while living in retreat at his hermitage, Kunzang Dechen Ösel Ling. When Kongtrul presented the manuscript to Kyentsé in 1862, the latter was highly impressed and said to Kongtrul:

> The success of this work is certainly due to the blessing of the spiritual masters and sky-dancers who have caused your inner energy pathways to open! This is a treasury of knowledge and must be considered the first of your five treasuries (*mdzo lnga*). You must be sure to write your own commentary to it.

It was Kyentsé himself who had previously prophesied that Kongtrul would write five treasury-like works. In 1863, Kongtrul composed his own three-volume commentary to his root text, entitled *The Infinite Ocean of Knowledge (Shes bya mtha' yas pa'i rgya mtsho)*, completing it in less than four months. The work was finally revised in 1864, with the help of Trashi Özer (bKra-shis 'Od-zer) (1836-1910), a scholar and abbot of Pelpung.

The Encompassment of All Knowledge consists of 154 pages in the modern edition[54] and of 78 folios in the Pelpung edition,[55] and it is written entirely in verse, with each line having nine syllables. It consists of ten sections (*gnas*), each of which has four chapters (*skabs*) of uneven lengths. Because Kongtrul touches on all Buddhist fields of knowledge as well as the related secular sciences known at his time, one must excuse the terse style of the composition. For the most part, it is impossible to understand the work without the aid of the commentary.

The Encompassment of All Knowledge, together with the commentary *The Infinite Ocean of Knowledge*, is often referred to as *The Treasury of Knowledge*, the first of Kongtrul's five treasuries. The commentary consists of 1936 pages in the modern edition and 992 folios in the Pelpung edition. The style is that of a "word commentary," in that the words of the root verses are used and expanded upon in the commentary. Even though it is not remarkable in its style, it is relatively clear and accessible. In some parts, the contemplative approach taken by Kongtrul serves to lead the reader into a contemplative state.

One's first impression of the work may be that its various subjects are surveyed superficially rather than explored in depth. This is partly true. A detailed survey of all Buddhist traditions and teachings would be endless; therefore, Kongtrul's treatment of each topic is brief. The way in which he deals with each topic, however, is anything but superficial. In fact, he demonstrates a remarkable gift for synthesis that is a natural consequence of his vast knowledge of Buddhism. The work should be viewed as an ideal starting point for further study.

In *The Encompassment of All Knowledge*, Kongtrul examines subjects, concepts, and terminology from the perspectives of different systems. He does so in order to demonstrate both the similarities and the differences of the various systems. This approach, in which different chapters are devoted to different systems, has a number of advantages. If the meaning of a subject, concept, or term is unclear in one system's exposition, for example, that meaning may be made clear in another system's exposition. An attentive reading of *The Encompassment of All Knowledge* will reveal the complex relationships that exist among its various subjects.

The order of the chapters within the sections is significant in that it reveals the level of importance that Kongtrul attaches to each system. He generally moves from lower levels of importance to higher levels, treating the subject first from the perspective of the Individual Way, next from the shared perspective of the Individual Way and the Universal Way, then from the exclusive perspective of the Universal Way, and finally from the perspective of the Dzog-chen system in particular or the Nyingma school in general. In fact, seven of the ten chapters that end the ten sections of the work utilize a Dzog-chen or Nyingma perspective. Kongtrul's nonsectarian and all-embracing attitude is exemplified by the work's ladder-like structure, in which the Individual and Universal Ways lead first to the Vajrayāna and ultimately to the Dzog-chen system, the peak of all spiritual pursuits. In moving from one system to the next, Kongtrul uses quotations that come mainly from the discourses of the Buddha, the tantras, and the treatises of the Indian sages, demonstrating in the process his exhaustive knowledge of the original sources.

In the philosophical chapters, Kongtrul is strictly scholastic but never argumentative and sophistic, and he never aligns himself with a particular point of view. He also defends, albeit humbly, philosophies, schools, and masters that had been attacked at times in the history of Tibetan Buddhism when conservative and absolutist attitudes held sway. Thus, in his treatment of the philosophical systems, he accorded a place equal to—if not higher than—those of the others to the "other emptiness" (*gzhan-stong*) school, which constitutes a link between the sūtra and tantra systems and facilitates the emergence of the experiential approach to the teachings.

Although Kongtrul wrote the most comprehensive piece of extant Tibetan literature, not everything that appears in *The Infinite Ocean of Knowledge* is his own writing. Entire pages and sections are copied from other sources, although Kongtrul often simplifies the original expositions in the process. In his treatment of the Dzog-chen system, for example, Kongtrul uses the work of Longchenpa, and when he discusses the history of Buddhism, he draws from the works of Butön (Bu-ston) (1290-1364), Tāranātha, and others. This borrowing does not, however, detract from the value of Kongtrul's work: such copying was common practice among Tibetan writers. This practice also indicates the various Tibetan masters who influenced Kongtrul, one of whom was undoubtedly the brilliant and eclectic Longchenpa.

Both editions of the text are presented in three volumes. The contents[56] of *The Encompassment of All Knowledge* and the corresponding commentary are as follows: In the first volume, Kongtrul deals with cosmology, the life of Buddha Śākyamuni, the teaching of Śākyamuni, and the history of Buddhism in India and Tibet. In the second, Kongtrul presents the three disciplines; the minor sciences (grammar, logic, arts, medicine, poetry, lexicography, literary composition, opera, and astrology); and the Buddhist paths and their practice. In the third, he presents the relative and ultimate truths and the various philosophical systems; the stages of meditation within sūtra and tantra, such as calm abiding and insight meditation, and the generation and completion stages of the Vajrayāna; a description of the tantras; and explanations of the secret instructions of the eight practice lineages of Tibet. Finally, he presents the stages and the path to be traveled and the goal to be attained: the three dimensions of awakening.

In particular, Kongtrul presents the oral instructions of various lineages, unfolding in very few words their experiential teachings. The editors of the Beijing edition described Kongtrul's work as follows:

> Without going through the trouble of finding many books, for those who wish to learn a single treatise that will free them from all ignorance, this work is like an ocean of reasoning; for those who wish to reflect it is like a boat (tak-

> ing one across the route) of reflection for the mind; for those who wish to meditate it is a jewel-like oral instruction; and for those who wish to engage in analysis it is like a clear crystal mirror.

This Book

Myriad Worlds discusses Buddhist cosmography and the genesis of beings who inhabit the universe. The descriptions of the universe that are given in the four chapters of the book are strikingly different. One universe is composed of a definite number of world-systems, one is composed of an infinite number of world-systems, and another is nothing but the play of the total and pure awareness of each and every being. Although they represent different approaches, these various cosmological systems do not contradict one another; instead, they are contained one within the other, like Chinese boxes. Each corresponds to the level of spiritual maturity of the individual for whom it is intended, and thus each one is built upon the foundation of another, the higher transcending rather than negating the lower.

The universe is considered from the point of view of its origin and its configuration. Its origin is explained in terms of a complex, transmutable relationship between mind and matter, a connection that becomes apparent as one progresses through the text. By contrast, the conclusive Dzog-chen treatment of the origin of the universe dispenses with the dualistic perspective, revealing the "Majestic Creative Principle of the Universe" to be intrinsic awareness alone. The configurations of the world-systems do not vary dramatically in the various cosmologies; they differ only in that they are described as having finite or infinite numbers of world-systems. These worlds are arranged in the same basic pattern of an *axis mundi* (Mount Meru), with surrounding mountain ranges, four continents, and so forth. Sentient beings are classified within a single world-system model. The various parts of Mount Meru, the continents, and the oceans are inhabited by beings whose lives are progressively more refined the closer their abodes are to the top of Mount Meru, with the highest worldly states of existence found in the form and formless realms above the mountain.

Kongtrul delineates four levels of cosmology: the numerically definite cosmology of the Individual Way, the cosmology of infinite buddha-fields of the Universal Way, the cosmology of the Tantra of the Wheel of Time (Kālacakra), and the noncosmology of the Dzog-chen, or Great Perfection, system. The author introduces the cosmology of infinite buddha-fields in the first chapter and then narrows the focus of his discussion to Endurance (Sahā), our own world-system, in the second chapter. In the third chapter, he begins his discussion of the perspective of the Wheel of Time; this he continues in part in the fourth chapter, where he also investigates the mechanisms of conditioned existence. In this way, he explains first the cosmology of infinite buddha-fields, then the numerically definite cosmologies, and finally the openness that constitutes the underlying reality of the universe, beings, and buddhas: the primordial purity of the universe that is presented in the Dzog-chen system.

The Numerically Definite Cosmology

When he was asked whether the world and the self were eternal or noneternal, both or neither, finite or infinite, the Buddha remained silent. His silence regarding such speculations about beginnings and ends was a denial of both absolutism and nihilism regarding the world and the self. On the one hand, this implies a denial that the world was created by Brahmā or any other supernatural being, and on the other, a denial that it came into being without causes. He also denied that the world emerged as the result of the transformation of a primordial substance (*prakṛti*), as was claimed by the Indian Sāṃkhya philosophy. In this respect, Buddhism is a truly nontheistic religion in which the concept of god as creator has no place. Buddhist cosmology recognizes a process of creation but does not acknowledge any sort of supernatural creator.

Who then created the world? The Buddhist reply is that the collective force of the evolutionary actions of sentient beings creates the world; therefore, all beings contribute to the creation of the world. "Evolutionary action" in this context refers to the cumulative potential that remains in the mind-stream after the performance of any physical, verbal, or mental action that is based on the underlying impulse of clinging to the idea of a self. According to the law of causality, this cumulative potential is able to produce specific results within the continuity of the subjective experience of each individual being, as well as producing the environment that that being inhabits. Thus, beings are related to their environments through causality, because the world is the result of the evolutionary actions of beings. In order to demonstrate that specific causes lead to specific results, Buddhist philosophy must postulate a linking factor and must also answer the question, What constitutes a person? Kongtrul briefly states the different views of various Buddhist schools regarding the nature of the linking factor. Centrists of the Consequential school, for example, regard this factor to be nothing other than the "mere person." ("Mere" indicates that the person exists only in a conventional sense.) Kongtrul points out that all these views are inadequate in some way, but he does not state his own views on the subject.

The creative relationship between mind and matter is the vital point in Kongtrul's treatment of the creation of the world. Certain "winds," or energies, are considered to be the potent agents of creation. These energies arise from the cumulative actions of beings who are about to take birth. Because they are the expressions of beings' actions, these energies are endowed with special potencies that are capable of shaping a new world. The energies of evolutionary actions thus form the bridge between mind and matter. Exactly how the cumulative potential of actions becomes external energy capable of contributing to creation constitutes the great mystery of how mind can create matter. In addition to energies, other factors are involved in the creation process. According to the Wheel of Time Tantra, scattered particles of matter remaining in space after a previous world-system has been destroyed are the "galactic seeds" that coalesce to form new planets, stars, and so forth, a process stimulated by the interplay of the five material elements. The Individualist cosmology states that energies arise from the ten directions and, through pressure and friction, produce primordial water. This primordial water element contains the seeds from which coarse matter arises, which is then shaped into various forms by the energy-winds generated by the past evolutionary actions of beings.

According to some commentators on Vasubandhu's *Treasury of Phenomenology*, generative seeds come from other world-systems; according to others, the seeds are contained within the primordial water; and according to others, the residual particles remaining after the destruction of an old world-system contribute to the formation of a new world-system. This creative process occurs throughout the entire universe, not only within our own world-system. Although the numerically definite cosmology is primarily concerned with a single world-system—our own—it clearly acknowledges the existence of a vast number of other worlds. In this scenario, there is no absolute beginning to the process of a world-system coming into being. Buddhist cosmology explains the creation of our world as an example of a timeless process in which mind and matter intermingle in a ceaseless flux of life and form. Worlds are created and destroyed endlessly within the infinity of time and space, and there is no edge to space and no beginning to time. What ensures the continuity of this process from eon to eon? Buddhists reply that the particular sphere of existence of beings who have attained the fourth meditative concentration is never destroyed by the cyclic fury of the elements, and that a special wind from this sphere becomes instrumental in the creation of new worlds.

It goes without saying that if the world is created by the evolutionary actions of beings, it is also destroyed by them.

In the numerically definite cosmology, the structure of the world is quite simple: a square *axis mundi*, like a mountain with terraces, surrounded by ranges of mountains and four main continents. The lowest types of beings, such as hell beings and starving spirits, dwell below Mount Meru. Superior beings dwell in places progressively higher up the mountain; the realms of the highest gods are in the skies above the summit of Mount Meru. This vision of the world is closely related to the spiritual path followed by the Individualists, who seek personal salvation from the cycle of lives. From the Individualist perspective, this world is created primarily by the evolutionary actions of beings, actions that are based on the concept of a self and the negative emotions that arise because of that concept; it is therefore a prison from which one must try to escape. It is a world of impure phenomena, an arena for the experience of suffering, which begins the moment a being takes physical form in that world. This cosmology reflects the ongoing drama of cyclic existence and the possibility of salvation from that existence. Freedom from cyclic existence means transcending the phenomenal world, never again to be born into its vale of suffering. This is the so-called perfect peace, or nirvāṇa, sought by the Individualists, who by virtue of their spiritual path aim to purify themselves of all defilements and become saints (*arhant*), and finally to extinguish themselves into a state of nonbeing, in much the same way that a flame dies out.

In this cosmological system, the lower states of life are filled with intense suffering and the higher ones are filled with distracting pleasures. None of these states is considered to be appropriate for the spiritual practice of those who seek liberation. Only the southern continent, which is known as the Land of Jambu, with its blend of suffering and pleasure, provides the rare circumstances in which people can conceive and practice the methods that lead to liberation. For this reason, the Land of Jambu is accorded a privileged place in Buddhist cosmology. It was there that the Buddha Śākyamuni attained enlightenment. Jambu is the land where the thousand buddhas of this Fortunate Age will appear. Therefore, the Land of Jambu is regarded as the best of all possible worlds in which to be born.

The Land of Jambu, in its original conception, probably referred to the Indian subcontinent. Considering the description given of its inhabitants, however, the details of the Land of Jambu may apply to our entire planet. The area associated with the jambu tree, from which this name for Earth comes, seems to be a blend of ancient myth and geographical fact. The sketchy descriptions provided by Kongtrul and other Buddhist sources place the jambu tree on the shore of a lake behind a range of snow mountains due north of the center of India. This naturally leads to the impression that the jambu tree is associated with sacred Lake Manasarovar, located high in the Himalayas at the foot of Mount Kailash. Providing further evidence of this connection, Kongtrul speaks of four rivers that originate in the vicinity of the lake, which might correspond to the four rivers that have their sources in the area of Lake Manasarovar and Mount Kailash. The fact that no jambu tree and associated wonders are found in this region, however, lends support to a mythical interpretation. The focus of the numerically definite cosmology on a single world-system is attributable to the Individualist ideal of personal freedom from the chain of births that is inherent in this cosmology. To attain liberation, realization of both personal and phenomenal selflessness is required. The principal goal of the spiritual practice of the Individualist, however, is the elimination of the tendency to cling to the idea of a personal self, which lies at the root of cyclic existence. Furthermore, Individualists do not fully cultivate the "skillful means" aspect of the spiritual path: compassion and love. These two factors account for the limited vision of the universe that is held by the Individualists. To fathom the magnitude of infinite numbers of world-systems being born and destroyed every moment requires a broader vision in one's spiritual view. It requires the courage of a bodhisattva, who cultivates great "protecting compassion" for the infinite numbers of beings who, at every moment, experience the misery of birth and death throughout infinite universes. Furthermore, the sheer magnitude of the apparent reality of such infinite universes would be difficult to conceive if one did not cultivate the understanding that not only oneself but also all the infinite worlds and all the beings who inhabit them are empty of intrinsic existence, nothing more than the magical play of relativity and emptiness.

Since the wider scope of the Universal Way is inconceivable to the Individualists, it stands to reason that their cosmology must be limited, accounting for only a limited number of world-systems. For the Individualists, the Buddha is simply a saint who is distinguished by the fact that he accumulated sufficient merit to exhibit the marks of a great being. Such buddhas can spread their beneficial and enlightening influence only within the limited sphere of a so-called third-order thousand world-system. Furthermore, only one such buddha can appear at any given time in such a system. After he has completed his work, such a buddha leaves the world and becomes extinct.

This cosmology, however, is not refuted by other Buddhist schools of thought. It is intended for the benefit of individuals with a lesser level of spiritual maturity, as a basis for subsequent higher understanding and as an integral part of a larger system of cosmology. As Kongtrul points out, every aspect of the Buddha's teaching is formulated for the benefit of a particular type of aspirant, and each is therefore valid by virtue of its efficacy in directing a different type of being onto the path of freedom. The wheel of the Buddha's teaching turns as a result of the force that is generated when the various needs and aspirations of living beings meet the compassion of the buddhas, but it is not a fixed, monolithic dogma.

The Cosmology of the Wheel of Time Tantra

The temporal and spatial presentation of the Tantra of the Wheel of Time[57] and its explanation of the origin of the universe are found in the third and fourth chapters of *Myriad Worlds.* The Tantra of the Wheel of Time is concerned with the integration of macrocosm and microcosm into a coherent system as a basis for the type of tantric spiritual development that it teaches, and therefore it focuses on our own world-system. It does not present a cosmos that differs significantly in configuration from that described in the Individualists' cosmology. The Wheel of Time cosmology differs from that of the Individualists in that it has different names for the continents and oceans, different shapes for Mount Meru and the encircling mountain ranges, and so forth. This cosmology also introduces an important and elaborate concept of the motion of the planets and the stars in conjunction with the human breath, the four eras, and so forth, which forms the basis for a form of astrology that belongs to this tantra. This concept, as well as some terminology, was probably borrowed from classical Indian thought and reworked. The Wheel of Time establishes a correspondence between the macrocosm and microcosm in terms of the formation of the universe and fetal development, and between the configuration of the universe and the shape and size of the human body. In the fourth chapter, the process involved in the creation of the world is described in more detail and is more refined than that described in the Individualist system of Vasubandhu.

The four eras (the eras of completion, three-quarters, two-quarters, and conflict) that mark the progressively descending vortex of time cycles in the Individualist system are associated in the Wheel of Time presentation with the country of Śambhala. In the third chapter of *Myriad Worlds,* Kongtrul cites the location of this country as being beyond the Himalayas, close to the northernmost extremity of the Land of Jambu. Wherever it may be, Śambhala is linked to the propagation of the Tantra of the Wheel of Time, one of the latest tantric systems to come to light. The first king of Śambhala, Sucandra, was said to have received the Wheel of Time Tantra from the Buddha himself at Dhānyakaṭaka in southern India; upon returning to his country, he made it the state religion. Kongtrul states that the kings of this country and their descendants will conquer the irreligious hordes of barbarians and reestablish the golden age throughout the twelve land masses of our world-system, one after the other. Only twenty-five kings of Śambhala are specifically mentioned in the *Wheel of Time Tantra,* and the names of their descendants are not given. The twenty-fifth king of Śambhala will ascend the throne in the year 2327 C.E., and in the ninetieth year of his rule, a war will be waged from Śambhala in which the barbarians will be defeated and the Wheel of Time teaching will spread throughout the world.

Kongtrul presents the information regarding Śambhala without commentary, relying on traditional sources. It is possible that Śambhala is not an actual place but an inner "pure land" symbolizing the spiritual wealth of our planet, which is constantly threatened by materialism. The wars periodically waged by the kings of Śambhala perhaps symbolize the desire of humanity to recover authentic values and spiritual insight.

The Cosmology of Infinite Buddha-Fields

The cosmology of infinite buddha-fields (*buddhakṣetra*) is unique to the Universal Way. Its sources can be found in a number of scriptures of the Universal Way, such as the *Avataṃsaka Scripture,* the *Saddharmapuṇḍarīka,* the *Pañcaviṃśatisāhasrikāprajñā-*

pāramitāsūtra, the *Vimalakīrtinirdeśasūtra*, and the *Acintyavimokṣa*. These scriptures convey the two most fundamental aspects of practice for those who aspire to the ideals of the bodhisattva: wisdom and skillful means. The transcendent wisdom (*prajñāpāramitā*) scriptures allude to this cosmology, but they are concerned with the nature of reality rather than its various manifestations. They transmit the essential teaching that "emptiness is (the ultimate nature of) form, and (the ultimate nature of) form is emptiness." This principle lays the foundation for the correct insight needed by bodhisattvas who are engaged in "oceans" of compassionate activity. The *Avataṃsaka Scripture* and other scriptures, however, introduce a grand cosmic play of infinite buddhas and bodhisattvas who are continuously engaged in teaching, demonstrating miracles, and practicing the ten perfections for the sake of others; they are concerned with the relative rather than with ultimate reality.

The reason that this cosmology presents world-systems as buddha-fields may be found in the first chapter of Kongtrul's book. Scriptures of the Universal Way state that the infinite world-systems come into being not only because of the evolutionary actions of beings but also because of the interconnections between buddhas and sentient beings. The scope of such vast and intricate interconnections is astounding. These interconnections involve the compassion of the buddhas, the dispositions and destinies of sentient beings, the natural laws of the universe, and the vows of the bodhisattvas. Through the interdependence of these factors (presumably including the creative mechanisms explained in the Individualist cosmology), myriad worlds appear in empty space. An absolute beginning of the universe is not posited in this system; instead, the universe is conceived as a cycle without commencement that repeats itself until all beings are liberated from the sufferings of cyclic existence.

The text clearly states that the buddhas and bodhisattvas are instrumental in the manifestation of the universe. According to this view, the universe is therefore the ground and agency for awakening rather than a prison from which to escape. It is the playground for the miraculous powers of enlightened beings, the amphitheater in which the bodhisattvas practice their skillful means to help others overcome their confusion. At this point, Kongtrul introduces the concept of "bodhisattvas purifying buddha-fields" (*bodhisattvānāṃ buddhakṣetrapariśodhana*) but does not explain it in detail. This is an important concept that is often discussed in reductive terms because its full import is otherwise difficult to grasp. It is explained to some extent by the Buddha in the scripture *The Holy Teachings of Vimalakīrti* (expertly translated into English by Robert Thurman). In that scripture, the Buddha states that the buddha-fields in which the bodhisattvas practice are fields of living beings. This would seem to indicate that the buddha-fields are the living beings themselves, as well as the environments that they inhabit. In the course of their practice of the ten perfections, the bodhisattvas work to lead others to spiritual maturity by various means. Consequently, the bodhisattvas' aspirations to lead all others to complete awakening constitute an important condition in the process of the formation of world-systems. Once the worlds arise, the bodhisattvas enter all of them for incalculable eons in order to benefit the beings who are born in those worlds. In stark contrast to the Individualist's intention to escape the world and terminate cyclic existence by means of personal awakening, bodhisattvas actually contribute to the creation of new worlds in which they may fulfill their heroic vows to liberate all beings. Beings see the purity of the realms in which they dwell according to their own levels of inner purity, but the realms themselves are pure from the very beginning. This fact is clearly illustrated in *The Holy Teachings of Vimalakīrti*, which states that the Buddha touched the ground with his big toes and our universe was transformed into radiant jewels of infinite light. The Buddha then informed Śāriputra that the universe is always pure, but in order to effect the spiritual maturity of beings, it appears to be flawed.

The primary element in the buddha-fields cosmology is the infinity of space and light, which replaces the static model of Mount Meru and the four continents that is expounded in the numerically definite world-systems cosmology. The former cosmology encompasses an infinite number of worlds in space, whose arrangement lies beyond the reach of rational thought.

These worlds appear in all conceivable, as well as inconceivable, dimensions and shapes, some resting on lotuses and jewels, others supported solely by the blessings of the buddhas. These worlds suffuse the ten directions; millions of worlds interpenetrate one another, and each world contains billions of others. Billions more are contained within each atom of each world. This is a cosmology whose monumental scope serves to open the mind to the unlimited, unfathomable, nonrational aspects of the universe. As a result, the mind breaks out of the cage of fixed concepts of definite space and existence and enters the open space of myriad worlds without beginning or end, beyond all fixed dimensions of size and shape. This cosmology also conveys the bodhisattva conception of enlightenment, which is the spiritual development of all living beings throughout the universe as the primary path of one's own search for awakening. It would have been appropriate for Kongtrul to begin his work with a description of Endurance, our own universe, and to have proceeded from the particular to the universal, from the limited cosmology of Mount Meru to the unlimited skies of the infinite buddha-fields. Out of respect for his own tradition, the Universal Way, however, he presents the mysterious space odyssey of infinite buddha-fields before exploring the particular details of our own world.

All that is described is contained within the "sphere of reality" (*dharmadhātu*), the ultimate realm that contains everything that exists. This sphere never changes, never becomes anything other than itself. It always remains empty of true existence. The countless realms that appear throughout the universe all manifest within this single realm: they exist within it and are destroyed within it. From the point of view of their ultimate nature, no realms have ever appeared, have ever been inhabited, have ever been destroyed. Nevertheless, in relative terms, infinite world-systems arise as phantom appearances based on interdependent connections, and these worlds serve the purposes of enlightened beings who act as spiritual guides, realizing that these realms have no ultimate reality. The unenlightened beings who inhabit these realms also have no ultimate reality; they cling, however, to the idea that they, their worlds, and their experiences are ultimately real. The sphere of reality and the interdependent manifestations within it can be perceived simultaneously only by the eye of a buddha.

The place of ordinary sentient beings in this display is explained by Kongtrul in the first chapter, where he states that the appearance of beings in these realms is the result of their failure to recognize their own nature—emptiness—a nature that they share with the realms into which they are born, the buddhas, and everything else that exists. The fundamental nature of each being is buddha-nature, the potential to awaken from the slumber of ignorance. The only difference between buddhas and sentient beings is that the former have attained freedom through their awareness of their original empty nature, while the latter remain imprisoned in their phantom worlds of suffering because of their lack of awareness of the empty nature of all phenomena. Misunderstanding their actual condition, sentient beings wander into realms that are the products of their own tendencies. The course of the experience of cyclic existence unfolds through the twelve links of interdependent origination, which Kongtrul delineates in detail, taking into account the perspectives of different Buddhist systems.

Within the Universalist cosmology of infinite buddha-fields, which is linked with the theory of the buddha-nature (*tathāgatagarbha*), it is apparent that the basis of the confusion experienced by beings, which has no fixed beginning in time, also forms the basis of awakening from that very confusion. In other words, one's actual state of being is the ground for both confusion and enlightenment. Each person must unearth the buddha-nature from the depths of delusion in the same way that a miner digs a precious jewel from the muck and mire of a mine. In order for that buddha-nature to reveal itself, however, two factors must coincide: the compassion of the buddhas, which takes the form of enlightened spiritual guides; and the practice of the spiritual path by sentient beings. The practice of the spiritual path is based on the understanding of one's limitations and potential as well as the defects of cyclic existence. For this reason, Kongtrul writes extensively on various causes and results that play a fundamental role in the deceptive state of existence, viewing them from the perspectives of both the Individualist and the Universalist systems.

Among the three dimensions of awakening (*kāya*), the enjoyment dimension (*saṃbhogakāya*) holds a special place in the Universal Way, reflecting the richness and fullness of the spiritual path of the Universal Way and its final result. The Universal Way is inspired by the resolve to attain enlightenment for the sake of all living beings, and therefore the welfare of others always takes priority over other more relative aspects of training, such as ethics. Thus, in pictorial representations, buddhas in the enjoyment dimension of awakening are depicted not as monks but as princes and princesses adorned with jewels and fine clothes. It is this form of the buddhas that plays such an important part in the Universalist cosmology. This form, or dimension, is associated with the pure realm called Unsurpassed (*Akaniṣṭha*). According to the teachings, the Unsurpassed realm is the "place" where every buddha attains enlightenment. Kongtrul, however, makes the remarkable statement that the Unsurpassed realm is "any place" where a being attains enlightenment. This statement sets the stage for Kongtrul's discussion of the Flower-Filled World, a world-system that contains our world, Endurance.

Kongtrul implies that wherever a being attains enlightenment, an Unsurpassed realm manifests spontaneously, complete with a palace, marvelously adorned with every imaginable precious ornament. The enlightened being becomes the lord of this realm, taking form as Buddha Illuminator (Vairocana), Great Glacial Lake of Wisdom, the enjoyment dimension of awakening, undifferentiated from all the buddhas of the ten directions. Illuminator also holds a special place in the Universalist cosmology, probably because he symbolizes purity of form, the form that constitutes the entire universe. The magnitude of this cosmology is apparent in the statement that within each pore of Illuminator's body, infinite world-systems appear, and within each atom of these worlds is an infinity of other worlds and infinite forms of Illuminator. Each form of Illuminator in turn contains infinite buddhas and buddha-fields. Illuminator encompasses the entire universe, and the entire universe constitutes Illuminator. If Kongtrul means to say that every being who attains enlightenment becomes the embodiment of this vast display of worlds and that all these worlds are encompassed by such a being, then in the light of the infinite number of buddhas of the ten directions, we are presented with an inconceivable, unfathomable image of a cosmos where the particular includes the universal and the universal is included within the particular; in other words, everything includes and is included within everything.

Our world, Endurance, is an infinitesimal part of this grand cosmic display, the thirteenth in a series of tiered world-systems that rest in an ocean of infinite world-systems, all of which rest in the palm of Buddha Illuminator. It is part of the universe called the Flower-Filled World, whose dimensions are billions of times greater than the third-order thousand world-system described in the numerically definite cosmology. It is the field of influence of a single manifest dimension of awakening (*nirmāṇakāya*). A distinction is made between Illuminator as the central figure in Unsurpassed and his manifestations throughout the other universes in order to emphasize that in the Universal Way, the primary method of bringing disciples to spiritual maturity is to explain the doctrine to them, which can only be accomplished by a buddha who manifests in a form that is visible to all beings.

In the fourth chapter of *Myriad Worlds*, Kongtrul explores the mechanisms through which beings experience the deception of cyclic existence from the Individualist, Universalist, and exceptional perspectives. He divides the exceptional perspective into two parts: the mechanism of cyclic existence, based on what he calls the "definite teaching" (which is probably derived from the third cycle of the Buddha's doctrine); and the view of Dzogchen, or the "Great Perfection."

Kongtrul states that in the first cycle of the Buddha's teaching, the primal cause of cyclic existence is cited as self-habit. This is basically the sense of a permanent identity, the habit of clinging to the idea of an independent self, whereas only a relative self, imputed on the basis of the five aggregates, actually exists. Not only is the self regarded as devoid of independent existence, but so is consciousness, which constitutes an important basis for the designation of the self and serves as the means whereby the person experiences the outer world. In the third cycle of the Buddha's teaching, the cause of this situation is held to be fundamental consciousness. Fundamental consciousness is a storehouse of imprints left by the actions of a person. These imprints produce a dualistic impression of a perceiving consciousness and perceived phenomena, perpetuating delusion.

The first part of the discussion of the exceptional system emphasizes the luminous and empty nature of the mind. The luminous and empty nature of the mind is the very buddha-nature that, when discovered within oneself, opens the gate to enlightenment. As long as this nature remains unrecognized, however, dualistic appearances continue to arise. Habitual involvement with these dualistic apprehensions produces "instincts" based on perceptions of external objects, subjective experiences, and the possession of a physical body. Later, these instincts express themselves in the outer world, in perceiving consciousness, and in embodied existence. Evolutionary actions performed during the course of life then produce further instincts that perpetuate cyclic life. The methods used to transcend cyclic life are not discussed extensively in these four chapters, since they are discussed in subsequent books of *The Infinite Ocean of Knowledge.* Kongtrul does, however, briefly mention the method of transcending cyclic life by terminating involvement in the twelve links through the realization that the idea of the self, which constitutes the first link of the chain of unawareness, is devoid of intrinsic reality.

The Non-Cosmology of the Dzog-chen System

In the last part of the fourth chapter of *Myriad Worlds* (presented as Chapter V in this translation), Kongtrul draws extensively from the *Tsig-dön-dzö (Tshig bdon mdzod)* of Longchenpa, providing a concise but highly illuminating account of the perspective held by followers of the Dzog-chen system. His discussion deals primarily with the mechanism of the arising of conditioned existence; he does not go into details about cosmology, which is not a major concern in the Dzog-chen system. The Dzog-chen presentation of the origin of cyclic existence is unique in that it defines the universe as primordial purity. Kongtrul clearly states that the Dzog-chen system stands at the summit of spirituality.

In the Dzog-chen system, the primal creative cause of the universe is neither the evolutionary actions of beings nor the interrelationships of the compassion of the buddhas and sentient beings, but *rigpa*, a state of pure and total awareness. This state of awareness is nothing other than the primordially pure ground of being itself (*gzhi*). Cyclic life is thus regarded as simply the arousal or excitement of the pure state of awareness "straying away from itself." The concept of awareness straying from itself is only a metaphor, because awareness can never stray from itself. When manifestations arise from the ground of being and are not recognized as the ground of being itself or the play of pure awareness, however, the delusion of cyclic existence begins. Failure to recognize the primordially pure nature of the ground of being is unawareness, which itself arises from intrinsic awareness. The process operates as follows: first, the ground of being manifests as five pure lights, but because of their unawareness, beings view these lights as concrete objects. For this reason, appearances themselves constitute deception.

Metaphorically speaking, when the seal that keeps the total and pure awareness in the original ground of being is broken, the creativity of intrinsic awareness arises and the entire universe, which is nothing more than the manifestation of one's intrinsic awareness, springs into being. This manifestation occurs in eight ways, which give rise to all the myriad realms of the buddhas' dimensions and of cyclic life. As the title of one of the principal tantras of Dzog-chen states, the total and pure state of awareness constitutes the "Majestic Creative Principle of the Universe."

It is believed in this system of thought that if the original ground of being is primordially pure, every sentient being is enlightened all along; therefore, beings are not impeded by any real limitations. All beings are by nature endowed with the same wisdom and other qualities that are possessed by buddhas, for in the state of pure and total awareness, everything is already complete and perfect. Both freedom and deception arise as the play of the excitement of the awareness, and the ground of being forms the basis for both without belonging to either state. One's own enlightened nature must, however, become revealed through a "reawakening." Drawing from Longchenpa, Kongtrul explains the method of awakening in the Dzog-chen system, calling it the "Liberation as Ever-Perfect," as the primordial buddha Samantabhadra. Awakening occurs in the following way: when objectifying thoughts, which are nothing more than the movement of pure and total intrinsic awareness, arise, one does not regard them as concrete, realizing instead that they are one's own inner radiance manifesting outwardly. When this insight dawns, the movements of thought cease spontaneously, without any need for meditation or other artificial techniques to transform or terminate them. At that instant, full realization is attained, and the wisdom and other qualities of a buddha are manifested.

Liberation as Ever-Perfect does not refer to the liberation of a buddha that has occurred in the past, such as that of Buddha Śākyamuni, but to the way in which countless beings are liberated right now and will continue to be liberated in the future simply by realizing their primordial purity. The basis, the path, and the ultimate result in this system are all of a singular, undifferentiated nature: total, pure awareness. Thus, the primordial freedom that one seeks to attain by practicing the spiritual path is something that one already possesses. Intrinsic freedom is itself the path that leads to the actualization of the goal.

The different systems of Buddhist cosmology are thus directly correlated with the ways in which sentient beings are drawn into cyclic existence, as well as with the various spiritual paths that provide the opportunity to be free. In the Individualist system, cyclic existence and the worlds in which it transpires must be transcended in order to attain the perfect peace of one's own liberation. By contrast, the followers of the Universal Way also aim to transcend cyclic existence, but not in order to abide eternally in a state of static peace; instead, they attain the "dynamic perfect peace" of a buddha in order to work unceasingly for the welfare of others. The Tantric Way symbolized by the Wheel of Time cosmology, however, goes a step further by teaching that cyclic life and transcendence of cyclic life have the same basis; therefore, cyclic life should be transformed rather than renounced. Tantra teaches that the actualization of the perfect peace of transcendence is found within the world itself and within the body, through the understanding that life and the transcendence of life are indivisible in the ultimate reality. Kongtrul states that an understanding of the Dzog-chen view of cyclic life is essential if one is to understand the path and the result of this system. The Dzog-chen perspective holds that everything emerges spontaneously from the primordially pure nature of being, that everything always remains primordially pure, and that when this truth is recognized within one's own natural awareness (*rang byung ye shes*), one instantly recovers one's original enlightened nature, which has been there all along.

Myriad Worlds contains invaluable material for study, reflection, and the refinement of one's mind. It provides an indispensable foundation for understanding Buddhist philosophy and practice, and it contains seeds of wisdom that are sure to sprout and blossom in the minds of spiritual aspirants and other attentive readers.

Root Verses from
The Encompassment of All Knowledge

Root Verses from *The Encompassment of All Knowledge*

In Sanskrit: *Yāna-sarva-mukhebhyaḥ samucchaya-pravacanaṃ-ratna-kośa-tri-śikṣa-sudeśika-śastraṃ sarvajñeya-spharaṇa-nāma*

The Encompassment of All Knowledge: A treasury of precious teachings compiled from all the approaches of the systems for spiritual development, a treatise that effectively transmits the three trainings

Namaḥ śrīmāṃ-sad-guru-pādāya

[Embodiment] of complete purity and ethics, you stand firm like the golden foundation.
Your beauty reflects your countless contemplations, like the distinct features of the mountains and continents.
Like the sun and moon, your brilliant wisdom illuminates all phenomena.
Supreme sage and achiever of all goals, I revere you.

With the heart of a great hero who protects beings for as long as they exist,
You suffused the universe with your excellent conduct.
Though father to the victorious ones, you manifest as the victorious ones' son.
Lion of Speech, grant me flawless intelligence.

You nurture the seed — the potential or nature of beings — by imparting instructions that mature and liberate them.

You cause others to purify incidental defilements through the twofold path,
And bestow the fruition, the four dimensions of awakening distinguished by great bliss.
To you, my mentor, and to the masters of the lineages, I bow.

Although I lack the intellectual capacity to compile knowledge correctly,
I shall compose a short, clear, comprehensive work
In order to ensure that those with insufficient knowledge or interest to understand the texts
Will not lose their opportunity on this isle of treasures.

* * *

This treatise [The Infinite Ocean of Knowledge] as a whole has [ten] divisions, equal in number to the ten perfections:
The realms that appear during the age of illumination; Buddha, the Teacher; the doctrine, both scriptural and experiential;
Its continuation and spread in the Land of Jambu;
Maintaining ethical conduct; learning; reflection; meditation;
Through successively engaging in these, progression through the paths; and realization of the ultimate result.

* * *

There are general and specific causes and conditions that initiate [the creation of realms]:
For as long as infinite space and sentient beings exist,
The compassion of the victorious ones and the actions of sentient beings continue without end.
Those to be guided and enlightened guides
Manifest through inconceivable interconnections.
When the characters and dispositions of those to be guided are activated,

[The compassion of] the guides [arises], and the configurations of the realms and the dimensions of awakening appear;
The miraculous methods of guiding others manifest beyond all bounds.
The sphere of reality never changes into something else;
Yet blessings, vows, actions, and natural laws
Cause oceans of realms to appear.
The realm Unsurpassed is free from incidental defilement
And transcends the experience of the three realms: it is indivisible pristine wisdom.
In this self-manifesting, spontaneously appearing [realm,] Richly Adorned,
Dwells Illuminator, Great Glacial Lake of Wisdom;
A billion realms in his every pore.
Their locations, shapes, sizes, durations, and arrangements are inconceivable.
Within the central minute particle in the palm of his hand lies the Oceanic World-System
That itself contains many world-systems, in the center of which
Lies the realm called Flower-Filled World.
Furthermore, [between the wind] and Unsurpassed lie one billion four-continent world-systems,
A great third-order thousand [world-system].
Multiplying that by factors of one billion
[Yields] Infinite Links, Continuums, Oceans,
And Flower-Filled World.
Each rests on an ocean and [is encircled by] an outer rim.
This is the sphere of influence of one supreme manifest dimension of awakening.
Inside the great outer rim, in a sea of scented water,
Four jewelled lotuses support
A tiered arrangement of twenty-five world-systems;
The thirteenth is known as Endurance.
This third-order thousand world-system
Is completely encircled by realms — Covered, Surpassing, Stainless, Variously Emerged, etc. —

Equal in number to the particles of this thirteenth world-system.
[Endurance] is spherical, has a four-vajra demarcation,
And rests on a multicolored configuration of wind and a network of lotuses.
Illuminator, the teacher in this [world-system],
Appears throughout the Unsurpassed realms of the pure domains.
This four-continent [world-system] called Destructible
Is surrounded by ten other four-continent [world-systems].
It is taught that these [world-systems] are formed and destroyed together;
This is the experiential domain solely of the lords of the tenth stage of awakening.

* * *

In our own world-system, four [ages] occur: formation, abiding, destruction, and vacuity.
Of the two, environment and inhabitants, [a description of] the environmental world [is presented first]:
After the age of vacuity had elapsed at the end of the previous age,
Winds arose from the ten directions, creating a configuration in the shape of a cross;
Rain fell from a cloud, and amidst a mass of water,
A thousand lotuses were seen; thus the Fortunate Age was proclaimed.
The churning of water by wind produced a golden disc,
Upon which rain fell; [this became] the great ocean.
The churning by wind developed the [ocean's] elements — superior, medium, and base;
These elements formed Mount Meru, the seven mountain ranges, the four continents and the outer rim.
The mountains and continents all extend eighty thousand [leagues] down into the ocean.
Mount Meru rises eighty thousand [leagues] above the ocean.

The four sides of Mount Meru are composed of crystal, blue beryl, ruby, and gold.
The sky [on each side] reflects these colors.
From sea level to half its height are four terraces.
Beyond it are seven golden mountain ranges, Yoke and the others.
The spaces between are filled with seas of enjoyment, which have eight qualities.
The four continents and the eight islands
Are semi-circular, trapezoidal, round, and square.
There are numerous unspecified little islands.
The outer rim consists of a mountain range composed of iron;
A salt-water ocean fills the area as far as this range.
North from the center of the Exalted Land, beyond nine black mountains,
Stand the Snowy Mountains, and north of these the Fragrant [Mountains].
Between these two mountain ranges lies Cool Lake; from its four sides
Four cascades flow in four directions toward the ocean.
A jambu tree adorns the lake's shore,
And so this continent is known as the land beautified by the jambu tree.
The names of Majestic Body and the others indicate their distinguishing features.
Tail-Fan Island is inhabited by cannibal demons, and the others, by humans.
The hells and the world of the starving spirits are located below the earth.
Animals, the inhabitants of the depths, dwell in the great ocean.
Demi-gods [live] in the crevices of Mount Meru from the water's edge down.
The Four Groups of the Great Kings reside mainly on the terraces of Mount Meru.
Beings may also dwell in various unspecified secondary abodes.

Above Mount Meru is the heaven of the Thirty-three
In which is found the Victorious Residence, the city called Lovely,
Parks, playing fields, the All-gathering tree, the fine stone slab,
The Assembly Hall of the Excellent Law, as well as the dwelling of the *yakṣas*.
Above, Conflict Free, Joyful, Enjoying Creations, and [Mastery Over] Others' [Creations]
Rest on riches like cloud formations in the sky.
There are sixteen heavens in the form realm, beginning with Group of the Pure;
Above them all is Lesser Unsurpassed.
The lord bodhisattvas reside above that, according to the *Five Treatises on the Stages*.
[The heavens] double in size and grow increasingly magnificent.
One third-order thousand world-system is fathomed by the vision of the proclaimers and solitary sages,
Who assert that it is composed of indivisible particles of matter.
The nature of each being is unobscured and undetermined.
The four absorptions of the formless realm and the other realms arise sequentially; [the beings within them]
Diffuse from higher to lower, down to the hells.
Moreover, the four levels of absorption of the formless realm
Are only distinctions in contemplation; they have no form or location.
The form realm: In the fourth level of meditative concentration, [there are] five pure domains and three heavens of ordinary beings.
Three [heavens] are located within each of the lower three levels of meditative concentration.
The desire realm comprises thirty-six types of beings:
Six groups of gods, [humans of the] four continents,
[Inhabitants of the] eight islands, animals and starving spirits,

[Beings in the] eight hot hells, and the eight cold hells.
The twenty existences, ten happy and ten miserable,
May also be classified as twenty-eight.
Within the happy existences — the form realm and the rest —
Lifespans and possessions decrease the lower the level.
In the miserable existences, suffering increases the lower the level.
The four [levels] of absorption, the four levels of meditative concentration, and the desire realm
Comprise nine levels. In terms of type, there are six [classes of] beings.
A classification of five — human, divine, and three miserable existences —
May be made in terms of paths and courses.
All these beings may be categorized according to the four modes of birth,
Or into pure, corrupt, and indeterminate groups.
During the time of abiding, most beings, except for animals,
Experience consequences that are predetermined.
In our world, humans have a wide variety of lifespans, wealth, and physical size.
Lifespan decreases from incalculable to ten,
And then increases to eighty thousand, and so on.
During a decline, a rise, and eighteen intermediate cycles,
There are fluctuations. The three continents are places where [consequences] are experienced;
Jambu Land, the most distinguished, is the place of action.
Beings in this world came down from the heaven of Clear Light.
The nourishment derived from meditative concentration and other [pristine] qualities gradually deteriorated due to craving.
The sun and moon provided light, and King Honored by Multitudes appeared.
Then, such distinctions as the four eras and four classes arose.

Wheel-monarchs, who [possess wheels of] gold, silver, copper, and iron,
Appear in this world only when the lifespan is no less than eighty thousand years.
Some say that they reign totally over the third-order thousand world-system.
There are many variations in food, hunger and thirst, color of clothing, night and day, etc.
Beings in lower [realm] do not see those in the higher.
At the time of destruction, the miserable realms, beginning with the hell realms, empty.
Gods and humans attain meditative concentration and are born in the form realm.
As the realms empty of inhabitants, the [beings of] the lower realms move higher.
The heavens of the first meditative concentration and below are destroyed by fire.
Space alone remains, a vacuity containing nothing at all.
Again formation occurs, and again abiding, and finally destruction by fire.
After seven such [sequences], a deluge at the end of the eighth
Destroys the second meditative concentration and below.
Seven destructions by fire alternating with one by water occur seven times,
Ending with another seven by fire.
Finally, intense wind destroys the third meditative concentration and below.
Because those three contemplations have imperfections [they are destroyed];
The fourth, being free of imperfection, is not destroyed by the elements.
Altogether, sixty-four great cycles of destruction occur.
Each of the ages of formation, abiding, destruction, and vacuity
Lasts for twenty intermediate ages; together, these [four] constitute one cosmic age.
Such statements as that in a single age seven fires,

One flood, and one wind arise, destroying the third level of meditative concentration and below,
Reflect different points of view of different systems.
The pure realms and the Seat of Enlightenment, etc., are not destroyed,
Since they are not the result of the origin [of suffering].

* * *

The *King of Tantras of the Primordial Buddha*
Refutes erroneous systems and integrates the outer, inner,
And alternative [levels]. In the center of space rest spherical foundations
Of wind, fire, water, and earth, [proportional in size to the measure between] the soles of the feet and the waist.
Mount Meru, its neck, face, and crowning protuberance
[Are proportional to the measure between] the waist and the crown of the head.
The center is green; the east, blue; the north, white; the south, red;
And the west, yellow. Each part is composed of a precious substance.
From the [edge of the] vast upper surface hang five indestructible enclosures
In a concentric arrangement; the outer ones are progressively longer.
At the base is a ledge which forms an indestructible perimeter.
Between the six continents — Moon, White, Most Excellent,
Kuśa Grass, Centaur, and Crane —
Are [six] oceans: Honey, Butter, Yogurt, Milk, Water, and Beer,
Encircled by the mountains Blue Radiance, Mandara Blossom,
Night, Jewel Radiance, Vessel, and Cool.
These are lands of experience. The seventh continent,
The Greater Land of Jambu, said to be the land of evolutionary action,

Is located between Cool Mountain Range and the edge of the salt water ocean.
The seventh mountain range forms the Impenetrable Perimeter,
Surrounded by the fire and wind arising from the respective spheres.
Beyond this is vacuity, devoid of any attributes.
The twelve lands of evolutionary action—the great continents of wind, fire, water, and earth—
Are situated in the center [of each] of the four directions.
They are semi-circular, triangular, round, and square in shape
And are flanked by smaller continents. All are positioned like lotus petals.
The Exalted Land is situated in the south of the Small Land of Jambu.
Situated to the north are, successively, Tibet, Khotan,
China, Śambhala, and the Great Snow Range.
Thirty-one existences — eleven desire, sixteen form, four [formless] —
Live within these [environments].
The celestial sphere pervades space between Mount Meru and the mountain of fire.
It is a belt of wind, within which the twelve houses
And the twenty-eight constellations formed first.
[The houses] are situated in a clockwise arrangement. Planets such as the sun and moon rise above them.
[Eight] move counter-clockwise; Eclipser [moves] clockwise.
A solar day is measured in terms of six breaths and sixty minor clepsydra measures constituting one major clepsydra measure of time.
Lunar, solar, and house days are determined
In relation to the movement of the moon, sun, and constellations.
The [three types of] days are equivalent to one fifteenth of a phase of the moon, one revolution of the sun around the continents,

And a thirtieth of the time [required for the sun] to move through a house.
Each is longer than the preceding one. Based on lunar months and house years,
The four seasons occur in natural sequence on earth.
Time-conjunctions affect the quality of life.
Explanations of the four eras of the doctrine
Of the wheel-holders, of the world-system, and of entering vacuity supplement the above.
The Victorious One did not base his teachings on the belief that a single system is the only valid one,
[But taught] in response to the interests and abilities of those he guided.
There are a variety of units for measuring space and time:
Eight minute particles equals one fine particle;
A hair-tip, ketsé seed, louse, barley seed, and finger-width [are determined] in a similar manner.
Twenty-four [finger-widths equals one] cubit; four cubits equals one bow-length;
Two thousand [bow-lengths equals one] ear-shot; four of those equals a league.
The phenomenology system presents units of form and time, and components of words.
Seven minute particles [equals] one fine particle;
Iron, water, rabbit, sheep, ox, and sun-ray particles
Louse egg, louse, barley seed, and finger-width are similarly determined.
Twenty-four finger-widths [equals] a cubit; four cubits, a bow-length;
Five hundred [bow-lengths], one ear-shot,
Or the measure to solitude; eight of those, a league.
The third-order thousand [world-system] is described and measured with these units.
One sixty-fourth of a finger-snap
Is the smallest unit of time. One hundred and twenty [of these units]
Equals an instant. Sixty instants [equals] one moment.
Thirty [moments equals] a period; thirty periods, a solar day;

Thirty solar days, a month; and twelve months, a year.
Based on these units, the measurable and the immeasurable are calculated.
Individual letters are the components of words.
[Groups of words] form sentences.
If examined, [words] do not capture [the essence, but are] deceptive.

* * *

What causes create the world?
The erroneous theories of the non-Buddhists claim that [the world]
Was created by Īśvara or the sage, or that it arose from the self or naturally.
It is taught in the scriptures that worlds and beings
Are created by various actions influenced by subtle and proliferating [emotions].
The factor ensuring actions' results is said to be acquired or inevitable,
The stream of mental consciousness, the fundamental consciousness,
The mere individual, clear light, and so forth.
The Analysts and Traditionists state that the environment is created from the wind at the peak [of existence] which remains from the time of destruction,
Or from five types of seeds carried from other worlds.
The stream [of phenomena] is undispersed and coheres through [the effect] of concordant actions.
Lasting form and time are deceptive impressions within naive minds;
It is taught that the exalted ones comprehend the cessation of particles and moments.
Most agree that in the formation [of the world] the mind is the agent, subtle particles and the moving and stationary winds are the objects acted upon,
And the [winds' motions] are the means of creation.
Six causes and four conditions produce conditioned phenomena;

Five results are produced by these [causes].
The Individualists' system of phenomenology follows these excellent explanations.
The productive cause of [a particular phenomenon] is that which is other than the conditioned phenomenon.
Coemergent causes are [conditioned phenomena] that are causes and results of one another.
Causes of the same outcome are preceding phenomena creating later similar phenomena.
Concomitant causes are mind and mental events that share five aspects.
Omnipresent causes are defiled phenomena.
Developing causes are non-virtue and contaminated virtue.
Developed results arise after their causes, pertain to a continuum,
And are unobscured and neutral.
Results concordant with the causes are of a type similar to same outcome and omnipresent [causes].
Freedom results are cessations attained through appreciative discernment.
Caused results are attainments through the power of the causes.
Owned results [which are exclusively] conditioned phenomena arise from non-hindering phenomena.
It is asserted that [results] are all conditioned phenomena, as well as the attainment of freedom,
And that the two unconditioned phenomena lack causes and results.
Developed [results] arise [from] the last [cause]; owned results from the first.
Results concordant with the cause [from] the third and fifth; caused [results] from the second and fourth.
Except for the productive cause, the five [other] causes are causal conditions.
Mind and mental factors producing results that arise immediately are immediate [conditions].
Phenomena suitable to be objects of the six consciousnesses are objective conditions.

Phenomena that do not obstruct arising are dominant conditions.
The arising, functioning, etc., [of conditions] can be learned from [Vasubandhu's] treatise.
Productive causes which produce [a result]; assisting, co-emergent [causes];
Expanding or same outcome [causes]; concomitant causes, sharing four factors;
Defiled omnipresent causes; developing causes of the body:
All may be categorized as productive causes,
Which the *Synthesis of Phenomenology* sets forth as twenty classes.
Causal conditions are the five causes and the fundamental consciousness.
The objective condition is the perceived object. The dominant condition is the support.
The immediate condition is asserted in the third way.
When four conditions are present, consciousness generates consciousness;
When there are two or three, consciousness produces coarse objects.
Freedom results are cessations without causes.
Owned results pertain to external phenomena.
Developed results pertain to the continuums of beings.
Caused results [arise from] creating causes; results concordant with causes [arise] from same outcome [causes].
Although cyclic life and actions do not exist ultimately,
Interdependent origination occurs superficially due to causes and conditions.
Thus, the wheel of twelve links continually turns.
Adherence to a self is the root of cyclic life.
Emotions produce actions and suffering.
These lead to [the cycle of suffering] which manifests like [dreams during] sleep.
The beginningless nature of mind is empty, clear, [and] unobstructed,

But its nature is not recognized.
[The fundamental consciousness], stirred by mental creations, produces dualistic appearances [and] the consciousnesses.
Feeling develops from acceptance and rejection; discernment, from objectification-habit.
[Discernment leads to] mental formations which are mental factors; habitual adherence creates form.
With attachment and grasping as a link, the wheel of existence turns.
In summation, three instincts imprinted on the fundamental consciousness
Cause three deceptive appearances: object, subject, and body.
The environmental world, the five objects such as form,
The eight consciousnesses, and virtuous and negative actions [develop from objective instincts].
[Adherence to] the forms of the six [types of] beings, and the object, agent, and action
Generate object and subject, which in turn produce emotions.
[Emotions] create cyclic life without beginning or end.
When the course of interdependent origination is reversed or its causes and conditions collapse from the inner core,
Deceptive [appearances] are exhausted and supreme liberation is attained.

* * *

The superior system of the Supreme Yoga is the culmination of all spiritual ways.
Six [claims] concerning the fundamental nature of the original ground are mistaken.
The correct [view is that the ground is] primordial purity, the common basis of both deception and freedom.
Two or three pristine wisdoms are inherent to the character [of the ground of being].

The spontaneity of the ground manifests as eight gates.
Three causes and four conditions [produce deception]: when the six cognitions arise,
The nature of the ground's manifestations is not realized; factors in groups of five [arise]
Based on subject and object. Through the course of the twelve links of interdependent origination, [the wheel] turns.
Object, body, and mind arise from the three bases of deception.
Mental, radiant, and material bodies develop in the three realms.
Womb-birth: from the penetrating, scattering, and equalizing [properties of the] elements,
The channels, syllables, energy-winds, and vital essences [form], and both the superficial and ultimate elements develop.
Through dependence on the former, the aggregates and so forth develop.
The latter serve as the cause of the four lamps which reveal the four visions.
Twenty-five elements generate the effulgence and creativity of pristine wisdom.
Buddha-nature pervades all sentient beings.
Its mode of appearance and mode of manifestation are taught in six sets of five.
Intrinsic awareness is present in the center of the heart, based on the three palaces.
The excellent vital essences abide in the four entrances of clear light.
The two eyes are the doors for the manifestation of external clarity;
[Depending on] objects and fulfilling crucial means, deception is ceased,
And one effortlessly attains the original place of freedom.

Prologue

Namaḥ śrīmāṃ-guru-mañjuśrī-nāthāya
[Reverence to the glorious spiritual master, the guide, Gentle Splendor!][1]

Glorious master, your profound and magnificent form is a treasury of abundant benefit for oneself and others.
[Your voice,] the drum of the highest doctrine,[2] resounds throughout space; [your] mind, bliss and emptiness, pervades all existence.
Source of oceans of the inconceivable qualities of enlightenment, your stream of awakened activity is effortless and spontaneous.
Sovereign of the Hundred Families,[3] remain forever as my crown, with your lotus feet touching my head.

Victorious One[4] who has attained the threefold greatness,[5] your symphony heralds the light of day,
Eliminates the darkness of the three worlds, and illuminates the path to liberation.
Lord of the doctrine, king of the doctrine, no one in the universe equals you;
Compassionate Sarvārthasiddha, with great devotion I revere you in thought, word, and deed.

Glorious Buddha born from a lotus, master of the miraculous powers of all the enlightened ones,
Embodiment of wisdom, your immortal form benefits [others] continually for as long as space exists;

Great bliss, adamantine speech, Padmākara[6] with your consort,
Even though I attain awakening, remain forever in the center of the beautiful lotus in my heart.

[Gentle Splendor], your name just falling upon one's ears topples the banners of a million hordes of demons;
Your resplendent sword of wisdom severs all webs of confusion with a single stroke.
Imparting with ease the brilliance of the two understandings,[7] you open the precious door to the ultimate good.
I bow to you, Gentle Splendor, and to your consort: grant me the supreme gift of flawless intelligence.

To the great pioneers appearing in the past, present, and future who illuminate the Buddha's teaching in India and Tibet,
And to those who uphold their instruction lineages,
To all without distinction, I bow a hundred times
With heartfelt devotion, free of all artifice.

Although my intelligence, narrow as the eye of a needle,
Cannot fathom the infinite depths of knowable phenomena,
I will elucidate this text, which summarizes the essential [points of knowledge],
So that those who share my good fortune may easily understand.

No one can estimate the furthest limits of infinite space and of phenomena;
Nevertheless, when a few essential points[8] have been revealed, the nature of all phenomena can be realized.
Thus, in a mere drop of water contained within the vase of an intelligent mind,
The wise taste the sublime flavor of the vast ocean of knowledge.

All [knowledge] verified by scriptural reference and
reason
Has been transmitted by authentic guides;
But since those of average intelligence may find it
difficult to comprehend,
I shall elucidate the meaning of this work through
commentary on its words.

To achieve liberation and omniscience, one must first traverse the ocean of learning. Then, through the wisdom derived from reflection and meditation, one will gradually and without difficulty attain unsurpassable awakening. This is the authentic path clearly revealed by the victorious ones and their heirs.[9]

In order that, at the very least, the entrance to this path may open easily to anyone whose intellect is as limited as mine, I will explain this treatise in three parts: the introduction, which provides the initial benefit of improving one's condition; the main body of the text, which has the subsequent benefit of leading one to freedom; and the conclusion, which has the final benefit of fulfilling the two objectives.[10]

Introduction

The introduction has three parts: (1) the presentation of the title [of the root verses] to describe this work as a whole and to explain its name; (2) expressions of reverence to ensure that obstacles to the composition of the commentary will not arise and that [the author] is known to be a follower of authentic teachers; and (3) the purpose of the composition and the author's resolve to complete it.

[I]
THE TITLE OF THE ROOT VERSES

This section has three parts: (1) presentation of the full title showing the correspondence between the two languages [Sanskrit and Tibetan]; (2) explanation of the meaning; and (3) elimination of doubts concerning the title.

[I.A]
The Title

> **In Sanskrit:** ***Yāna-sarva-mukhebhyaḥ samucchaya-pravacanaṃ ratna-kośa-tri-śikṣa-sudeśikā-śāstraṃ sarvajñeya-spharaṇa-nāma***

In the land known as White Expanse (India) because it is a vast land where the clothing is predominantly white, or Exalted Land because it is the land where the exalted Buddha appeared, there are four great language groups: Sanskrit (literally "perfected"), Prākṛit ("ordinary"), Apabhraṃśa ("corrupted"), and Piśāci ("demons'").[1] The title is rendered in the principal one among these, Sanskrit, the divine language.

In Tibetan: *Theg pa'i sgo thams cad las kun tu btus pa gsung rab rin po che'i mdzod bslab pa gsum legs par ston pa'i bstan bcos shes bya kun khyab zhes bya ba*

The Encompassment of All Knowledge: A treasury of precious teachings compiled from all the approaches of the systems for spiritual development, a treatise that effectively transmits the three trainings

Yāna (*theg pa*) means "system for spiritual development"; *sarva mukhebhyaḥ* (*sgo thams cad las*) means "from all approaches"; *samucchaya* (*kun tu btus pa*) means "compiled"; *pravacanaṃ* (*gsung rab*) means "teachings"; *ratna-kośa* (*rin po che'i mdzod*) means "precious treasury"; *tri-śikṣa* (*bslab pa gsum*) means "three trainings"[2]; *sudeśikā* (*legs par ston pa*) means "effectively transmits"; *śāstraṃ* (*bstan bcos*) means "treatise"; *sarvajñeya* (*shes bya kun nam thams cad*) means "all knowledge"; *spharaṇa* (*khyab*) or (*'phro ba*) means "encompass" or "unfold"; *nāma* (*zhes bya ba*) means "thus titled."[3]

[I.B]
The Title's Meaning

This section has three parts: (1) an explanation of the title's literal meaning; (2) fulfillment of five essential observations; and (3) identification of the style of the commentary, *The Infinite Ocean of Knowledge*.

[I.B.1]
The Title's Literal Meaning

With regard to its structure, *The Encompassment of All Knowledge* is a *compilation* of the essentials *from all* treatises that present the distinct *systems* for spiritual development of gods and humans and the Buddha's three- or nine-stage *system*.[4] [In the title,] *approaches* refers to these systems.

In nature, *The Encompassment of All Knowledge* is a comprehensive collection of the most important explanations from the Transcendent One's own *teachings* and from the treatises commenting on them. Therefore, this work is called *treasury* because those precious teachings are contained within it, or because this [treasury] is inherent within [those teachings].

In character, this *treatise*[5] clearly, thoroughly, and *effectively transmits the three trainings* of higher ethics, meditation, and wisdom. It has the qualities that enable one to overcome the enemy of emotions, and to protect oneself from [rebirth in] miserable existences. It is distinct from the six [types of] flawed treatises and possesses the qualities of the three [types of] valid treatises.[6]

These latter words, "*treatise that effectively transmits the three trainings*," refer principally to the subject matter [of the work].

Just as space makes it possible for an observer to discern objects, the contents of this treatise make it possible for the intellect to discern all objects of knowledge. Therefore, the contents are *an encompassment of all knowledge*. Alternatively, just as space is the medium through which the universe and beings unfold, this [work] allows the three kinds of wisdom[7] to *unfold*.

This [part of the title] refers principally to [the words] that convey the contents.

[I.B.2]
The Five Essential Observations

The resident scholars of Vikramaśīla Monastery[8] expounded treatises by making five kinds of essential observations:

(1) Who the author [of the treatise] is
(2) What its scriptural sources are
(3) How it is classified
(4) For whose benefit it is written
(5) What the import of the work as a whole is

These observations may be made with regard to the present work. First, the identity of the author is stated at the end of the work; in the colophon, his various names are stated. The second is explained by [the words of the title,] *compiled from the approaches of all the systems of spiritual development*. The third is indicated by [the words] *a treasury of precious teachings*.

Fourth, there are two [possible motivations for composing such a work]: to benefit oneself or to benefit others. I have not composed this work in response to others' requests. Instead, I have been motivated by the noblest intention to benefit others and by [the wish] to refine my own understanding of all knowledge. This is implied by the words, *the encompassment of all knowledge*. Fifth, the nature of the content is conveyed by the words *the treatise that effectively transmits the three trainings*.

[I.B.3]
The Style of the Commentary, The Infinite Ocean of Knowledge

A treatise may be classified [as one of] two kinds of commentary on the words of the Buddha: general or specific. Since this work encompasses all fields of knowledge, it should be regarded as a general commentary.

[I.C]
Elimination of Doubts Concerning the Title

One might question whether it is logical to give a Sanskrit title to a Tibetan treatise because it is not a translation from that language. However, there is no fault in doing so. Such a title is both logical and meaningful because this work is based on the teachings of the Buddha and commentaries originating in India. This is comparable to calling Indian a person who is ethnically Indian but has been born in Tibet.

In doing so, I have imitated the works of the Tibetan scholar Thumi, the writings of the sagacious Longchenpa, and others. Although this is like a firefly [trying to] imitate the sun, there is no wrong in my wish to emulate [these masters] because my intention is pure.

[II]
EXPRESSIONS OF REVERENCE

This section has four parts: (1) reverence to the illustrious spiritual master, composed in Sanskrit; (2) reverence to the Lord of Sages (Buddha Śākyamuni), based on the three trainings; (3) praise and supplication for the fulfillment of my wishes to the Lion of Speech (Mañjuśrī), based on the path of the perfections[9]; and (4) bowing with devotion to the master and the lineage, based on the stages of the Secret Mantra path.[10]

[II.A]
Reverence to the Illustrious Spiritual Master

Namaḥ śrīmāṃ-sad-guru-pādāya

This reverence, in Tibetan *dPal ldan bla ma dam pa'i zhabs la phyag tsal lo*, means "I bow at the feet of the illustrious[11] and genuine master."

There are two parts [to the discussion of these words of reverence]: (1) their context, and (2) an explanation of their meaning.

[II.A.1]
Context

Appropriate circumstances for expressing reverence include to serve a purpose, for a [particular] reason, to resolve contradictory opinions, to respond to a question, and so forth. These words of reverence are written to serve a particular purpose.

The explanation of the purpose served by this reverence is based on the [words] "I bow at the feet." To whom is reverence expressed? It is expressed to the illustrious and genuine master who embodies the perfection of all refuges. Who is expressing reverence? The author of the treatise is expressing reverence with great devotion in thought, word, and deed. What is the purpose of expressing reverence? Those who read the praise of such a unique individual will develop faith in that person. Furthermore, discerning readers will first develop confidence in the person who expresses such respect, because by doing so, he is following [the example of] authentic masters. Consequently, they will consider the treatise composed by this person worth studying and will do so. The expression of reverence serves the additional purposes of completing the cultivation of merit and pristine wisdom and of preventing interruptions to the completion of the composition. At what point in the treatise is reverence expressed? It is expressed at the beginning of the composition. In what way is reverence expressed? With great devotion in thought, word, and deed.

[II.A.2]

The Meaning of the Words of Reverence

Śrī means "glory," signifying both non-dual pristine wisdom and the [spiritual master] who should be relied upon. Grounded in the [experience of the union of] emptiness and appearance, the master has travelled the path, using skillful means and wisdom. As a result, he or she "possesses" (*-mant*) the fruition [of the path], the unity of pristine wisdom and the dimensions of awakening, and leads disciples to the same attainment. Master in [Sanskrit] is *guru*, which means laden with good qualities, and *uttara*, [which means] "highest."

The [Sanskrit] word *sat* has many meanings, but in this case denotes "genuine." Since this signifies perfection, [it describes] one who is master of masters. From the *King of Tantras*[12]:

> An illustrious master is one in whose mind and speech the face of the Buddha is present.

The Buddha [referred to in this quote] is Wheel of Time (Kālacakra). His four faces symbolize the four successive empowerments, the fourth of which is the co-emergent pristine wisdom [empowerment]. One who embodies this wisdom is known as an illustrious master since he or she has realized it and reveals it to disciples through speech.

The above words of reverence are addressed to my own spiritual master from whom I have obtained a measure of his kindness [through receiving such instruction]. The words *at the feet* indicate that I bow [before him] and show reverence with heartfelt devotion.

[II.B]

Reverence to the Lord of Sages, Buddha Śākyamuni

> **[Embodiment] of complete purity and ethics, you stand firm like the golden foundation.**
> **Your beauty reflects your countless contemplations, like the distinct features of the mountains and continents.**
> **Like the sun and moon, your brilliant wisdom illuminates all phenomena.**
> **Supreme sage and achiever of all goals, I revere you.**

Completely purified of all the faults of worldly and inferior spiritual ways, you are the embodiment of the ethics of the three disciplines[13] and stand firm as the basis for all good qualities, like the golden foundation of the universe.

Transcending all mental states that exist from the peak of existence downward, you are the embodiment of incalculable contemplations,[14] such as the contemplation that develops courage. Your beauty is a reflection of these contemplations, distinct like the features of [the universe], Mount Meru, the four continents and their islands.

With unmistaken understanding of the general and specific characteristics [of phenomena], you are the embodiment of wisdom, whose realization has penetrated the two kinds of selflessness.[15] You illuminate all phenomena as they are and as they appear, like the brilliance of the sun and moon illuminating the world.

Unrivalled in any way by anyone renowned in the world as a sage, such as Kapila,[16] you are the supreme embodiment of complete liberation, perfect peace without remainder.[17]

Perfected in the four pristine wisdoms,[18] you are the embodiment of the vision of the pristine wisdom of complete liberation. Thus you fulfill your enlightened intentions for the benefit of those to be spiritually transformed in this age of conflict.[19] Recalling your kindness, I revere you with sincere devotion.

These words of reverence explicitly present the three types of training that constitute the principal qualities of a buddha, along with a subsidiary explanation of the five [aspects of] the embodiment of complete purity and a summary of the contents of this treatise.

The three types of training are common denominators in the three systems of spiritual development. The sequence of the three trainings in the words of reverence above corresponds to the tradition most accessible to ordinary people, that of the proclaimers.[20] Therefore, it would have been appropriate for me to compose the commentary, *The Infinite Ocean of Knowledge,* based on this tradition.[21] [However, my commentary presents the trainings] in the sequence followed by the Buddha's Way [the Universal Way].[22]

[II.C]

Praise and Supplication to the Lion of Speech, Mañjuśrī

With the heart of a great hero who protects beings for as long as they exist,
You suffused the universe with your excellent conduct.
Though father to the victorious ones, you manifest as the victorious ones' son.
Lion of Speech, grant me flawless intelligence.

First, you developed the mind of supreme awakening, the excellent seed [of enlightenment]. Of the three ways[23] to accomplish this, you chose the path of the shepherd, the awakening mind of [bodhisattvas of] the highest capacity. With this attitude, you protect beings with compassion for as long as they exist, forfeiting your own buddhahood. While on the path, the power of your mind, great as that of a peerless hero, suffused the universe with an ocean of excellent conduct, such as the ten perfections,[24] which no other bodhisattva[25] can match, even partly. As the result [of the path], you are father to all the victorious ones, for you were perfectly awakened from the very beginning. Neverthless, you now appear as the youthful son of the Victorious Ones, working for the benefit of others without weariness or woe, until cyclic existence has ceased.

Gentle Splendor, Lion of Speech, grant me and all who hear or teach the doctrine perfect memory and intelligence free from the flaws of attachment and impediment.[26]

This praise mentions briefly the import of the perfections of the Universal Way.

[II.D]

Bowing to the Master and the Lineage

You nurture the seed — the potential or nature of beings — by imparting instructions that mature and liberate them.
You cause others to purify incidental defilements through the twofold path,
And bestow the fruition, the four dimensions of awakening distinguished by great bliss.
To you, my mentor, and to the masters of the lineages, I bow.

> You understand that the ground continuity [for spiritual development]—the potential for awakening and the radiant awareness nature of mind—is naturally present, like a seed, in every sentient being. Thus, you bestow the empowerments that bring them to spiritual maturity and impart the instructions that liberate them. In these distinctive ways, you nurture their [potential] for freedom.
>
> You cause others to attain the realizations of the path through [their practice of] the two phases of creation and completion, the path continuity. Consequently, they purify all their incidental defilements—experienced, but without intrinsic reality—of emotions, cognitive obscurations, and [the obscuration to] transition.[27]
>
> You bestow or cause others to attain in their present lifetimes the fruition continuity, the four dimensions of awakening[28] distinguished by great bliss.
>
> To you, master of indestructible reality, my principal mentor and spiritual guide who is kind in these three ways, and to the masters of the lineages of the three disciplines, I bow with heartfelt devotion.

This [homage] presents all the stages of the path of the Way of Indestructible Reality.

[III]
THE AUTHOR'S RESOLVE TO COMPLETE THIS WORK

This section has two parts: (1) the main discussion; and (2) a supplementary discussion of the four components [necessary for composing a treatise], purpose, etc.

[IIIA]
Main Discussion

> **Although I lack the intellectual capacity to compile knowledge correctly,**
> **I shall compose a short, clear, comprehensive work**
> **In order to ensure that those with insufficient knowledge or interest to understand the texts**
> **Will not lose their opportunity on this isle of treasures.**

> I lack both the natural and acquired wisdom gained from learning, reflection, and meditation, and I do not have even the slightest fraction of the intellectual capacity [required to]

compile correctly the vastness of knowledge. Therefore, I am not worthy to compose this work. Nevertheless, individuals debased by these degenerate times have resorted to corrupt forms of livelihood, using the Three Jewels[29] for their own ends, and have little knowledge or diligence. Seeing this, I have been motivated by the noble intention to benefit myself and others, who like me have neither sufficient good fortune nor power of intelligence to comprehend even minor texts,[30] let alone the voluminous scriptures of the Buddha.

Due to good propensities developed in the past, we have landed on this treasure-island of precious discourses and tantras. To ensure that not even a fraction of this opportunity to understand, experience, and realize be lost, I hereby resolve to compose a short explanatory text on a vast subject. It will be clear because the words and their meanings will be easy to understand. In only a few verses, I will discuss exhaustively all fields of knowledge.

[IIIB]
The Four Components Necessary for Composing a Treatise

The master Vasubandhu instructed [his students] to include five elements when composing a treatise. [As stated in his *Principles of Elucidation*][31]:

> The following should be expressed:
> The purpose, a synopsis,
> An explanation, connections,
> And counter-arguments.

The first element presented should be the purpose of the treatise. A synopsis should then summarize what fulfills that purpose, while the explanation itself presents in detail the meaning of [what is summarized in] the synopsis. The connections, which should not contradict the sequence [of the subjects], and counter-arguments, which should not contradict reason, are discussed wherever appropriate.

For the first of these, [purpose, Vasubandhu presented] an elaborate analysis of the purpose, the connections, [etc.,] in which each of the four points are divided into three parts. Presented here is a condensation of this [twelve-part] scheme into four [main components (subject matter, purpose, ultimate purpose, and connections) applied to this work]:

First is the subject matter: This treatise [presents] a comprehensive description of the realms where those to be spiritually guided live; their guide, the Buddha, and his teaching; the fields that constitute the progressive practice of the [Buddha's] teachings—ethics, learning, reflection, and meditation; and the complete fruition of travelling the path, the achievement of freedom.

Second is the purpose: By studying and expounding these subjects, one becomes well-versed in them. This education results in the wisdom that allows one to understand the levels of the Buddha's teachings and his systems for spiritual development. This understanding in turn facilitates the development of the authentic wisdom born from reflection and meditation.

Third is the ultimate purpose: Through this [wisdom], one easily attains the state of freedom and omniscience.

Fourth are the connections: The ultimate purpose is connected with the purpose, and the purpose with the subject matter. Each is related in turn to that which precedes it.

Overview of *The Infinite Ocean of Knowledge*

This treatise [*The Infinite Ocean of Knowledge*] as a whole has [ten] divisions, equal in number to the ten perfections:
The realms that appear during the age of illumination; Buddha, the Teacher; the doctrine, both scriptural and experiential;
Its continuation and spread in the Land of Jambu;
Maintaining ethical conduct; learning; reflection; meditation;
Through successively engaging in these, progression through the paths; and realization of the ultimate result.

The body of the treatise [*The Infinite Ocean of Knowledge*] has [ten] integral divisions, to be equal in number to the ten perfections:

Book I. The realms that appear during the Fortunate Age of Illumination, the precondition for the arising of the precious Jewels [of Buddhism]

Book II. Advent of Buddha the Teacher, the principal Jewel, who transforms beings within those realms

Book III. Origin of the [Buddha's] doctrine, both the scriptural and experiential aspects of his cycles of teaching

Book IV. Extent of the spread and flourishing of the doctrine in this supreme Land of Jambu

Book V. Training in and maintaining of the ethical systems of personal liberation, of awakening mind, and of mantra, these being the initial stages of spiritual practice while the Buddha's doctrine remains in the world

Book VI. Elimination of misconceptions through learning, after having taken these systems of ethics as the basis of practice

Book VII. Ascertainment of the doctrine through reflection

Book VIII. Verification of the doctrine through meditation

Book IX. Complete progression through the stages and paths of spiritual development by successively engaging in [ethical conduct, learning, reflection, and meditation]

Book X. Realization of the ultimate result, liberation and omniscience

The brief overview of the work [*The Infinite Ocean of Knowledge*] includes four points: the subject of each division, the specification of number, the order, and a synopsis.

The first, [the subject of each division,] will be explained extensively in the individual chapters of the divisions which follow.

Second, the fields of knowledge that should be known by novices — those unfamiliar with these subjects — are presented in ten divisions within this work. These are enhanced by a structure of four chapters each. The number is specific because more [chapters are] unnecessary, and fewer would not be comprehensive.

Third, the justification for such a systematic order is [evident in the enumeration of the books] as outlined above.

Fourth, these forty chapters together comprise an explanation of the three trainings. Training in higher ethics is explained by the fifth division; training in wisdom, by the sixth and seventh; and training in meditation, principally by the eighth. The first through the fourth divisions are branches of training in wisdom. The ninth and tenth are related to the eighth division because [their subjects] are derived from the perfection of [meditation].

Therefore, [it is fitting] that this [work] be called "a treatise that effectively transmits the three trainings."

Myriad Worlds

Chapter I
The Cosmology of the Universal Way

This chapter has two main sections: (1) an explanation of the causes and conditions that create the [realms of existence], and (2) a presentation of the arrangement of the realms.

[I]
THE CAUSES AND CONDITIONS THAT CREATE THE REALMS OF EXISTENCE

This section has two parts: (1) a concise presentation, and (2) an extensive explanation.

[I.A]
Concise Presentation

> **There are general and specific causes and conditions that initiate [the creation of realms]:**

Oceans of realms have arisen from the relationships between those to be guided to enlightenment [sentient beings], and the enlightened guides [the buddhas]. The general and specific causes and conditions for the initial creation of [these] realms [are explained below].

[I.B]
Extensive Explanation

This section has two parts: (1) a general presentation of the relationships between those to be guided and the enlightened guides, and (2) a discussion of the particular causes and conditions from which realms arise.

[I.B.1]

The Relationships Between Those to be Guided and the Enlightened Guides

For as long as infinite space and sentient beings exist,
The compassion of the victorious ones and the actions of sentient beings continue without end.
Those to be guided and enlightened guides
Manifest through inconceivable interconnections.
When the characters and dispositions of those to be guided are activated,
[The compassion of] the guides [arises], and the configurations of the realms and the dimensions of awakening appear;
The miraculous methods of guiding others manifest beyond all bounds.

For as long as infinite space and the countless dispositions of sentient beings exist, the compassionate strength of the victorious ones [buddhas] and the actions and emotions of beings will never end. The [variety of] characters and dispositions of beings (those to be guided to enlightenment) and the expressions of the compassion of buddhas (those who guide them) manifest fully due to the inconceivable power of natural interconnections.

By way of explanation, sentient beings [are unaware[1] of the pure nature] of the [mind's] sphere of reality.[2] Consequently, their characters and dispositions [begin to manifest]. That is to say, instinctive unawareness acts as the principal cause and adventitious conceptualization as the contributing factor in activating the propensities of beings. Craving and grasping cause beings to form a connection with the three realms.[3]

The compassion of buddhas arises in response to this: inconceivable configurations of realms and the dimensions of awakening within those realms manifest spontaneously and effortlessly. The [buddhas'] methods of guiding beings, such as the four great miracles[4] perceived by all, arise in an immeasurable and inconceivable display.

[I.B.2]
Particular Causes and Conditions

> **The sphere of reality never changes into something else;**
> **Yet blessings, vows, actions, and natural laws**
> **Cause oceans of realms to appear.**

The sphere of reality, the sphere of vision of each of the joyful ones,[5] completely transcends the limited domain of thought, expression, etc., and can be neither measured nor located. It never becomes anything other than itself, even to the slightest degree, nor is it affected by any other substance. At the same time, various causes and conditions — the blessings of the transcendent ones,[6] the extraordinary vows made by bodhisattvas to purify realms, the convergence of sentient beings' multitudinous actions, and natural law — cause oceans of realms to appear. The *Flower Ornament Scripture*[7] states:

> The boundless oceans of realms that I have described
> Have been purified by the Illuminator's own qualities.
> This buddha's world of pristine wisdom is inconceivable,
> As are his blessings and miraculous displays.
>
> The bodhisattvas' inconceivable oceans of vows,
> Cultivated in response to the inclinations of [beings],
> And the inconceivable oceans of beings' actions
> Cause oceans of realms to manifest in all directions.
>
> The miraculous powers of the bodhisattvas
> And their intention to attain omniscience
> Cause their oceans of vows to reach fulfillment
> And limitless realms to appear throughout infinite space.
>
> While cultivating boundless oceans of excellent conduct,
> [Bodhisattvas] enter the infinite sphere of the joyful ones.
> They spend endless eons in each realm
> And purify all oceans of realms in all directions.
> Actions generated by the inconceivable range of beings' mentalities
> Cause oceans of realms to arise.

[II]
THE ARRANGEMENT OF THE REALMS

This section has three parts: (1) a presentation of the realm called Richly Adorned; (2) a detailed explanation of the realm called Flower-Filled World; and (3) a description of the distinctive features of our own world-system, known as Endurance.

[II.A]
The Richly Adorned Realm

This section has two parts: (1) a general description of the realm Richly Adorned, and (2) a description of the distinctive features of the realms within Richly Adorned.

[II.A.1]
A Description of Richly Adorned

The realm Unsurpassed is free from incidental defilement
And transcends the experience of the three realms: it is indivisible pristine wisdom.
In this self-manifesting, spontaneously appearing [realm,] Richly Adorned,
Dwells Illuminator, Great Glacial Lake of Wisdom;
A billion realms in his every pore.

Enlightenment is attained when the naturally pure sphere of reality [of the mind] is freed of adventitious defilement, and the sphere of reality becomes inseparable from pristine wisdom. The place where this occurs is called Unsurpassed.[8] It is not limited to any one place or direction, just as the images of one's dream are experienced wherever one falls asleep.

The "Unsurpassed" place of enlightenment is not part of the confused, habitual experience of unenlightened beings, but transcends [everything experienced] in the three realms. This natural expression [of enlightenment] is a pure realm and has a celestial palace of pristine wisdom, without direction or division, adorned with an endless array of ornaments. Clouds of offerings and adornments of complete enjoyment appear naturally and fill all space.

In this place so "richly adorned" dwells the expression of the effortless complete enjoyment of all buddhas, known as Illuminator, Appearing Everywhere, Great Glacial Lake of Wisdom. Each pore of his body contains hundreds of billions of realms, not to mention the infinite oceans of realms that exist within his whole body. Moreover, realms as numerous as the atoms in the [entire] realm appear within each atom [of each realm]. Infinite oceans of [Illuminator's] forms appear within his one form. Each form appears as though it were pervading all of the infinite oceans of his forms and realms. This exists by virtue of a great miracle that transcends the sphere of [ordinary] experience. [The *Prayer for Excellence*[9]] states:

> In as little as [the space of] a hair-breadth in every region without exception,
> Rest oceans of buddhas and oceans of realms,
> As many as exist throughout all time.
> As I engage in [excellent] conduct for an ocean of eons, I resolve to enter them all!

[II.A.2]

The Distinctive Features of the Realms within Richly Adorned

> **Their locations, shapes, sizes, durations, and arrangements are inconceivable.**

First, distinctions according to location [and configuration]: The *Flower Ornament Scripture*[10] states:

> Some oceans of realms of pure light rest within the infinity of space;
> Others have a luminous nature and rest in oceans of jewels.

Further:

> Many oceans of realms exceed all boundaries and rest in a vast sea of lotuses.

Further:

> Vast oceans of realms rest within the buddhas' blessing.

The existence of these realms depends upon the four elements, the actions of sentient beings, the blessings of the buddhas, and so forth. These realms appear in a variety of configurations such as intersecting, upside-down, and right-side-up.

Second, distinctions according to shape[11] :

> Some realms are round, some are triangular,
> Some appear square,

> Some are [shaped like] eight-spoked wheels, jewels, or lotuses;
> All are designed by the oceans of actions [of beings].

Third, [distinctions according to] size:

> Each of the ten world-systems from Saffron Banner up to Resplendent Lotus increases in size and qualities by factors of ten. [Certain realms] that are manifesting now, such as Delightful[12] and Blissful,[13] are vast, whereas our own realm, Endurance, and even more so Thumb-Size[14] (the realm of the buddha called Delight in Stars), and other [realms], are extremely small. The realm of All-Seeing Guide that will manifest in the future, Pure Cluster, will be immeasurably vast. There are many [descriptions] such as these.

Fourth, [distinctions according to] duration[15]:

> Some realms [endure] for just an eon,
> Some for ten eons,
> Some realms are said [to endure
> For] ten million eons times the number of their particles.

Fifth, distinctions according to the arrangements of the decorations[16]:

> Some realms are richly embellished
> With the millions of realm-adornments.
> These diversified ornaments of various styles
> Appear as myriad optical illusions.

Some distinctions according to the presence of buddhas are expressed in these words[17]:

> In some realms, there are no buddhas;
> In some realms, there are buddhas;
> In some realms, there is one buddha;
> In some, many buddhas.

[Concerning distinctions according to] light,[18]

> In some realms, there is no light.

Beginning with this reference to realms that are dark, fearsome, and terrifying, there follows[19]:

> In some, the light of the gods,

Similarly,[20] [some realms are illuminated by]

> ... the light of palaces,
> ... the light of the sun and moon,

> ... natural light, light of trees,
> ... light of mountains,
> ... light of jewels,
> ... light of lamps,
> ... light of buddhas.

Further[21]

> In some realms, there is the light of lotuses.

And:

> In [others], the light of fragrant waters.

And:

> These realms have been purified through the power of bodhisattvas' vows.

Whether or not [a world-system] comprises four continents forms another distinction. Our own third-order thousand world-system[22] is divided into many four-continent [world-systems], whereas Blissful, as well as some other realms, are flat like the palm of a hand. Among those that comprise [four continents], there are many different sizes [of continents].

There are also distinctions regarding enjoyment. In Truly Joyous, for instance, the gods wish to be human. The massive mountain [that forms the axis of a four-continent world-system] can differ [from one realm to another]. Differences also exist in the forms of life: some beings have emotions, while others embody purity, and so on. Worlds exist in an inconceivable variety of ways.

[II.B]
The Flower-Filled World

This section has two parts: (1) an overall explanation, and (2) a detailed explanation.

[II.B.1]
Overall Explanation

> **Within the central minute particle in the palm of his hand lies the Oceanic World-System**
> **That itself contains many world-systems, in the center of which**
> **Lies the realm called Flower-Filled World.**

Within the single minute particle in the very center of the palm of the hand of [the Buddha] Illuminator, Great Glacial Lake of Wisdom, lies the Oceanic World-System which rests in the center of the Enlightened One's palm. Furthermore, Great Glacial Lake of Wisdom himself manifests throughout this world-system as an enlightened teacher. The magnitude of this inconceivable place is the sphere of experience solely of buddhas and bodhisattvas who dwell on the [three] higher stages [of awakening].

Numerous world-systems are found within the Oceanic World-System. In the center of these lies Flower-Filled World,[23] the realm of the manifest dimension of awakening of Buddha Illuminator.

[II.B.2]
Detailed Explanation

> **Furthermore, [between the wind] and Unsurpassed lie one billion four-continent world-systems,**
> **A great third-order thousand [world-system].**
> **Multiplying that by factors of one billion**
> **[Yields] Infinite Links, Continuums, Oceans,**
> **And Flower-Filled World.**
> **Each rests on an ocean and [is encircled by] an outer rim.**
> **This is the sphere of influence of one supreme manifest dimension of awakening.**

The extent of the realm Flower-Filled World is determined in the following way:

First of all, the area that includes the four continents, Mount Meru, and the outer rim of mountains — everything from the underlying configuration of wind[24] up to Unsurpassed, the peak of existence — is referred to as a four-continent world-system. An identical world-system is located in space at a distance of one thousand times the magnitude of that world-system. A total of one thousand such world-systems [evenly distributed in space], encircled by a rim, is referred to as a first-order thousand world-system. This considered as a single unit, replicated one thousand times and surrounded by a perimeter, is referred to as a second-order thousand world-system. One thousand [second-order thousand world-systems] enclosed by a great rim is called a third-order thousand world-system. Thus, one billion four-continent world-systems is called one great thousand third-order thousand world-system.

(Although teachers of phenomenology[25] base their calculations on the area from the heaven [called] The Pure downwards, the description given here is based on the *Marvellous Life of the Buddha*, the *Pure Golden Light Scripture*, and other sources.)

The total number of world-systems comprising one Flower-Filled World is calculated by progressively multiplying by factors of one billion: One billion great thousand third-order thousand world-systems constitutes the world-system Infinite Links. A billion of those is the world-system Infinite Continuums. A billion of those is the world-system Oceanic Infinity. One billion of those is the extent of one Flower-Filled World. Each world-system rests on its own great ocean and is encircled by a rim. At the same time, one great rim encircles them all.

One [arrangement] of such dimension constitutes the sphere of influence of a single supreme manifest dimension of awakening. To those of limited intelligence, [the sphere of influence] is taught to be only a third-order thousand world-system.

[II.C]
Distinctive Features of Our Own World-System, Endurance

This section has two parts: (1) identification of Endurance, and (2) a supplementary explanation.

[I.C.1]
Identification of Endurance

> **Inside the great outer rim, within seas of scented waters,**
> **Four jewelled lotuses support**
> **A tiered arrangement of twenty-five world-systems;**
> **The thirteenth is known as Endurance.**

Within the great outer rim of that [arrangement of one] Flower-Filled World are the indescribable oceans of fragrant waters [descending from] the body of Great Glacial Lake, as numerous as the particles in all the buddha realms. In the center of these oceans are seas of scented waters filled with beautiful anthers on which rest four immense jewelled lotuses.

A tiered arrangement of twenty-five world-systems is supported by these [lotuses]. In the spaces between each [of these world-systems] are infinite tiers of world-systems, which define their boundaries. The thirteenth of these [twenty-five world-systems] is our own third-order thousand world-system, known as Endurance.

The Sanskrit term for Endurance is *sahā*, which denotes possession, forbearance, or capacity. All sentient beings who have taken birth in this realm endure emotions and sufferings. In other words, beings possess these [afflictions] in great measure. "Endurance" also signifies the forbearance of hardship. The bodhisattvas of this realm patiently endure [hardship] with exceptional courage and excel in bravery. Thus, this realm is known as Endurance.

[I.C.2]
The Supplementary Explanation

> **This third-order thousand world-system**
> **Is completely encircled by realms — Covered, Surpassing, Stainless, Variously Emerged, etc. —**
> **Equal in number to the particles of this thirteenth world-system.**
> **[Endurance] is spherical, has a four-vajra demarcation,**
> **And rests on a multicolored configuration of wind and a network of lotuses.**

This third-order thousand world-system of Endurance alone is encircled by buddha realms equal in number to the particles of this thirteenth world-system. To the east is Covered; to the south, Surpassing; to the west, Stainless; and to the north, Variously Emerged. In the intermediate directions are Benefitting, Variously Appeared, Complete Joy, and Activator. Above and below are found Resounding Melody, Not Great, and others. Endurance is spherical and has a four-vajra boundary demarcation. It is supported by a multicolored configuration of wind and rests on a network of lotuses.

> **Illuminator, the teacher in this [world-system],**
> **Appears throughout the Unsurpassed realms of the pure domains.**

The enlightened teacher in our third-order thousand world-system [Endurance] is an emanation of the enjoyment dimension of awakening, the great Illuminator. This is a single form whose vast emanations appear throughout all the Unsurpassed realms in the pure domains and teach the Dharma in the midst of all the powerful [bodhisattvas].[26] The Centrist scholar Dharmamitra explains[27]:

> This form, differentiated [from others] by vows, the power of cultivation [of merit and pristine wisdom], and intention, has attained complete enlightenment in one Unsurpassed domain alone. Therefore, the myriad forms of the enjoyment dimension of awakening that dwell in all the [other] Unsurpassed realms are solely his apparition manifesting in a vast [display].[28]

> **This four-continent [world-system] called Destructible**
> **Is surrounded by ten other four-continent [world-systems].**

Our four-continent world-system, which is situated in the center of Endurance, is known as Destructible. It is said that even this [world-system] alone is surrounded by ten other satellite four-continent world-systems. Beginning from the East, these are, respectively, Well Protected, Joyful, Unbearable, Excellent Essence, Befriended, Fine Land, Lion Inhabited, Well Formed. Above is Bearing Wealth, and below, Radiant Light.

> **It is taught that these [world-systems] are formed and destroyed together;**
> **This is the experiential domain solely of the lords of the tenth stage of awakening.**

The view most widely shared by Buddhist systems is that [the worlds within] any single third-order thousand world-system are formed together and destroyed [together]. Another view states that all the realms of the emanations of a single supreme manifest dimension of awakening (such as the oceans of realms that are located in the Flower-Filled World) are formed and destroyed together. The magnitude of this latter view is unfathomable to proclaimers and others; it remains the domain of experience solely of the lord [bodhisattvas] of the tenth stage [of awakening].

Chapter II

Our Universe according to the Individual and Universal Ways

The second chapter, an explication of our universe, the world-system known as Endurance, has two parts: (1) a preamble, and (2) an extensive presentation.

[I] THE PREAMBLE

In our own world-system, four [ages] occur: formation, abiding, destruction, and vacuity.

Our own world-system, composed of four continents, is subject to four great ages: the age of formation, the age of abiding, the age of destruction, and the age of vacuity.[1]

[II] THE EXTENSIVE PRESENTATION

This section has three parts: (1) the age of the initial formation of our world-system, (2) the age of its interim abiding, and (3) the ages of its final destruction and vacuity.

[II.A] The Age of the Initial Formation of our World-System

Of the two, environment and inhabitants, [a description of] the environmental world [is presented first]:

The lands that appear when four ages occur have both environment and inhabitants; of these two, the environment is described first.

The discussion of the initial formation of our world-system has two parts: (1) a description of the environment, and (2) a description of the inhabitants.

[II.A.1]
The Environment

This section has two parts: (1) the main explanation, and (2) a supplementary discussion of the viewpoint of the proclaimers and solitary sages.[2] [The main explanation] has five parts: (1) the origin of the Fortunate Age, (2) the arrangement of the mountains and continents, (3) the meanings of the names of the continents, (4) [descriptions of] the three miserable realms and the demi-gods' realm, and (5) the realm of the gods.

[II.A.1.a.i]
The Origin of the Fortunate Age

After the age of vacuity had elapsed at the end of the previous age,
Winds arose from the ten directions, creating a configuration in the shape of a cross;
Rain fell from a cloud, and amidst a mass of water,
A thousand lotuses were seen; thus the Fortunate Age was proclaimed.

The collective actions of beings and the power of the vows to purify realms[3] made by the bodhisattvas of the present Fortunate Age produced the following sequence of events:

After the previous age had reached completion and the twenty intermediate ages [that constitute] the age of vacuity had elapsed, winds arose from each of the ten directions.[4] The powerful convergence and compression of these winds created a configuration of wind in the shape of a cross — solid, extremely hard, and indestructible. In the space above the wind, a thick cloud resembling a golden yoke formed. From this cloud, rain fell continuously over a long period of time. The size of raindrops ranged from large [ones to raindrops as big as the diameter of] the main shaft of a chariot. This deluge produced an immense mass of water, supported by the wind. At the center of this great ocean, a thousand golden lotuses appeared. Upon seeing this, the gods and goddesses of the pure domains[5] knew it to be a sign that one thousand buddhas would appear, and so they declared: "How wonderful! This is the dawn of the Fortunate Age!" According to the *White Lotus of Compassion Scripture*, this age is known as a fortunate one because the gods and goddesses made this announcement. Similarly, the *Blossomed Wisdom Scripture* refers to this age as "the age when one thousand lotuses are seen."

[II.A.1.a.ii]
Arrangement of the Mountains and Continents

The churning of water by wind produced a golden disc,
Upon which rain fell; [this became] the great ocean.
The churning by wind developed the [ocean's] elements — superior, medium, and base;
These elements formed Mount Meru, the seven mountain ranges, the four continents and the outer rim.

The churning of the great mass of water by the wind produced a golden foundation[6] above the water while rain continued to fall uninterruptedly. As a result, a great outer ocean [which contained various elements] formed above the golden disc. Intense churning of the ocean by winds [arising from] various directions gradually developed the three grades of elements—superior, medium, and base. The superior elements became the central, massive Mount Meru, which is made of four precious substances. The elements of medium quality formed the seven ranges of golden mountains. The base elements formed the four continents, surrounded by the eight neighboring islands and many other islands, as well as the outer rim of iron mountains.

On this subject, the master Vasubandhu explains in detail that the waters [of the ocean] contained only various potentials for the elements, [not the actual elements]. When these seeds were driven apart by winds with special agencies, the different types [of elements] were produced.

The mountains and continents all extend eighty thousand [leagues] down into the ocean.
Mount Meru rises eighty thousand [leagues] above the ocean.

The base of Mount Meru and the bases of each of the seven mountain [ranges], the four continents, and the outer rim [of mountains] extend eighty thousand leagues[7] below the ocean's surface and rest on [the golden disc called] Mighty. Mount Meru rises eighty thousand leagues above the surface of the ocean.

The four sides of Mount Meru are composed of crystal, blue beryl, ruby, and gold.
The sky [on each side] reflects these colors.
From sea level to half its height are four terraces.

[Viewed from above,] Mount Meru is square, with four square slabs [of decreasing size in ascending order]. The eastern face of Mount Meru is composed of crystal; the southern, blue beryl; the western, ruby; and the northern, gold. The color of each face is clearly reflected in the sky around it. Four [square] slabs form four tiers of terraces around Mount Meru, beginning at sea level and reaching halfway up its height.

Beyond it are seven golden mountain ranges, Yoke and the others.
The spaces between are filled with seas of enjoyment, which have eight qualities.

Beyond Mount Meru and completely surrounding it like curtains are seven mountain ranges, each forming a square. These seven golden mountain ranges [are named according to the shape of their peaks:] Yoke, Plough, Acacia Forest, Pleasing-to-the-Eye, Horse's Ear, Bent, and Rim.

The spaces between [the mountain ranges] are filled with what are known as the seven seas enjoyed [by the *nāgas*[8]], the waters of which have eight qualities: cool, tasty, light, soft, clear, odorless, harmless to the throat if swallowed, and harmless to the stomach.

The four continents and the eight islands
Are semi-circular, trapezoidal, round, and square.

The four continents are [situated in the outer ocean]. Majestic Body lies east of Mount Meru; the Land of Jambu is south; Bountiful Cow is west; and Unpleasant Sound is north. Adjacent to these are eight islands: Body and Majestic Body are situated [near Majestic Body] in the East; Tail-Fan and Other Tail-Fan, [near the Land of Jambu] in the South; Crafty and Treading the Perfect Path, [near Bountiful Cow] in the West; and Unpleasant Sound and Moon of Unpleasant Sound, [near Unpleasant Sound] in the North.

The four main continents have the following shapes: semicircular, trapezoidal, round, and square, respectively. Moreover, the eight islands have the same shape as the principal continent in their respective directions.

There are numerous unspecified little islands.

Only these twelve land masses are mentioned in the discourses of the Buddha since these are the principal ones. The *Brāhmaṇa Vyāsa Scripture,* however, enumerates sixteen large regions that surround the Land of Jambu alone, such as Siṃhala, Suvarṇadvīpa, Tāmradvīpa, Togar, Kamboja.[9] Moreover, the *Inconceivable Secrets of the Transcendent Ones Scripture* and other sources state that there are a thousand small lands [in this four-continent world-system]. In fact, an inestimable number of little islands whose names, dimensions, and shapes are not specified [in the scriptures] are located adjacent to each of the four continents.

The outer rim consists of a mountain range composed of iron;
A salt-water ocean fills the area as far as this range.

The outer iron mountain range, [called the Horse-faced] Mountain Range, surrounds the continents and forms the outer border or outer rim [of this world-system]. This range is composed of volcanic iron. Except for the continents, the area beyond the golden mountains as far as the outer rim is filled with salt water and is known as the Salt Water Ocean. Furthermore, the edge of this ocean touches the Horse-faced Mountain Range; the volcanic fires of this mountain range cause the ocean [to evaporate so that it does] not exceed its limits.

[II.A.1.a.iii]
The Meanings of the Names of the Continents

North from the center of the Exalted Land, beyond nine black mountains,

Stand the Snowy Mountains, and north of these the Fragrant [Mountains].
Between these two mountain ranges lies Cool Lake; from its four sides
Four cascades flow in four directions toward the ocean.
A jambu tree adorns the lake's shore,
And so this continent is known as the land beautified by the jambu tree.

Why is the Land of Jambu known by this name? Situated to the north of the center[10] of the Exalted Land (India), in the region beyond nine black mountain ranges, stands a snow-peaked mountain range called the Snowy Mountains[11] and further north, the Fragrant Mountain Range.[12] Between these two mountain ranges lies a lake that is the dwelling place of the *nāga* king, Cool. The lake itself is known as Cool[13] for [this reason:] In the past, a brahmin named Seer [encouraged a wheel-monarch[14]] to make offerings in order to attain [rebirth as] a god or as a wheel-monarch. [During a twelve-year period of cooking rice for offerings,] the wheel-monarch poured the warm rice-water [into a pit] where it [eventually] lost its warmth. Cool Lake formed [from this cooled rice-water]. The lake, the source of all rivers, forests, jewels, and medicines, is fifty leagues in depth and breadth.

The four cascades issue from mouths on each of the four sides of the lake. On the eastern side, from a cliff shaped like an elephant's head, falls the river Gaṅga, drawing along with it silver particles. On the southern side, from a cliff the shape of a bull's head, falls the river Sindhu, carrying particles of blue beryl. On the western side, from a cliff the shape of a horse's head, falls the river Vakṣu, carrying crystal particles. On the northern side, from a rock the shape of a lion's head, the river Sītā[15] descends, carrying gold particles. Moreover, each of these four rivers has five hundred tributaries, and all flow seven times in a clockwise direction around Cool Lake before continuing in the four directions toward the great ocean.

At the shore of the lake stands a fruit tree called the jambu,[16] which bears a sweet fruit the size of a clay pot, named "jambu" from the sound made by the ripened fruit falling into the water. Since this continent is adorned by this tree, it is known as the Land of Jambu. It is said that the *nāga* kings, appearing as fish, eat the jambu fruit; what remains uneaten becomes the gold of the rivers of Jambu.

The names of Majestic Body and the others indicate their distinguishing features.

The names of the three other continents — Majestic Body, etc. — indicate their distinguishing features. [In the eastern continent, Majestic Body,] the human body is remarkably majestic. [In the western continent, Bountiful Cow,] the wish-fulfilling cow provides an abundance of wealth. [In the northern continent, Unpleasant Sound,] the sun sometimes becomes covered with clouds due to the mischief of unruly *nāgas*. Consequently, drums and stringed instruments, etc., sound unpleasant: their appealing music becomes a cacophony. For these reasons, the continents are known by their respective names.

Tail-Fan Island is inhabited by cannibal demons, and the others, by humans.

Among the twelve continents and islands, Tail-Fan Island, one of the islands of Jambu, is inhabited only by cannibal demons,[17] while all the rest are populated by humans. The humans on these islands resemble those living on their adjacent principal continent.

The Tibetan term for human, *mi*, principally implies mental capacity or aptitude and is derived from the [Sanskrit] *manuṣya*, which denotes aptitude or discernment.

[II.A.1.a.iv]
The Three Miserable Realms and the Demi-gods' Realm

The hells and the world of the starving spirits are located below the earth.
Animals, the inhabitants of the depths, dwell in the great ocean.
Demi-gods [live] in the crevices of Mount Meru from the water's edge down.

Of the six kinds of beings, the human realm has been discussed [above]; a description of the three miserable existences now follows:

The hells and [the world of] the starving spirits[18] are located mainly below the surface of the earth. The eight hot hells are situated [in the lowest positions]. The most intense hot hell, Ceaseless Torture, is located twenty thousand leagues below the Land of Jambu. Above this hell, the other seven hot hells are situated one above the other: Extreme Heat, Heat, Loud Shrieking, Shrieking, Crushing, Black Lines, and Reviving.

On each of the four sides of each of the eight hells are the four neighboring hells: [1] Pit of Live Embers, [2] Swamp of Filth, [3] Road of Razor Blades, [Forest with] Leaves Like Swords, Forest of Iron Spikes, and [4] River Without Ford.

The eight cold hells are located beyond the neighboring hells. Their names are Blistering, Blisters Bursting, Teeth Chattering, Moaning with Cold, Wailing with Cold, Splitting Like a Blue Lotus, Splitting Like a Lotus, Splitting Widely Like a [Great] Lotus.

Since the continents resemble piles of grain, much larger at the bottom, there is no inconsistency in accommodating these [hells below this Land of Jambu]. Moreover, it is unnecessary to strictly define the size of these formations since the hells, according to the Universal Way, are simply projections of one's own mind.

Hells of shorter duration may be either isolated from one another or clustered together and have no fixed location. Their variety is due to specific acts particular to an individual.

The Sanskrit word for hell, *naraka,* is constructed by affixing the negative particle *na* to the word *raka,* which means "pleasurable." This implies that there is no vestige of pleasure [in the hells]. Alternatively, if *raka* is interpreted as "to take," [the term] means "hell" because one is led there as a consequence of unwholesome actions.

The king of the starving spirits, Lord of the Dead, lives five hundred leagues below the Land of Jambu. According to the *Great Mindfulness Scripture,* he rules over thirty-six [types of] starving spirits: those with drooping stomachs, those with mouths as minute as the eye of a needle, etc. [The abode of the Lord of the Dead] is their principal habitat, but they live in many other places. Furthermore, [the *Mindfulness Scripture* states that] some starving spirits who possess miraculous powers (such as the demi-gods who are classified as starving spirits) experience splendorous lives like those of the gods.

The Tibetan term for starving spirit, *yi dwags*, corresponds to the [Sanskrit] *preta*. *Preta* means completely gone, in other words, departed [from this life] without possibility of return. Alternatively, [*yi dwags* denotes] suffering greatly from hunger and thirst.

Animals inhabit the sky, the water, and vast stretches of the earth. Their principal habitat, however, is the great ocean where animals such as *nāgas* inhabit the depths, living [crowded together], like fermenting grains of beer.

[The abode of] the demi-gods is not explicitly mentioned in Vasubandhu's *Treasury of Phenomenology*. However, the *Great Mindfulness Scripture* states that the demi-gods dwell in crevices in the base of Mount Meru below the water level. A particular kind of demi-god classified as an animal lives at the bottom of the ocean; the chief demi-gods — Rāhu, Garland Necklace, and others — live at [different] levels above the ocean floor.

The [Tibetan] term for animal, *dud 'gro*, means "moving stooped over," because animals move around in a bent-over position. The [Sanskrit] word *tiras* [from which *tiryañc* (animal) is derived] seems to refer to the predominant postures for locomotion since the term denotes being bent over, crooked, or horizontal.

The Tibetan term for demi-god, *lha min*, is derived from the [Sanskrit] *asura*, meaning "deprived of the essence." The demigods are said to lack the ambrosia of the gods. Alternatively, *sura* means "god," to which the negative particle *a* is affixed to imply inferiority, [i.e., less than a god].

[II.A.1.a.v]
The Realm of the Gods

The Four Groups of the Great Kings reside mainly on the terraces of Mount Meru.
Beings may also dwell in various unspecified secondary abodes.

The Four Groups of the Great Kings constitutes the first [i.e., the lowest] of the six classes of gods of the desire realm.[19] The gods of this class reside mainly on the terraces of Mount Meru. The Vessel-Bearers live on the first terrace; Garland-Bearers, on the second; and Inebriates, on the third. Their kings, the four great kings, reside in the four directions of the fourth terrace. The gods in the kings' entourage generally reside [in the same place as the kings], but may also dwell in various other places, wherever suitable, be it in space or on one of the seven mountain ranges, such as Yoke.

In brief, the beings [commonly associated] with environments from the hell-realm to this level of heaven may dwell in various other unspecified secondary abodes. Even the mountains, cliffs, trees, temples, and homes of this human realm, wherever suitable, may serve as the habitat or environment for any of these forms of life.

Above Mount Meru is the heaven of the Thirty-three
In which is found the Victorious Residence, the city called Lovely,
Parks, playing fields, the All-gathering Tree, the fine stone slab,
The Assembly Hall of the Excellent Law, as well as the dwelling of the *yakṣas*.

The heaven known as the Thirty-three [Groups of] Gods is located on the summit of the massive Meru. The chiefs of these Thirty-three Groups are enumerated as follows: the eight gods of wealth, the two Aśvins, the eleven wrathful ones, and the twelve suns. One of the twelve suns, Śakra[20] himself, rules as the principal chief—the Powerful One—of the [Thirty-three]; the remaining thirty-two lesser chiefs are designated by the title Nearly as Powerful.

The Thirty-three Groups of Gods constituting this heaven are enumerated in the *Great Mindfulness Scripture*[21] as follows:

Dwelling at [the Assembly Hall of the] Excellent Law [1], on the Heights [2], at the Peak of the Mountain [3], and at the Place of Auspicious Vision [4];
Dwelling in One Region [5], in the Cluster of Trees [6], and in the Park of Various Chariots [7];

Dwelling at Delightful [8], at Beautiful [9], by the All-gathering [Tree] [10];
Dwelling Near the [Park of] Various Activities [11], Near the Thicket [12];
Dwelling in the Heart of the Jewel [13], Living in Space [14];
Dwelling in the Golden Cave [15], in the Garland's Shadow [16];
Travelling High and Low [17], Entertained by Various Radiances [18],
Subtle Enjoyment [19], Attached to Melodies [20], Blazing Splendor [21],
Full like the Moon [22], Pair of Sala Trees [23],
Walking in Pairs With Open Eyes [24], Walking with Closed Eyes [25],
Having Superior Body and Complexion [26], Having Dangling Jewels [27],
Living Communally [28], Living with an Entourage [29], Acting With Dignity [30],
Having Splendor [31], Having Splendid Garlands [32], Unmixed [33].
In this way, the Thirty-three [Groups of Gods] are enumerated.

Indra's court, the Victorious Residence, stands at the centre [of this heaven]. This palace is four-sided; each side is fifty leagues [wide] and four and one half high. One hundred and one jewelled turrets encircle the palace. [The palace grounds] are encompassed by a golden wall, each side of which extends two thousand five hundred leagues wide and one and a half leagues high. The ground, as soft as cotton, is made of gold beautified by an assortment of jewels of a hundred and one different hues. Sixteen thousand jewelled columns delineate the terraces [of the palace]. Above them, beams and cross-members support the protecting roofs. Five hundred armored young gods stand guard at each of the gates in the four directions. The palace and its grounds, the four great highways, and many smaller roads are all located within the city called Lovely.

The Park of Various Chariots is found to the east of the city; the Park of Armory, to the south; the Park of Various Activities, to the west; and the Park of Delights, to the north. All four parks are one thousand leagues in circumference. Playing fields [border these parks].

Beyond these parks and northeast of Lovely grows the All-gathering Tree. This tree, the source of the fulfillment of all wishes, grows to a height of one hundred leagues and has branches that reach fifty leagues in length. Its roots extend fifty leagues under the earth. Below the tree lies a square stone slab known as Armoniga,[22] which looks like a white blanket. Each of its sides is fifty leagues long, making it two hundred leagues in perimeter.

The circular Gathering Place Where the Gods Hear the Excellent Law, nine hundred leagues in circumference, is located southwest of Lovely. In its center is the golden throne on which Indra teaches the law of the gods and the seats arranged for the thirty-two Nearly as Powerful chiefs.

Moreover, astounding things are found in this heaven, such as the drumbeat that naturally reverberates with the [sound that proclaims the] four insignia of the Buddhist teaching,[23] urging the gods away from unwholesome ways; the vase of ambrosia which protects the gods from sickness, aging, and untimely death; the elephants [called] Sturdy and Son of the Land Guardian; the horse called Thunder-Cloud with hundreds and thousands of attendants. Secretive *yakṣas*[24] known as vajra-holders reside on four mounds [located at the corners of the top of Mount Meru].

Above, Conflict Free, Joyful, Enjoying Creations, and [Mastery Over] Others' [Creations]
Rest on riches like cloud formations in the sky.

Above the heaven of the Thirty-three, gods live on levels one above the other, supported by magnificent divine riches resembling cloud formations in the sky. [These riches,] celestial palaces and so on, have been created by the previous actions particular to each type of god.

On the first of these levels is Free From Conflict, which, although included within the desire realm, remains free from any conflict with the demi-gods. This [level] is also called Twins: the gods here are born (in the miraculous mode of birth)[25] in pairs. Above Free From Conflict are located the other heavens of the desire realm: Joyful, where the gods are [filled] with joy [at hearing] the teaching of the victorious one, Invincible[26]; Enjoying Creations, where the gods can freely enjoy pleasures that they themselves have created; and Mastery Over Others' Creations, where the gods have power over the enjoyments that other gods have created. These [four, along with the heaven of the four Great Kings and the Thirty-three], constitute the six classes of gods of the desire realm.

There are sixteen heavens in the form realm, beginning with Group of the Pure;
Above them all is Lesser Unsurpassed.
The lord bodhisattvas reside above that, according to the *Five Treatises on the Stages*.

The sixteen heavens of the form realm,[27] [beginning with] Group of the Pure, are situated above the desire realm and are tiered one above the other. The heaven called Lesser Unsurpassed is located above all of these, for a total of seventeen classes of form realm heavens. These seventeen, [grouped according to the four levels of meditative concentration of their respective resident gods], are described here in ascending order, beginning with the first level of meditative concentration.

The first level comprises three heavens: Group of the Pure, Priests of Brahmā,[28] and Great Pure Ones. Group of the Pure is called "pure" because the gods there have eradicated evil and non-virtue, and "group" because they are considered collectively. Priests of Brahmā is so named because the gods there recite prayers before Brahmā. Great Pure Ones, lords of this third-order thousand Endurance World-System, surpass others in terms of lifespan, physical dimensions, and so on, due to their great virtue.

Three heavens are found within the second level of meditative concentration: Dim Light, Measureless Light, and Clear Light. In Dim Light, both the magnitude and the strength of the light seem feeble compared to those of higher heavens. In Measureless Light, the magnitude of light appears immeasurably greater than that of lower heavens. In Clear Light, the magnitude and brilliance of the light illuminates all other heavens [below].

The third level of meditative concentration is composed of three heavens: Lesser Virtue, Limitless Virtue, and Flourishing Virtue. Lesser Virtue is so named because the bliss of the gods at this level of meditative concentration is completely peaceful, hence "virtuous," but less than that of the higher levels, hence "lesser." In Limitless Virtue, the bliss is immeasurably greater than that of lower levels. In Flourishing Virtue, the bliss of the gods increases greatly; no class of gods embodies greater virtue than this one.

The fourth level of meditative concentration is divided into [eight heavens]: Cloudless, Merit-Born, Great Result, Not Greater, Without Distress, Manifest Richness, Good Vision, and Unsurpassed. The first three are the heavens of ordinary beings: Cloudless lacks a basis of billowing, clustering clouds [that all the other heavens have]. Gods are born in Merit-Born due to the merit of their unwavering [contemplation].[29] In Great Result, the conditions of life ("the result") are superior to those of ordinary beings in other heavens.

[The latter five heavens are the] "pure domains." Not Greater has no qualities greater than those of the higher pure heavens. Owing to their attainment of a unique state of contemplation, the gods of Without Distress remain free of the distress of emotions and regret. Manifest Richness reflects perfect tranquillity and unmatched beauty. In Good Vision, the gods' outlook or vision is correct and good. Unsurpassed is so called because within this group of heavens no other heaven surpasses the qualities of this one. This heaven is also known as Final Gathering since it is the final form composed of particles of matter.

It is said that all gods who do not possess the power of discernment inhabit one area of Great Result. The gods of the fourth meditative concentration who share a common environment do not share a common fate: each god undergoes a solitary birth and death, including [the appearance and dissolution of] the celestial palace and possessions. Within the fourth level of meditative concentration, Not Greater to Unsurpassed are known as the pure domains because only exalted ones[30] are born there. Many scriptures, such as the *Descent into Laṅka Scripture*, as well as some tantras, concur that Unsurpassed is the abode of the enjoyment dimension of awakening. Moreover, Asaṅga's *Five Treatises on the Stages* states that the Place of the Great Lords, where [bodhisattvas] who have attained mastery of the tenth stage [of awakening] take birth, is located above Unsurpassed.

> **[The heavens] double in size and grow increasingly magnificent.**

The dimensions and shapes of these realms are all precisely described in the Buddha's teaching on phenomenology and in other sources. Generally speaking, however, [most sources] maintain that the heavens double in size in ascending order and are proportionally more magnificent in terms of power and wealth.

The term "god" in Sanskrit, *divaukas,* denotes sky dwellers or dwelling in the higher realms because the homes of these gods are in the higher realms. Another Sanskrit word for god is *deva,* meaning play or sport, since gods frolic about, amusing themselves.

[II.A.1.b]

Supplementary Discussion of the Viewpoint of the Proclaimers and the Solitary Sages

> **One third-order thousand world-system is fathomed by the vision of the proclaimers and solitary sages,**
> **Who assert that it is composed of indivisible particles of matter.**

The precise arrangement of just a single second-order thousand world-system or the great thousand third-order thousand world-system as explained above is fathomed by the sublime vision of the exalted proclaimers and solitary sages. Beyond that, the configuration of the realms of the Infinite Oceans world-system remains the field of experience solely of buddhas and the bodhisattvas who have attained the pure stages.[31] [The *Treasury of Phenomenology*] states:

> The saintly [proclaimers],[32] the rhinoceros [-like solitary sages],[33] and the buddhas
> Have seen, [respectively,] the second-order thousand, third-order thousand, and countless world-systems.

The proclaimers and solitary sages assert that the coarse environmental world is composed of an agglomerate formed of the eight constituents of particles, that is, the indivisible minute particles of the four [elements] — earth, water, fire, wind — as well as smell, taste, texture, and form. However, they do not share the opinion held by some non-Buddhists[34] that infinitesimal, indivisible particles of matter remain in empty space following the destruction [of the world-system] of the previous age. Rather, they assert that the collective actions of beings who are to take birth in this world-system produce energy-winds capable of generating the manifold [world] as their coarse result. Thus, they consider these energy-winds to be the initial cause [for the creation of the world]. This view and others will be discussed in detail below (in Chapter Four).

[II.A.2]
The Inhabitants, Sentient Beings

This section has four parts: (1) the nature of every sentient being, (2) the manner of diffusion of beings, (3) their experiences of happiness and suffering, and (4) categorization.

[II.A.2.a]
The Nature of Every Sentient Being

The nature of each being is unobscured and undetermined.

The basis for all life, the environmental world, has been described above. The nature of every being who lives in that environment remains unaffected by actions or emotions and is neither virtuous nor evil. The theories unique to the Universalists—that fundamental consciousness,[35] radiant awareness, etc., [is the nature of every being]—will be discussed in Chapter Four.

[II.A.2.b]
The Manner of Diffusion

This section has parts: (1) a concise presentation, and (2) an extensive explanation.

[II.A.2.b.i]
The Concise Presentation

> **The four absorptions of the formless realm and the other realms arise sequentially; [the beings within them]**
> **Diffuse from higher to lower, down to the hells.**

From beginningless time, every sentient being has been in a state of delusion. This instinctive unawareness of the nature of being serves as the concomitant cause that activates the propensity for dualistic experience. This causes a being to wander astray in the three realms [of existence].

Initially, the four levels of absorption[36] of the formless realm come into existence (beginning with Neither [Discernment] nor No [Discernment]) followed sequentially by the form realm and the desire realm. In short, beings diffuse from higher forms of life to lower; thus, all the [different] realms, from the highest down to the hells, come into existence.

[II.A.2.b.ii]
The Extensive Explanation

> **Moreover, the four levels of absorption of the formless realm**
> **Are only distinctions in contemplation; they have no form or location.**

The formless realm refers to the four levels of meditative absorption.

Some masters discuss these four levels in descending order, in keeping with the way beings first take birth [and then diffuse downward throughout] cyclic existence. Although that approach is appropriate, the four levels are presented here in ascending order to facilitate understanding.

When an individual first achieves contemplative absorption, the thought occurs, "This is infinite like space." Once this experience arises, it grows and develops. This path results in a birth having the same name, Absorption of Infinite Space. The other three levels follow the same pattern: the Absorption of Infinite Consciousness is so named because of the initial thought, "This is infinite consciousness." The Absorption of Nothing Whatever is so named because of the initial thought, "This is nothing at all." The Absorption of Neither Discernment nor No Discernment is so named because of a feeble discernment, an initial thought: "Discernment is like a sickness, tumor, or pain; no discernment is total numbness."

During the period of the initial delusion [in which beings do not recognize their own natures] that impels them to take birth in the three realms, beings move from the highest [levels] of the formless realm levels down to the lowest. Subsequently, as beings take birth within the various realms of cyclic life, they are born wherever appropriate, according to which of the four meditative absorptions they developed in a previous existence. Some individuals who have attained the highest [of the four levels] gradually descend from one level to the one below. Others may move from whatever [state] they have attained to any other form of existence. These changes do not follow any fixed pattern.

Generally speaking, however, the majority of beings who attain the four [levels] of this formless realm fall gradually lower and lower. [This process takes place as follows]: When a god [of the highest level] dies, the contemplation of Neither Discernment nor No Discernment—the peak of existence—dissolves, and the discernment of Nothing Whatever arises. This absorption is slightly coarser than the previous one. Since that experience feels blissful, attachment to that state develops and the god falls to that level.

In the same way, at the time of death of [a god in the Infinite] Consciousness [realm], the consciousness of Infinite Space arises. That experience causes the god to be born in the equivalent state. This occurs because long habituation to abiding in a specific state of contemplation facilitates re-entering that state of mind.

The gods of the four formless levels described here are classified simply according to differences in their contemplation rather than according to higher and lower locations since they have neither fixed locations nor physical forms of particular sizes. Wherever a being achieves a [specific] state of absorption, that being attains the same state after death in the same place.

Some specialists in phenomenology assert that the formless levels do have forms and locations in a tiered arrangement above Unsurpassed. They contend that the expression "formless" is a term used simply as a negation of inferior states. Further, the *Flower Ornament Scripture* makes repeated use of terms that imply that the formless realm has physical structure. For example[37]:

> The formless realm has location, ...a basis, ...an environment, ...and shape.

Similarly, according to Vimalamitra and Padmasaṃbhava, and according to the views expressed in Early Translation[38] texts such as the *Great Array: The Tantra of Supreme Wish-Fulfillment*, four [realms] such as Sky of Tiered Lotuses are located in space high above the form realm, and these serve as the basis for the forms of beings absorbed in contemplation.

> **The form realm: In the fourth level of meditative concentration, [there are] five pure domains and three heavens of ordinary beings.**
> **Three [heavens] are located within each of the lower three levels of meditative concentration.**

The realm of form is so named because beings within it are free from the attachment endemic to the desire realm but still have attachment to form. This realm's seventeen heavens can be grouped into what are known as the four levels of meditative concentration. Five pure domains — Unsurpassed, etc. — and three heavens for ordinary beings, such as Great Result, are located at the fourth and highest level of meditative concentration. As previously described, three heavens are located at each of the three lower levels of meditative concentrations: Flourishing Virtue, etc., at the third; Clear Light, etc., at the second; and Great Pure Ones, etc., at the first.

At the beginning of the formation of a [new] world, if the previous world has been destroyed by fire, a god of the second level of meditative concentration dies and takes birth in the empty celestial residence of Brahmā [that is, on the first level]. From that point onward, beings diffuse progressively [throughout the realms] in descending order, so that all realms of existence from Priests of Brahmā and Group of the Pure down to and including the hells [fill with life]. In the case of the previous world having been destroyed by water, [this process] begins by [a god] of the third level of contemplation being born at the level below, and so on.

The desire realm comprises thirty-six types of beings:
Six groups of gods, [humans of the] four continents,
[Inhabitants of the] eight islands, animals and starving spirits,
[Beings in the] eight hot hells, and the eight cold hells.

The desire realm is so named because beings of this realm are preoccupied with sensual pleasures, mainly sexual intercourse, and crave coarse foods.[39] It comprises the six classes of desire realm gods (dwelling in Mastery Over Others' Creations and the others), the [beings that inhabit] the four great continents (Unpleasant Sound, Bountiful Cow, Majestic Body, Land of Jambu) and their eight islands, and the eighteen [types of beings in the] miserable existences (the animals, the starving spirits, and the beings of the eight hot and the eight cold hells.) Together these are known as thirty-six types of beings of the desire realm. At the time of the initial formation of the world, these existences formed as beings descended and diffused from higher states in the order explained above.

The twenty existences, ten happy and ten miserable,
May also be classified as twenty-eight.

In other classifications, the gods of the six heavens of the desire realm and the humans of the four continents constitute the "ten happy existences." The [beings of the] eight hells, the animals, and the starving spirits make up the "ten miserable existences." Together these are known as the "twenty existences of the desire realm." If the [beings of the] eight islands are counted separately, there are then twenty-eight existences within the desire realm.

Although the demi-gods may be included in the category of animals, their habitat, physical form, possessions, and so on are qualitatively so similar to those of the gods that they are classified as gods. As the *Five Treatises on the Stages* and the *Wish-Fulfilling Scripture* confirm, the negative *a* in *asura*, the Sanskrit word for demi-god, denotes inferiority, not a denial of status as a god (*sura*).

[II.A.2.c]
Happiness and Suffering

> **Within the happy existences — the form realm and the rest —**
> **Lifespans and possessions decrease the lower the level.**
> **In the miserable existences, suffering increases the lower the level.**

The lifespans and possessions of the gods in the seventeen heavens of the form realm, of the six classes of the gods of the desire realm, and of humans of the four continents decrease in the descending order described in the previous section (on diffusion). Conversely, the higher [realms] experience much greater lifespans and enjoyments than the lower.

The intensity of suffering and the span of life experienced by beings in the miserable existences increase progressively in descending order: starving spirits suffer more than animals, hell beings more than starving spirits, and beings in lower hells more than those in higher hells.

[II.A.2.d]
Categorization

> **The four [levels] of absorption, the four levels of meditative concentration, and the desire realm**
> **Comprise nine levels. In terms of type, there are six [classes of] beings.**
> **A classification of five — human, divine, and three miserable existences —**
> **May be made in terms of paths and courses.**

The three realms are divided into nine levels according to different mental states: four levels of the formless realm, differentiated by the four levels of meditative absorption; four levels of the form realm, differentiated by the four levels of meditative concentration; and one level for the desire realm, since there is no such differentiation within it.

When sentient beings are grouped according to their types, there are six distinct groups. The *Reunion of Father and Son Scripture*[40] states:

> The Lion of Humanity taught that
> The six classes of living beings —
> Hell beings, animals, starving spirits,
> Demi-gods, humans, and gods — are superficial [reality].

Moreover, the *Marvellous Life of the Buddha Scripture*[41] states:

> Through the forces of craving, becoming, and unawareness,
> Ordinary beings foolishly spin through the five existences —
> Human, god, and the three miserable existences —
> Just like a potter's wheel spinning 'round.

This fivefold classification is based on the courses of birth and paths of migration experienced by beings. Alternatively, the five paths are explained as the path of dream, the path of instincts, the path of evolutionary actions, the path of unpredictable and deceptive cyclic life, and the path of unpredictable and distinct causes and effects.

> **All these beings may be categorized according to the four modes of birth,**
> **Or into pure, corrupt, and indeterminate groups.**

All beings may be categorized according to their modes of birth, of which there are four possibilities: womb birth, egg birth, birth through heat and moisture, and miraculous birth. Gods, hell beings, and beings in the intermediate state[42] are said to experience miraculous birth; humans and animals experience all four modes of birth; and starving spirits undergo both womb and miraculous births.

Moreover, all who are born, live, and die within this type of world of sentient beings may be included within one of three groups: the definitely pure, the definitely corrupt, and the indeterminate. The first consists of exalted ones; the second, of those who have committed [evil] acts that bring immediate results[43]; and the third includes all other beings.

[II.B]
The Interim Abiding of Our World-System

The explanation of the way the world abides in the interim phase has four parts: (1) a general explanation of beings, (2) a particular explanation of the Land of Jambu, (3) the origin of the wheel-monarchs, and (4) [a description of the] features of life.

[II.B.1]
The Beings of Our World-System

> **During the time of abiding, most beings, except for animals,**
> **Experience consequences that are predetermined.**

After the world-system has formed completely and has entered its period of abiding, all beings of the lower realms (with the exception of the animals) and most beings of the higher realms generally experience only the consequences of virtuous or unvirtuous actions committed in previous existences. Thus, their happiness and suffering, their lifespans and enjoyments, and other aspects of their lives are all predetermined.

Although animals experience the results of their previous negative actions, they have indefinite lifespans, etc. At one extreme, the great *nāgas* and certain other animals live for an entire intermediate age[44]; at the other extreme, some organisms live for only an instant. Moreover, there are innumerable possibilities with respect to their physical shapes and features. The domesticated animals have some vestige of happiness, but those born in the darkness of the areas between continents, as well as some other animals, are tormented by unremitting suffering.

A correlation exists between the lifespans of beings in the six hot hells in descending order (beginning with Reviving) and time as experienced in the six desire realm heavens in ascending order: The number of years in the lifespan of a being in a certain hell equals the number of years in the lifespan of a god in the corresponding heaven. However, what counts as one day in the life of a hell being is equivalent to the entire lifespan of a god.

For example, a being in the Reviving Hell lives for five hundred years, during which period each day is equal to the entire lifespan of the gods of the Four Groups of the Great Kings. The lifespan in Extreme Heat is said to last half an intermediate age, and that of Ceaseless Torture, one full cosmic age. Within the cold hells, the lifespan in Blistering is equal to the time necessary to exhaust the sesame seed stock of Magadhā when it is reduced at the rate of one seed per hundred years. The lifespans of the others increase proportionally, each one twenty times more than the previous.

The lifespan of starving spirits lasts five hundred years, one day in their life being equal to a month in the human realms.

Asaṅga's *Facts of the Stages* states that the physical size and lifespan of a demi-god are equivalent to those of a god of the Thirty-three Groups of Gods. Within the three miserable realms there is a great variety of physical sizes. The stature of humans in Majestic Body is equal to eight cubits measured on a human in the Land of Jambu; the stature of humans in Bountiful Cow is double that of Majestic Body; and that of Unpleasant Sound is double that of Bountiful Cow. The stature of the six desire gods increases proportionally from one quarter of an earshot in the lowest heaven to one and a half earshots[45] in the highest.

A human being in Majestic Body lives two hundred and fifty years; in Bountiful Cow, five hundred years; and in Unpleasant Sound, one thousand years. For gods in the Four Groups of the Great Kings, a single day is equal to fifty human years, and they live for five hundred years. In the heaven called Thirty-three Groups of Gods, one day is equal to one hundred human years, and the gods there live one thousand years. Lifespan for gods in the heavens above the Thirty-three, up to and including Mastery Over Others' Creations, doubles from heaven to heaven in ascending order.

The gods of the form realm live for ages equal to the number of leagues of their stature. Lifespans range from half an age for a god of Group of the Pure to sixteen thousand ages for a god of Unsurpassed.

The gods of the four formless realms, beginning with Infinite Space, enjoy lifespans of twenty thousand, forty thousand, sixty thousand, and eighty thousand ages, respectively. In these figures, "age" refers to a cosmic age for every level above Faint Light and half a cosmic age for every level below.

[II.B.2]
The Land of Jambu

In our world, humans have a wide variety of lifespans, wealth, and physical size.
Lifespan decreases from incalculable to ten,
And then increases to eighty thousand, and so on.
During a decline, a rise, and eighteen intermediate cycles,
There are fluctuations. The three continents are places where [consequences] are experienced;
Jambu Land, the most distinguished, is the place of action.

In this land of Jambu, humans mainly engage in evolutionary actions.[46] Consequently, there is nothing fixed or definitive regarding their lifespans, wealth, and physical size.

Initially, human lifespan was measureless, but gradually it became calculable; eventually, lifespan will decrease to ten years. This long age concludes with the three periods of famine, plague, and war. Specifically, when lifespan is thirty years, there will be a period of famine lasting for seven years, seven months, and seven days; when twenty years, a period of plague lasting seven months and seven days; and when ten years, a period of war lasting seven days. This entire sequence [during which lifespan decreases from countless to ten years] is termed a long decline.[47]

One cycle refers to a rise and decline together, i.e., the time required for lifespan to rise from ten to eighty thousand years, and then to decline from eighty thousand to ten years. Eighteen such periods are referred to as the eighteen intermediate cycles. Each of these cycles concludes with [periods of] famine, plague, and war. Finally, the period during which lifespan increases from ten to eighty thousand years is called a long rise.[48] Altogether, these are referred to as the twenty intermediate ages. Because of the slower pace during the rise and decline at the beginning and end of the ages, the length of time of each is equal to one intermediate cycle, as pointed out in Purṇavardhana's *Commentary [to the Treasury of Phenomenology]* and other texts. The *Facts of the Stages* also refers to the long decline and long rise at the beginning and end of the ages as being each equal to one cycle.

According to the sagacious Longchenpa, after the human lifespan has increased to measureless (during the long rise) and has then begun to decline again, the buddha Inspired[49] will appear [in this world] just as the lifespan first becomes calculable. This statement agrees, for the most part, [with predictions found in] the Universal Way [scriptures].

During both the long rise and decline as well as the eighteen intermediate cycles, the lifespans, physical sizes, and wealth of beings undergo various fluctuations.

One is mistaken if one believes that human life in this world is inferior to others. Since humans of the three other continents experience [only] the results of their past [actions], they have no possibility of performing new evolutionary actions. Therefore, these places are inferior to Jambu.

The Land of Jambu is a place for new evolutionary actions. Therefore, any action performed by persons born here has especially powerful [effects]. Moreover, people feel sad when hearing accounts of impermanence, etc., and so are easily guided [onto the spiritual path]. For these reasons, supreme emanations of awakening—spiritual guides, including our own teacher Śākyamuni—demonstrate enlightenment in this world and become the teachers [of humanity]. Therefore, human life in the Land of Jambu is superior to that on the other continents. The *Great Mindfulness Scripture*[50] states:

> Compared to the other three continents, this is a place for evolutionary action. Here, people are inspired to practice the ten virtues. Here, buddhas appear. All four places of humans depend on this one. Here, people are conscientious about the ten virtuous actions and are inspired to practice them. This is a place for pure conduct. Here, there is an awareness of birth and death. Here, there is the indestructible seat of enlightenment.[51]

From the same source:

> Among the four continents of our universe inhabited by humans, the Land of Jambu is the most important.

Beings in this world came down from the heaven of Clear Light.
The nourishment derived from meditative concentration and other [pristine] qualities gradually deteriorated due to craving.

The sun and moon provided light, and King Honored by Multitudes appeared.
Then, such distinctions as the four eras and four classes arose.

The genesis of humans on this continent occurred when a god in [the heaven of] Clear Light died and took miraculous birth here. A second, then a third followed, and their numbers increased progressively until there were many, all of whom took miraculous birth here like the first. All could travel through space, had radiant bodies, and were sustained by the nourishment of meditative concentration, like gods of the form realm.

Later, a white earth-nectar that tasted like honey appeared. Eating copiously of this, they began to crave it. Consequently, the nourishment of meditative concentration and other qualities, including miraculous powers and even the earth-nectar itself, disappeared. Then appeared a creamy orange earth-food, and they ate that. Because they began to crave it, both the food and the radiance of their bodies gradually deteriorated. At that point, due to the forces of collective evolutionary actions and the natural laws of existence,[52] the sun and moon began to illuminate the world. In the same way, other earth-nectars as well as fields of sprouts appeared and disappeared. Subsequently, fields of huskless *śāli* rice grew[53]; reaped in the morning the crop could grow [again] in the evening. Digestion of this rice produced bodily wastes such as feces and urine.

Eating these coarse foods caused the male and female genitals to appear. Gradually, opposite genders became attracted to each other and engaged in sexual intercourse. Others reviled and threw mud at them, whereupon they became ashamed; regarding their sexual activity as inappropriate, they abandoned it for periods of up to seven days. Some of the most depraved individuals constructed houses in order to protect themselves from the embarrassment of being observed while copulating.

Then, because people stored and hoarded the grain, even the *śāli* rice, which required no cultivation, disappeared. In its place grew a grain with a husk. Because this grain, once harvested, had to be planted again, land was apportioned and fields were farmed. Eventually, [people] began to steal one another's crops and disputes erupted. Consequently, a person of fine physical stature known for his outstanding qualities was chosen from the community to be master of the fields. Honored by everyone, he was offered a portion of the produce, and came to be known as King Honored by Multitudes; he was the [world's] first king. [His descendants] were referred to as royalty because they were lords of the fields, and also because they safeguarded [the well-being of society].

Gradually, people became predominately evil and violated the king's laws. Regardless how stringent the disciplinary measures, people failed to obey the laws, and so capital punishment was instituted. Fearing death, people began to lie and commit other evil acts. Eventually, the five forms of degeneration[54] evolved, culminating in periods of plague, war, and famine.

The history of our continent unfolded in four distinct eras.[55] The first era is called the era of completeness [because splendor and enjoyments were complete]. The second is the era of three-quarters, so called because theft and sexual intercourse reduced the splendor and wealth of the environment and its inhabitants by one quarter. Then, due to lying, the splendor and enjoyments were reduced to one half, and so the third era is referred to as the era of two-quarters. The fourth and final period is the era of conflict, during which even the remnant quarter of wealth and splendor gradually diminishes due to murder and the other forms of non-virtue committed by humans.

Human beings became divided into four classes[56]: royalty descended from the lineage of King Honored by Multitudes; brahmins came from those who were disillusioned by the shortcomings of household life; merchants descended from those who did not steal or commit other forms of non-virtue; and the menial class came from those who engaged in theft and other non-virtuous activities.

[II.B.3]
The Origin of the Wheel-Monarchs

> **Wheel-monarchs, who [possess wheels of] gold, silver, copper, and iron,**
> **Appear in this world only when the lifespan is no less than eighty thousand years.**

Some say that they reign totally over the third-order thousand world-system.

Wheel-monarchs, who reign over the four continents [by virtue of their possession of] a gold, silver, copper or iron wheel, are said to appear in this world whenever the lifespan rises above eighty thousand years. The origin of the line of wheel-monarchs of the present age is explained as follows:

According to the *Supreme Essence Commentary on Transcendent Wisdom in Eight Thousand Lines*, the court of King Honored by Multitudes was established at Rājagṛha.[57] King Honored by Multitudes married a queen named Upper River Maiden who bore a son named Beautiful Light. Beautiful Light's queen, named Born from a Mountain, begat a son named Virtue. Virtue's queen, Voice of the Clouds, begat Perfect Virtue. Perfect Virtue's queen, Palm Legs, gave birth to Noble Purification. These are known as the five kings of the Fortunate Age.

A protuberance grew on the crown of the head of the king Noble Purification, and from it sprang [a child] named Suckle Me,[58] [who inherited the throne]. [One day] when he was standing on the terrace of his residence, a gold wheel appeared in space before him. He flung the wheel with the command, "Conquer the East!" The wheel moved in that direction, carrying the king's attendants upon it. In succession, [the inhabitants of] the four continents as well as [the heaven of] the Thirty-three Groups of Gods welcomed them and thus became subjects of the king. That's how Suckle Me became a great wheel-monarch. His physical form and his activities equalled Indra's; however, his lifespan exceeded Indra's by one hundred and forty times.

The son of Suckle Me, called Handsome, possessed a silver wheel; he gained control of three continents — the eastern, southern, and western — simply by advancing in their direction. The son of Handsome, named Very Handsome, possessed a copper wheel; he gained power over the eastern and southern continents simply by preparing for battle. Very Handsome's son, called Having Beauty, possessed an iron wheel; he gained control of the southern continent by brandishing weapons. His son, known as Having Great Beauty, also possessed an iron wheel; by simply brandishing weapons, he too gained control of the southern continent.[59]

All subsequent wheel-monarchs held power over only a single continent. Furthermore, two wheel-monarchs never appeared simultaneously because buddhas, indras, and wheel-monarchs have not performed the actions that cause rivals to appear. Wheel-monarchs exhibit the characteristic marks and signs [of great beings][60] similar to those of a buddha, but not as obvious and complete. For the most part, they are exalted ones. They appear when the [human] lifespan is not less than eighty thousand years, i.e., during the era of completeness, because all ten virtues are practiced. After the era of completeness has ended, their power and prosperity become depleted. However, there are some rulers who are referred to as wheel-monarchs because they reign over most of the Land of Jambu, even though they lack such attributes as the seven precious articles. These monarchs appear whenever [conditions are] appropriate, but only until [human] lifespan has decreased to one hundred years.

Wheel-monarchs own three sets of seven articles endowed with extraordinary characteristics. The first [of these three sets] consists of the seven supremely precious articles, which are described in the *Great Mindfulness Scripture*[61]:

> [1] The precious wheel is made of gold, is five hundred leagues [in diameter] and has one thousand spokes. Within a day it can travel one thousand leagues. By the power of the wheel, the king's attendants, the elephant and so on, are able to travel anywhere through space up to [the heaven of] the Thirty-three and can hear what the king does not hear. The wheel eliminates rivals. It appeared from space.
>
> [2] The precious jewel has eight facets and equals the size of a large man's thigh. It illuminates the night up to a distance of one hundred leagues, and if the day is hot, it provides cooling water of eight qualities. Within a radius of one hundred leagues, this jewel eliminates all diseases and fulfills all wishes. It was presented by Indra.
>
> [3] The precious queen's body exudes the fragrance of sandalwood; the scent of the blue lotus flower issues from her mouth. Contact with her provokes no passions; all men regard her as a mother or sister. Within the kingdom she elimi-

> nates all hunger and thirst and lives in harmony with everyone. She gives birth to many sons. When her husband is absent, [she maintains chastity] and never succumbs to the pleasures of the five senses. She was presented by the minister.
>
> [4] The precious minister is free of disturbing emotions and has forsaken all unvirtuous actions. He is proficient in everything he does, even without training. He is like a loving parent toward all beings.
>
> [5] The precious elephant is wise and obedient. In a single day, he can circle the Land of Jambu three times. When mounted by the king, he goes wherever the king wishes, without being prompted. He defeats the king's adversaries.
>
> [6] The precious horse is bluish-green in color, like the neck of a peacock, and has qualities similar to those of the elephant. Both [the elephant and the horse] were given by Śakra.
>
> [7] The precious general has the power to conquer all enemies, yet he causes no harm to others. Alternatively, the seventh precious article is the precious chamberlain, who obeys the king's commands and keeps his treasury full. Experts on this topic say that a gold wheel-monarch has no general because he does not need to prepare for battle; in that case, the seventh article is the chamberlain, who also serves as treasurer. Since the other three [types of wheel-monarch] must prepare for battle, for them the general is counted as the seventh.

The second set of possessions, the seven semi-precious articles, consists of the following: [The first is] the sword whose mere presence intimidates those who contravene the king's laws. [The second is] the hide canopy, which is ten leagues in length and five in width, impervious to rain and unruffled by wind. It serves as a residence for the king and the members of his entourage wherever they go, providing warmth in cold weather and coolness in the heat. It was offered by a merchant and is said to be the hide of a *nāga* that came from the ocean. [The third is] the mansion, twelve leagues in length and seven in width, which is warm in the cold and cool in the heat. Goddesses gather there to play music, and from the mansion one can see whatever one wishes—the moon, the constellations, or precious gems. [The fourth is] the garment that is impenetrable to weapons and fire; it is soft and never soils, and whoever wears it remains unaffected by heat, cold, hunger, thirst, and weariness. [The fifth is] the pleasure garden, where young gods and goddesses, birds and other creatures gather at the time of royal visits. [The sixth is] the bedding that frees one from disturbing emotions and clears the mind, and if one cultivates contemplation, it also effects liberation. [The seventh is] the pair of boots that allows the wearer to walk on water and to travel a hundred leagues in an instant, without weariness. [Additional semi-precious articles] include the thousand sons who have renounced the ten unvirtuous actions and the bow and arrow that overpower the enemy.

The last set of possessions, the seven types of jewels, are mentioned in [Haribhadra's] *Discussion on the Scripture of Transcendent Wisdom in Eight Thousand Lines*[62]:

> Seven substances—coral, blue beryl,
> Silver, gold, crystal,
> Pink pearl, and emerald—are [called] precious
> Because they are universally considered valuable.

Moreover, the *Questions of Gaganagañja Scripture* mentions that there are wheel-monarchs who control our entire third-order thousand world-system. Further, the *Scripture Revealing Dharma and its Meaning*[63] states:

> In the world-system called Source of Flowers, there appeared a ruler of humanity, a wheel-monarch called Victorious, who was sovereign of this great thousand third-order thousand world system.

[II.B.4]
Features of Life

> **There are many variations in food, hunger and thirst,**
> **color of clothing, night and day, etc.**
> **Beings in lower [realms] do not see those in the higher.**

Beings living in their respective realms are [nourished by a variety of foods]. Many kinds of food are eaten in three of the human continents, while in the northern continent only an uncultivated grain is consumed. The gods of the desire realm live on ambrosia, and those of the form realm, on the nourishment of contemplation. These are some of the differences with respect to food. Hunger and thirst are experienced in the desire realm, but not in the two higher realms.

Styles of clothing also distinguish [the different realms]. In the three continents, humans wear clothes in a variety of colors, whereas clothing in the northern continent is exclusively white. In the six [heavens of] the desire realm, the gods wear clothes of multi-colored cloth—white, yellow, blue, and red; in the form realm, all clothing is white. Garments in the three continents are very heavy, being made of silk, cotton, etc.; garments in the northern continent and desire gods' realm are fashioned from the bark of a wish-fulfilling tree, and are soft, supple, and light. Garments in the northern continent weigh only an ounce[64]; [they decrease progressively in weight up to] Unsurpassed, where they are weightless.

In the four continents, the distinction between night and day depends on the light of the sun and moon. Because of the natural radiance [of realms] above [the highest of the golden mountain ranges,] Yoke, there is no variation in light and dark; the inhabitants of these regions distinguish day from night by the opening and closing of flowers.

A corpse remains after the death of a being born in any mode except miraculous birth. In the latter case, no corpse remains after death.

In three of the continents, humans attach great importance to the amount of rainfall and the quality of the harvest, while humans in the northern continent and the gods feel no such [concern]. Many such features distinguish life in the higher realms.

Except for those who have attained miraculous powers or those who are guided by gods of higher realms, those in lower realms are not able to travel to or to see realms above their own. However, just the opposite applies for those of the higher realms. The gods of the form realm, such as those of the Group of the Pure, can travel to the Land of Jambu. At that time, their bodies do not leave their own abodes, but emanate into our world in a [human] form as a result of having previously experienced this level of existence. Because [the gods of] Mastery Over Others' Creations and [heavens] below it are on the same level—the desire realm—gods [of those realms] travel to our world in their own form.

[II.C]
The Ages of the Final Destruction and Vacuity of Our World-System

This section has two parts: (1) the main [discussion], and (2) a supplementary [discussion].

[II.C.1]
The Main Discussion

This section has two parts: (1) an explanation of the emptying of the world-system of inhabitants, and (2) an explanation of the destruction of the environment.

[II.C.1.a]
The Emptying of the World-System of Inhabitants

> **At the time of destruction, the miserable realms, beginning with the hell realms, empty.**
> **Gods and humans attain meditative concentration and are born in the form realm.**
> **As the realms empty of inhabitants, the [beings of] the lower realms move higher.**

When the period of abiding comes to an end and the period of destruction begins, all those in the hell realm who have exhausted the causes [for the hell experience] move to higher realms. Those who have not exhausted the causes [for the hell experience] remain and experience suffering when this world is destroyed. Finally they move on, and take birth in the hell of another world. No beings are born anew in the hell realms of this world; in this way the hell realms are emptied. This marks the beginning of the process of destruction; subsequently, the principal habitations of starving spirits and animals are similarly emptied.

Next, one human being of the Land of Jambu, by his own inherent qualities, attains the second level of meditative concentration and remains in that state. Then, arising [from that meditative concentration], he says, "This is the bliss and joy that has come from isolation[65]!" His words instantly pervade the Land of Jambu. Immediately upon hearing these words, others follow the same training, achieve the second level of meditative concentration, and take birth among the class of gods of Clear Light.

When there is no longer a single human left in the Land of Jambu, all the humans of the eastern continent, Majestic Body, and the western, Bountiful Cow, undergo the same change. Those of Unpleasant Sound take birth in the heaven of the Thirty-three. Humans inhabiting the islands follow [a pattern] similar to those of their adjacent continent. In this way, the human world empties. Subsequently, a single god announces the way to attain the second level of meditative concentration, and gradually the [gods below the second level] attain higher levels and are born in the form realm. They then move from lower to higher levels by attaining progressively higher meditative concentrations. When there is no longer a single being left in the heaven of the Pure and below, the destruction (emptying) of the inhabitants is complete.

[II.C.1.b]
Environment

> **The heavens of the first meditative concentration and below are destroyed by fire.**
> **Space alone remains, a vacuity containing nothing at all.**
> **Again formation occurs, and again abiding, and finally destruction by fire.**

After the emptying of the world's inhabitants, no rain falls. Seven suns begin to blaze, eventually drying up everything from plants and trees to forests and great oceans. Finally, all becomes a single tongue of fire which burns and destroys everything from the hell of Unceasing Torment up to and including the first level of meditative concentration. Below the second level of the form realm, only space remains, a vacuity containing nothing whatsoever. Again, as before, a new world-system comes into existence. Finally, at the completion of its period of abiding, it is similarly destroyed by fire.

After seven such [sequences], a deluge at the end of the eighth
Destroys the second meditative concentration and below.

This sequence of formation and destruction takes place seven times; at the end of the eighth [period of abiding], a great cloud gathers in the heaven of Clear Light. A deluge pours down, dissolving this world just as salt dissolves into water. Even this [mass of water] evaporates, so that the [level of] the second meditative concentration and everything below is destroyed.

Seven destructions by fires alternating with one by water occur seven times,
Ending with another seven by fire.
Finally, intense wind destroys the third meditative concentration and below.

When the sequence of seven destructions by fire, alternating with one destruction by water, has occurred seven times, again there are seven destructions by fire. At the end of that entire process, a wind arises which pulverizes even Mount Meru, the king of mountains, and destroys the third level of meditative concentration and everything below.

Because those three contemplations have imperfections, [they are destroyed];
The fourth, being free of imperfection, is not destroyed by the elements.

The lower three levels of meditative concentrations are destroyed by fire, water, and wind because these contemplations are imperfect. The imperfection of the first level of meditative concentration, the presence of investigation and examination, resembles fire. The imperfection of the second, the presence of joy and bliss, resembles water. The imperfection of the meditative concentration in the third, the inhalation and exhalation of the breath, resembles wind. Because of these [imperfections], [each meditative concentration] is destroyed by [the element corresponding to its imperfection].

Because the fourth meditative concentration has none of these imperfections, it is not destroyed by external elements. However, sentient beings [of this level of meditative concentration] are said to undergo birth and destruction together with their mentally created celestial palaces and other possessions.

The earth element is not a contributing factor in [these cycles of] destruction because the environmental world itself is composed primarily of the element earth.

[II.C.2]
Supplementary Discussion

This section has three parts: (1) an enumeration of ages, (2) other patterns of destruction, and (3) places that are not destroyed.

[II.C.2.a]
Enumeration of Ages

> **Altogether, sixty-four great cycles of destruction occur.**

All these cycles of destruction and reformation of the world-system yielding a total of sixty-four great cycles occur in succession. This is equal to the lifespan of the gods in Virtue Increasing.

> **Each of the ages of formation, abiding, destruction, and vacuity**
> **Lasts for twenty intermediate ages; together, these [four] constitute one cosmic age.**

The duration of the age of formation equals the time between the initial stage of [the formation] of the wind configuration and the formation of the hells. It also equals the time required for the human lifespan in the Land of Jambu to decrease from incalculable to eighty thousand years. The age of formation comprises twenty intermediate ages: one intermediate age is required for the formation of the environment and nineteen for the inhabitants.

The first intermediate age of the period of abiding is the period during which the lifespan decreases from eighty thousand to ten years. Then, the period of increasing to eighty thousand and the period of again decreasing to ten, taken together, equals one intermediate cycle; eighteen repetitions of this are called the eighteen intermediate cycles. Again, the increase [of lifespan] from ten years to eighty thousand or an incalculable number constitutes the final intermediate age. In total, the period of abiding lasts twenty intermediate ages.

The period of destruction lasts twenty intermediate ages: the destruction of the inhabitants lasts nineteen intermediate ages and the destruction of the environment lasts for one.

The period of vacuity, the period of darkness between the previous world's destruction and the next world's formation, lasts twenty intermediate ages.

In summary, each of the four periods—formation, abiding, destruction, and vacuity—lasts twenty intermediate ages, which, when added together, make eighty intermediate ages; these constitute one cosmic age. These [calculations] have been made from the perspective of our [world-system,] Endurance. In general, however, the length of days and ages is not precisely fixed. The *Inconceivable King Scripture*[66] states that for the buddhas Sage of the Śākyas, Infinite Life, Vajra Conqueror, Radiant Fully Bloomed Lotus Form, Dharma Banner, Lion, Illuminator, Dharma Radiance Fully Bloomed Flower Form, King of Wisdom Light, Moon[-like] Intelligence, and Splendor of Excellence, an age in the former buddha's period is merely a single day for the following.

[II.C.2.b]
Other Patterns of Destruction

> **Such statements as that in a single age seven fires,**
> **One flood, and one wind arise, destroying the third level of meditative concentration and below,**
> **Reflect different points of view of different systems.**

The sagacious Drimé Özer (Longchenpa) and others assert that destruction occurs in a single great cycle [as opposed to the sixty-four cycles of destruction described above]. During this cycle of destruction, everything from the third level of meditative concentration down is destroyed by seven fires of destruction and one deluge, followed by destruction by wind, in the same order of destruction as described above. Because this is a different view according to a different system, it does not coincide with the view expressed in the Individualists' [system of] phenomenology. It should not, however, be considered wrong.

Generally, while this third-order thousand world-system is undergoing formation and destruction, there are inestimable world-systems like ours that exist in other parts of the universe. Even now, periods of destruction, vacuity, formation, and abiding of world-systems in the ten directions are occurring continuously, beyond measure or limit. There are also numerous different patterns of formation and destruction.

[II.C.2.c]
Places That Are Not Destroyed

> **The pure realms and the Seat of Enlightenment, etc., are not destroyed,**
> **Since they are not the result of the origin [of suffering].**

Are there places in this world-system not subject to formation and destruction? The pure realms of the enjoyment dimension of awakening, the natural radiance of the pristine wisdom of the exalted ones, are such places. The realms that arise from the force of the bodhisattvas' inconceivable virtue and vows to purify all realms—Blissful[67] and Delightful, for example—belong to the same category. These realms are not subject to formation and destruction until the activity of the buddhas has been completed.

The Seat of Enlightenment, Vulture's Peak,[68] and other sacred places are not destroyed along with this world. Although they are [part of] this world, they have not originated from [evolutionary actions and emotions that are] the origin of suffering.

Chapter III

Space and Time in the Tantra of the Wheel of Time

The third chapter describes our universe according to the special system of the *Tantra of the Wheel of Time*.[1] It is presented in two parts: (1) the main explanation, and (2) a supplementary explanation of the measures of space and time.

[I] MAIN EXPLANATION

The main explanation consists of three parts: (1) the description of space, (2) the description of time, and (3) a conclusive summary.

[I.A] **Space**

This section has seven parts: (1) the source and reason for this description of space and time, (2) Mount Meru and its foundations, (3) the mountains and continents, (4) the twelve lands of evolutionary action, (5) the Small Land of Jambu and its six regions, (6) the types of beings, and (7) the celestial sphere and time-conjunctions.

[I.A.1] *The Source and Reason for this Description of Space and Time*

> ***The King of Tantras of the Primordial Buddha***
> **Refutes erroneous systems and integrates the outer, inner,**
> **And alternative [levels].**

[The source for this description of space and time] is the *Great King of Tantras of the Sacred Primordial Buddha,*[2] the [tantra] of the Glorious Wheel of Time, the pinnacle of all Buddhist systems. This tantra refutes the erroneous descriptions of space and time based on incomplete or one-sided perspectives found in the systems of non-Buddhists and the common systems of the proclaimers and solitary sages.

[The outer Wheel of Time denotes] our world-system, which reaches a height of 400,000 leagues. The inner [Wheel of Time] is the adamantine body[3] which is four of one's own cubits [in height]. The alternative [Wheel of Time] consists of the four parts of the maṇḍalas[4] [of the Wheel of Time,[5]] which are of equal dimensions. Based on these levels, the ultimate [Wheel of Time] (the four branches of familiarization and accomplishment[6] or the binding of the crucial four indestructible states[7]) purifies what must be purified—the impurities of the four states.[8] The result of that purification is the actualization of the four pure dimensions of awakening. Therefore, these levels are unified into a single comprehensive system. The following descriptions of space and time are based on that integration.

[I.A.2]
Mount Meru and its Foundations

> **In the center of space rest spherical foundations**
> **Of wind, fire, water, and earth, [proportional in size to**
> **the measure between] the soles of the feet and the waist.**
> **Mount Meru, its neck, face, and crowning protuberance**
> **[Are proportional to the measure between] the waist and**
> **the crown of the head.**

In the middle of space rests a spherical foundation of dark wind, 50,000 leagues in thickness. Above that rest the spheres of fire, water, and earth, [one directly on the top of the other]. All are completely circular, of the same thickness [as the wind], and [arranged one within the other, like bowls placed one inside the next, the upper rims of each being level]. The thickness of each of these [four spheres] corresponds proportionally to each of the four hand spans (two cubits) that the human body measures from the soles of the feet to the waist.

The diameters of the spheres are as follows: the wind extends 400,000 leagues; the fire, 300,000; the water, 200,000; and the earth, 100,000. All four are [semi-]spherical; their outer circumference is three times their diameter.

Above these stands Mount Meru, 100,000 leagues in height, [corresponding to] the one full cubit measure from the waist to the base of the neck [of a human body]. This mountain is the basis of the celestial spheres and the axis of their rotation.

Above Mount Meru, its "neck" reaches 25,000 leagues in height; its "face," 50,000 leagues; and its "crown protuberance," 25,000 leagues, totalling 100,000. These [three, Mount Meru's neck, face, and crown protuberance] have no physical forms. However, the names "neck," etc., are used to indicate their imaginary forms. These higher levels [of the world-system] are constituted of only the most subtle elements, whereas the lower levels are composed of all the coarse elements—earth, water, fire, wind, and space. The coarser elements are not found [at the higher levels]; only the last two—wind and space—of the five elements remain [in the higher parts of Mount Meru].

The proportions [of the upper parts of Mount Meru] correspond to those of the human body: the neck is six finger-widths, the face is a hand-span, and from the hairline to the crown of the head is six finger-widths. Altogether, this equals one full cubit. Thus, two cubits [is the measure] from the waist to the crown of the head [of a human being].

The center is green; the east, blue; the north, white; the south, red;
And the west, yellow. Each part is composed of a precious substance.

The center of Mount Meru is green in color; the east side is blue; the north, white; the south, red; the west, yellow. Each part is composed of a precious substance—emerald, blue beryl, crystal, ruby, and topaz. These jewels are coarse elements formed from the six [basic] elements—space, wind, fire, earth, water, and pervasive pristine wisdom.

From the [edge of the] vast upper surface hang five indestructible enclosures

In a concentric arrangement; the outer ones are progressively longer.

The top of Mount Meru measures 50,000 [leagues] in diameter. The base (where the mountain meets the earth sphere) measures 16,000 [leagues] in diameter. Thus, Mount Meru is shaped like a porcelain cup, with a vast upper surface. Five concentric enclosures hang from the edge of this vast upper surface, like ornamental curtains, completely encircling the mountain.

From the innermost outward, the enclosures are progressively longer, the outermost enclosure being even with the peak of Cool Mountain Range. As a result, the light of the sun and moon does not strike the continents within this enclosure. However, the human inhabitants there are sustained by their own natural luminosity. (Details of these continents will be presented below.)

The illustrious Tsuglag Trengwa taught that the central of the five [enclosures] of Mount Meru resembles a main axis and that the four remaining [enclosures] hang down, giving the appearance of a five-pointed scepter.

There are evidently many different models of this world-system. This explanation is based upon the most prevalent model.

At the base is a ledge which forms an indestructible perimeter.

The base of Mount Meru is encircled by a ledge which forms an impenetrable perimeter 1000 leagues wide. The distance between the outer boundary of this ledge and [the point on the surface of the earth sphere in a direct line below] the outer limit of the upper surface of Mount Meru is 16,000 leagues. In this area are situated alternating [rings] of continents, oceans, and mountain ranges.

[I.A.3]
The Mountains and the Continents

Between the six continents—Moon, White, Most Excellent, Kuśa Grass, Centaur, and Crane—
Are [six] oceans: Honey, Butter, Yogurt, Milk, Water, and Beer,

Encircled by the mountains Blue Radiance, Mandara Blossom, Night, Jewel Radiance, Vessel, and Cool.

Six [concentric rings of] continents are situated around Mount Meru [and] within the outermost of the five indestructible enclosures. In outward succession, these are known as Moon, White, Most Excellent, Kuśa Grass,[9] Centaur,[10] and Crane. Between these, in the same order, lie rings of oceans—Honey, Butter, Yogurt, Milk, Water, and Beer. An enclosing mountain range is situated at the edge of each of these [oceans]; these six are called Blue Radiance, Mandara Blossom,[11] Night, Jewel Radiance, Vessel,[12] and Cool. Each [ring of] mountains, continent, and ocean has the same width—888 leagues, three earshots, 1,111 bow-lengths, ten finger-widths, and five and one-third barley seeds.

These are lands of experience. The seventh continent,
The Greater Land of Jambu, said to be the land of evolutionary action,
Is located between Cool Mountain Range and the edge of the salt water ocean.
The seventh mountain range forms the Indestructible Perimeter,
Surrounded by the fire and wind arising from the respective spheres.
Beyond this is vacuity, devoid of any attributes.

[The lands between Meru] and the Cool Mountain Range are known as lands [where beings] experience [the results of their past actions, without the possibility of performing new evolutionary actions]. The area between the outer side of Cool Mountain Range and the inner border of the salt water ocean defines the seventh continent ring, known as the Greater Land of Jambu, the land of evolutionary action. The Greater Land of Jambu comprises twelve land masses, evenly distributed in the cardinal and intermediate directions, [with seas surrounding them]. These twelve land masses [plus the seas] form a ring 25,000 leagues wide.

A salt water ocean, 50,000 leagues wide, surrounds this continent ring. Beyond the ocean stands the seventh mountain [ring], the Great Indestructible Perimeter. This in turn is surrounded by the fire rising from the sphere of fire (the Horse-faced Fire), which itself is surrounded by the wind rising from the sphere of wind. The width of each of these two extends 50,000 [leagues]. The four spheres of wind, fire, water, and earth [are arranged] one within the other, the outer edge of each turning upward. The upper exposed surfaces of all [four spheres] rest evenly with one another.

The full height [of our world-system] is the distance between the pinnacle of existence [that is, the crown protuberance of Mount Meru] and the [lower limit of] the wind sphere. The breadth of the world-system is [the distance between the two outer extremities of the wind sphere]. These two dimensions of height and breadth both measure [400,000] leagues. Surrounding this world-system is only vacuity, devoid of attributes of motility, darkness, and lightness.[13]

[I.A.4]
The Twelve Lands of Evolutionary Action

> **The twelve lands of evolutionary action—the great continents of wind, fire, water, and earth—**
> **Are situated in the center [of each] of the four directions.**
> **They are semi-circular, triangular, round, and square in shape**
> **And are flanked by smaller continents. All are positioned like lotus petals.**

The area of evolutionary action, the seventh continent ring, the Greater Land of Jambu, is divided into twelve land masses. Each of these is encircled by a large sea that merges with the [surrounding salt water] ocean. The four great continents occupy the central positions in the four cardinal directions: to the east is situated the continent of wind, semi-circular [in shape]; to the south, the continent of fire, triangular; to the west, the continent of water, round; to the north, the continent of earth, square. The size [of these] is, respectively, seven thousand, eight thousand, nine thousand, and ten thousand leagues in breadth. Each of the great continents is flanked by two smaller continents; [all twelve] are positioned in a circular arrangement, like the petals of a lotus. Thus, [there are] three southern continents, three western continents, three northern continents, and three eastern continents. The three southern continents are referred to as "the eastern southern continent," "the central [southern continent]," and "the western [southern continent]." The terms used in the *[Treasury of] Phenomenology* (such as "Tail-Fan [Island]"), references to small islands, and so forth, are not found in this [system].

[I.A.5]
The Small Land of Jambu and its Six Regions

> **The Exalted Land is situated in the south of the Small Land of Jambu.**
> **Situated to the north are, successively, Tibet, Khotan, China, Śambhala, and the Great Snow Range.**

The three southern continents together are called the Small Land of Jambu, a land of evolutionary action. The central southern continent contains six regions. The first is Exalted Land (India), which comprises six cities—Magadhā[14] (where the seat of enlightenment, the place where bodhisattvas develop adamantine contemplation,[15] is located), Vaiśālī,[16] Śrāvastī,[17] Kormo Jig,[18] Sāketa,[19] and Campāka[20]—and many surrounding provinces such as Baṅgala, Kauśāmbi, and Kashmir.

A succession of other countries is found to the north of the Exalted Land. In closest proximity is Tibet, the country that the bodhisattva Mighty Lord of the World[21] made his own. Next is Khotan,[22] the land that the exalted Śāriputra and Vaiśravaṇa[23] created by releasing the [waters of a] lake and where the Gomasalakanda Stūpa[24] is found. Next is China, a land enhanced by the four great mountains such as Five-Peaked Mountain (Wu-Tai Shan), where the exalted Mañjuśrī dwells, appearing as a youth. Next is the country of Śambhala, protected by the thirty-two chieftains,[25] Buddhist kings who are emanations of bodhisattvas and wrathful deities. This country has nine hundred and seventy million cities, principal among which is Kalāpa.[26] [Most distant from the Exalted Land] lies the Great Snow Mountain Range that joins the northern snow mountains of Śambhala and is situated at the northernmost extremity of this continent of Jambu.

[I.A.6]
The Types of Beings

> **Thirty-one existences—eleven desire, sixteen form, four [formless]—**
> **Live within these [environments].**

The [Wheel of Time] Tantra does not enumerate sentient beings, the inhabitants of this world-system, in the conventional way. It teaches that thirty-one [types of] beings—eleven in the desire realm, sixteen in the form realm, and four in the formless realm—live within the cosmological features described above ([i.e.,] Mount Meru and the surrounding regions).

First, eleven [types of beings] live in the desire realm. These are summarized as follows:

> Hell [beings], starving spirits, animals,
> Humans, demi-gods, and six types of gods in the desire realm.

A hell is located in each half (of the thickness dimension) of the four spherical foundations of this world-system, beginning in the lower half of the spherical foundation of earth. These seven parts, in descending order, are the locations for the following hells:

> Pebbles, Sand, Swamp,
> Smoke, Fire, Great Darkness,
> And Great Wailing—the seven [hells].

The eighth, the Indestructible Flame Hell, is not found in a location separate from that of the seventh hell, but it is considered as a separate hell because a different experience of suffering characterizes it.

The two parts of the upper half of the spherical foundation of earth provide the locations for the realms of the demi-gods and the *nāgas*. The demi-gods inhabit the upper part; the *nāgas*, the lower.

Humans [inhabit] various continents, some of which are places where only the results of past actions are experienced; others are places where new evolutionary actions can be performed. Starving spirits and animals also inhabit these places;

this Tantra does not specify any other habitats for these forms of life.

There are six [classes of] desire realm gods—the heaven of the Four Groups of the Great Kings is located between the "shoulder" level of Mount Meru and the ground level [where Mount Meru meets the spherical foundation of earth]. The heaven of the Thirty-three rests on the top of Mount Meru. Four heavens are situated above that—Free from Conflict, Joyful, Enjoying Creations, and Mastery Over Others' Creations. Each occupies one quarter of the lower third of the neck of Mount Meru.

Second, the sixteen states of existence of the form realm [are situated as follows]: The four [realms of] wind are located at the four parts of the forehead of Mount Meru—Unsurpassed, Good Vision, Without Distress, and Not Greater. The four [realms of] fire are situated at [the four parts of] the nose area of Mount Meru—Great Results, Merit-Born, Cloudless, and Flourishing Virtue. The four [realms of] water are located at the chin area—Limitless Virtue, Lesser Virtue, Clear Light, and Measureless Light. The four [realms of] earth are located at the two [remaining] thirds of the neck [of Mount Meru]—Dim Light, Great Pure Ones, Chanting in the Presence [of Brahma], and Group of the Pure Ones.

Third, in the formless realm, there are four types of beings. Sentient beings absorbed in the four [states]—Infinite Space, Infinite Consciousness, Nothing Whatever, and Neither Discernment nor No Discernment—are said to live in levels from the crown protuberance of Mount Meru down to the hairline.

The three realms, consisting of the thirty-one existences of our world-system [mentioned above], are formed in temporal sequence. Because the three realms have the nature of enlightened mind, speech, and body, their development follows a parallel sequence: the formless realm [enlightened mind] comes into existence first, followed by the form realm and the desire realm. Furthermore, life within the desire realm comes into existence following the same sequence: life first forms below the earth, then on it, then above it.

[I.A.7]
The Celestial Sphere and Time-Conjunctions

> **The celestial sphere pervades space between Mount Meru and the mountain of fire.**
> **It is a belt of wind, within which the twelve houses**
> **And the twenty-eight constellations formed first.**

The celestial sphere[27] pervades the space between the outer circumference at which the [outermost impenetrable] enclosure of Mount Meru meets Cool Mountain Range and the inner circumference of the mountainous [ring] of fire [i.e., Horse-faced Fire]. The celestial sphere is a circular belt possessing the nature of wind that supports [all] the celestial palaces of the gods. Since it is slightly higher near Mount Meru, it has the bent shape of a bow. Near the mountainous [ring] of fire, it is slightly lower, resembling a lotus petal. It forms a complete circle [around Mount Meru].

Concerning the meaning of the word,

> The [Sanskrit] term *gola* (celestial sphere) may be translated
> As hollow, concave and convex, circular, heavy and light, and so forth.
> Translated precisely, it denotes "that which holds up the heavens."

The form [of the celestial sphere] is described differently by different scholars—as resembling the spokes of a wheel; rising up or spreading out; as resembling a stack of helmets, a chain, or a shield. [These descriptions] are based on reason and scriptural reference. The view that the celestial sphere is shaped like a cluster of boats eventually became the most prevalent. The eighth lord [Karmapa] Mikyö Dorjé, with some amusement, provided a clear description of this in the *Ocean of the Mind*.

The term "house," from the [Sanskrit] *rāśi*, denotes a gathering or cluster. The *Fundamental Tantra of Mañjuśrī*[28] states that there are thirty-six houses; other sources present different enumerations. Regardless of how many houses have formed on the celestial sphere, twelve houses exert the most pronounced influence—both positive and negative—on [the affairs of] this world. They are:

Aries, Taurus, Gemini, Cancer,
Leo, Virgo, Libra, Scorpio,
Sagittarius, Capricorn,[29] Aquarius, Pisces.

Infinite numbers of stars are contained within the houses, which are the area of their rotation. The sage Delight in Stars (Jyotirāma) has stated:

Know that the number of stars
Is two hundred and eighty-five million.

Further,

In some discussions related to phenomenology, it is said
That in the sky of six empty spheres,
Nāga eyes see the number of stars.[30]

Thus, there are [many viewpoints] such as [this one that asserts] that there are 28,000,000 [stars]. In the center of all stars is the pole-star and Canopus, which are shaped like a top ornament and its surrounding canopy. In addition, twenty-seven constellations are considered in astrological calculations to predict the outcomes of specific actions:

[1] Beta Arietis
[2] Thirty-five Arietis
[3] Eta Tauri
[4] Aldebaran
[5] Lambda Orionis
[6] Alpha Orionis
[7] Beta Geminorum
[8] Delta Cancri
[9] Alpha Hydroe
[10] Regulus
[11] Delta Leonis
[12] Beta Leonis
[13] Delta Corvi
[14] Spica Virgis
[15] Arcturus
[16] Alpha Libroe
[17] Delta Scorpio
[18] Antares
[19] Lambda Scorpii
[20] Delta Sagittari
[21] Sigma Sagittari
[22] Alpha Aquiloe
[23] Beta Delphinum
[24] Lambda Aquarius
[25] Alpha Pegasi
[26] Gama Pegasi
[27] Zeta Piscum

The constellations called Lyra and Alpha Aquiloe are both situated in one star cluster; however, they may be counted separately to make twenty-eight. Concisely expressed, the houses, the twenty-eight constellations, and so on formed [before the planets].

[The houses] are situated in a clockwise arrangement.
Planets such as the sun and moon rise above them.
[Eight] move counter-clockwise; Eclipser [moves] clockwise.

Each constellation is divided into four quarters, nine such quarters situated in each house. Thus, Beta Arietis, Thirty-five Arietis, and one quarter of Eta Tauri are situated in Aries House, and so on. [The houses and constellations] are situated in a clockwise arrangement. The first of these houses is Aries, and the first constellation is Beta Arietis, since this is where the movement of the sun begins [at the beginning of the year].

The planets rise above the stars[31] that are positioned within their respective houses. These include the Sun in the last quarter of Beta Geminorum[32] and the Moon in the first [quarter] of Beta Arietis,[33] and so forth. These planets govern the houses and constellations like lords.

The ten planets are Sun, Moon, Mars, Mercury,
Jupiter, Venus, Saturn,
Long Tail [of Smoke], Eclipser, and Fire of Time.[34]

The eight from the Sun to Long Tail begin their natural movement counterclockwise around Mount Meru, and Eclipser and Fire of Time clockwise. Four of these—Sun, Mars, Jupiter, and Saturn—are called malefic planets because they are right branches; and the four—Moon, Mercury, Venus, and Long Tail—are called benefic planets because they are left branches.

[I.B]
Time

This section has two parts: (1) the three types of days, and (2) different ways of explaining the four eras.

[I.B.1]
The Three Types of Days

A solar day is measured in terms of six breaths and sixty minor clepsydra measures constituting one major clepsydra measure of time.
Lunar, solar, and house days are determined
In relation to the movement of the moon, sun, and constellations.

One breath refers to one complete breath—the inhalation, pause, and exhalation—of a healthy young person. Six breaths [equals] one minor clepsydra measure, [24 seconds]; sixty minor clepsydra measures [equals] one major clepsydra measure of time [24 minutes][35]; and the time required for sixty major clepsydra measures of time [to elapse] equals one solar day [a 24-hour cycle]. 21,600 breaths are taken within the period of a solar day. [In one solar day,] twelve movements[36] or time-conjunctions occur, each time-conjunction being equivalent to 1,800 breaths or five major clepsydra measures. A time-conjunction is the basis for all calculations of time. The three types of days —lunar day, solar day, and house day[37]—are determined in relation to the movement of the moon, sun, and constellations.

The [three types of] days are equivalent to one fifteenth of a phase of the moon, one revolution of the sun around the continents,
And a thirtieth of the time [required for the sun] to move through a house.
Each is longer than the preceding one. Based on lunar months and house years,
The four seasons occur in natural sequence on earth.

A lunar day is equal to one fifteenth of the waxing or of the waning phase of the moon and is a period of time slightly longer than fifty-nine major clepsydra measures of time. A solar day is equal to one [complete] revolution of the sun around the four continents, from the dawn of one day until the dawn of the next, or one complete cycle of the major clepsydra measures for a day of the week, a period of time equal to sixty major clepsydra measures of time. A house day is equal to one thirtieth of the time [it takes] the sun to move through one of the [twelve] houses, a period of time slightly longer than sixty major clepsydra measures of time. Therefore, the solar day is longer than the lunar day, and the house day is longer than the solar day.

One of these three [days] is used as the basic unit for calculating a month or a year, [depending] on the relative length of time [to be determined]. For a period up to a month, the principal [measure used] is the solar day because both lunar and house days must be calculated in relation to the solar day. For a month, the principal measure is the lunar day. Although the passing of thirty lunar days does not equal thirty solar days, the moon completes its cycle in this period. Therefore, it is necessary to use the lunar day as the basic measure for a month.

[On the other hand], the lunar day is not used as a measure for the year. The reason is that when one subtracts the three hundred and sixty-five solar days from the three hundred and seventy-one lunar days [in a year,] an excess of six days remains. Because of this extra portion, [a lunar day] does not equal a day of the year. On this point, the *Commentary to the Treasury of Phenomenology*[38] states:

> After the two halves of each month
> Of winter, spring and summer have elapsed,
> An extra half day remains in the month.
> Since it does not equal a day of the year, the learned reject
> [the lunar day as a measure for a year].

The house day is used as the principal unit of measure for a year. This is because a full year equals the time required for one full cycle of the four seasons of equal duration. To complete such a cycle, the sun must make a full revolution through the twelve house months, each consisting of thirty house days. The *Vajra Ḍāka Tantra*[39] states:

> The journey of the sun, going and returning,
> Is referred to as one year.

Thus, the year consists of neither more nor less than three hundred and sixty house days or twelve house months.

A period of twelve [solar or lunar] months, each month consisting of either thirty solar days or thirty lunar days, does not constitute a house year. Eleven days would have to be added [to a year of three hundred and sixty lunar days] for it to equal a house year. Similarly, slightly more than five solar days must be added [to a year of three hundred and sixty solar days] for it to equal a house year.

The completion of the period in which the moon waxes fifteen [days] and wanes fifteen [days] constitutes one month, known as a lunar month. One year, as determined by one complete [cycle of] summer, fall, winter, and spring, is known as a house year.

Stellar houses are the loci for the transits of the nine planets. The effect of these transits on earth is the occurrence of the four seasons. When it is spring in the three southern land masses, it is summer in the eastern continents, autumn in the northern continents, and winter in the western continents. [In other words, the four seasons in the four continents] are occurring in a counterclockwise arrangement. In each of the land masses, however, the seasons occur in their natural sequence (i.e., clockwise): first spring, then summer, autumn, and winter.

Twelve time-conjunctions occur in space. One time-conjunction is defined as the time it takes the planets to transit a single house. [As mentioned above, each constellation has four quarters;] a house is composed of nine such quarters. Eventually all the planets complete the twelve time-conjunctions. However, the statement that all the houses of the twelve time-conjunctions are transited [in exactly] one year applies only to the sun's movement.[40] Similarly, only the sun transits the twelve time-conjunctions, whereas the houses appear in their entirety once each day.

Time-conjunctions affect the quality of life.

Inherent to the human body, which is composed of six elements, are the internal energy-winds of the twelve personal time-conjunctions. When these energy-winds circulate in harmony with their natural patterns, the body remains in good health. Discomfort results when these energy-winds are out of harmony with their natural patterns. Similarly, when the external energy-winds of the twelve time-conjunctions move in harmony with their natural patterns, the quality of the environment improves. The *Tantra of Wheel of Time*[41] states:

> Grain will grow in secluded regions, and trees will be laden with firm fruit.

Moreover, [due to their influence,] the human lifespan increases from 100 years to 800,000 [years].

When these winds move out of harmony with their natural patterns, the quality of [both] the environment and beings deteriorates, and the lifespan decreases from 800,000 years to 100. Thus, depending upon the relative harmony or disharmony with natural patterns, the quality of life fluctuates through time in general and during specific periods—the seasons, etc.

[I.B.2]
Different Ways of Explaining the Four Eras

> **Explanations of the four eras of the doctrine**
> **Of the wheel-holders, of the world-system, and of entering vacuity supplement the above.**

In addition to the above description of time, scholars with broad knowledge of the scriptures have presented explanations [on the following topics]: (1) the four eras of the Buddha's doctrine, (2) the four eras of the wheel-holders,[42] lords over humanity, (3) the four eras of our world-system, and (4) the four eras of the planets entering vacuity. Numerous presentations of these subjects have been provided by Indian and Tibetan scholars; to elaborate on these would lead to an endless discussion. The following brief explanation accords with that of the eighth lord [Karmapa], the venerable Mikyö Dorjé.

[I.B.2.a]
The Four Eras of the Buddha's Doctrine

The doctrine of the Buddha endures for ten 500-year periods [following his passing from this world]. The first [era], composed of three periods of spiritual attainment, is considered [the era of] completeness. The second, composed of three periods of spiritual practice, is considered [the era of] three-quarters. The third, composed of three periods of theoretical teaching, is called [the era of] two-quarters. The fourth, the one period of time [when] only the outward appearance [of the religious order] is maintained, is called [the era of] conflict.

The division [of the Buddha's doctrine concerning] discipline[43] designates the era of completeness as the period [from the Buddha's passing into perfect peace] until the occasion of the formal testimony [in the presence of the monastic community] of the first defeating act.[44] The era of three-quarters is designated as the subsequent period lasting until the occasion of the testimony of the second defeating act, and so on. This is essentially the same theory as that proposed by the scholar

[*Daṃṣṭrāsena*] in his *Commentary to the Large, [Medium and Small] Transcendent Wisdom Scriptures.*[45] Similarly, the *Concise Tantra [of the Wheel of Time]*[46] provides a source for this classification [of the four eras], implicit in the following:

> It is as the Protector of the World [taught].

[I.B.2.b]
The Four Eras of the Wheel-Holders

In our land, [the central of the three southern continents,] the four eras [of the wheel-holders] lasts for a total of 21,600 years. Completeness, three-quarters, and two-quarters each lasts 5,400 years. The initial stage of the conflict [era] lasts for 3,600 years. This period, added to the total of the former three eras, totals 19,800 years, the time period during which Buddhism prevails. The remaining 1,800 [years is] the time during which barbaric religions prevail.

Fifty-one years after the chieftain Hidden Omnipresent One[47] ascended the lion throne [of the kingdom of Śambhala], the 1,800-year period of barbarism began. It will end fifty-one years after Forceful [Wheel-Holder][48] ascends the lion throne. Forceful [Wheel-Holder] will conquer the arrogant barbarians[49] with the four divisions of his army[50] and convert them to Buddhism. At that point, the era of completeness will begin again, and the human lifespan will gradually increase to 1,800 years. The year that the era of completeness begins [here] corresponds to the first year of the 1,800-year barbaric period on the western of the three southern continents.

At the same time, of the two sons of Forceful [Wheel-Holder], The Pure and the Chief of the Gods, The Pure will ascend to power in this land. Other kings descended from the family of the Chief of the Gods will defeat the barbarians of the western southern continent 1,800 years after the era of completeness has begun here. [This victory will mark] the beginning of the era of completeness on that continent.

At that time, the 1,800-year barbaric period begins on the southern of the three western continents. At the end of that period, Buddhist kings descended from the family of Chief of the Gods will defeat the barbarians, and the era of completeness will begin [there]. Following this pattern, the other nine land masses, in succession, enter the 1,800-year period of barbarism. The barbarians are [then] defeated by Buddhist kings and the era of completeness begins. Starting with Chief of the Gods, [wheel-holders] of that lineage appear in a clockwise manner through the twelve lands. When they have all made their appearance, a chieftain also known as Forceful [Wheel-Holder] will once again defeat the barbarians in this land, and the era of completeness will begin.

In brief, the era of completeness is experienced in the land that is the residence of a chieftain who subdues the non-Buddhist barbarians. The adjacent land, in a clockwise direction, experiences the era of conflict; the next experiences two-quarters; and the next to that, three-quarters.

[I.B.2.c]
The Four Eras of Our World-System

These can be understood from the description given [in the previous chapter]. The number of years constituting the eras and other details will not be discussed here.

[I.B.2.d]
The Four Eras of the Planets Entering Vacuity

The following quote from the *Wheel of Time Tantra*[51] states the duration of the four eras of the planets' entering vacuity and how this occurs:

> Empty, empty, space, *nāga,* and hand, the sage, and the moon are the duration of the era of completeness.
> Space, empty, flavor, nine, and the sun are known as the number of years of the era of three-quarters.
> Empty, space, the Vedas, flavor, and snake [are] in fact the years of the era of two-quarters.
> Empty, space, space, eyes, qualities, and sea-treasure are the number of years of the era of conflict.
> At the end of these years, the group of planets dwell in pure vacuity devoid of houses.[52]

A complete transit of the seven planets of the week[53] (the sun and the others) and Eclipser through the twenty-seven constellations is known as one great planetary day. This lasts approximately sixty-four years and seven months. One and a half planetary days lasts ninety-six years, ten and a half months. The *Tantra of the Wheel of Time* designates this a lesser century. A Wheel of Time year is the length of time in a one-hundred-year period that the pristine wisdom aspect is accumulated: three years and three half-months. This is calculated in the following way: one thirty-second of the 36,000 days of a century is 1,125 days; converted to years and months, this period equals three years and three half-months.

A hundred-year period, which includes a Wheel of Time year, is equal to three planetary half days. The first [planetary] half-day embodies lightness; the second, motility; and the third, darkness. These are related, in corresponding order, to the external phenomena of phlegm, bile, and wind. When these three —phlegm, bile, and wind—as internal constituents of the human body, are in balance, physical health is maintained. Imbalance [of these constituents] causes disease and deterioration of health. Similarly, even in the world, balance [of these elements] preserves [the environment]; imbalance has a destructive influence. Although there may be some imbalance [in our physical health], the aspect of pristine wisdom [nevertheless enters] the central [channel in the proportion appropriate to] the Wheel of Time year.

Three planetary days, together with the corresponding [two] Wheel of Time years, equals two hundred years. Each day within this period consists of sixty major clepsydra measures of time; this entire period consists of 4,320,000 major clepsydra measures. In terms of the human body, 4,320,000 breaths are taken during a 200-day period. At the end of this time, some small amount of wind will have entered the central [channel] of even an ordinary individual. In the external [universe], at the end of 4,320,000 years (a period numerically equivalent to the number of major clepsydra measures and breaths), all the planets will enter the vacuity [beyond our universe], completing one great [cycle of] the four eras. Then, beginning with the specific transits, the era of completeness again arises, and so on. This cycle of the four eras thus repeats itself again and again.

[I.C]
A Conclusive Summary

> **The Victorious One did not base his teachings on the belief that a single system is the only valid one,**
> **[But taught] in response to the interests and abilities of those he guided.**

One may wonder why this description of the universe does not accord with that of phenomenology and other systems. The omniscient Victorious One did not view any aspect of either the environment or the inhabitants of our world-system as ultimately real. Therefore, his teaching is not one that, based on a belief in a single view, sets forth a particular system as the only valid one. Instead, the Buddha spoke in response to the various levels of capabilities, interests, and dispositions of those to be guided [to enlightenment].

All [the different teachings given by the Buddha] are true. However, the Wheel of Time description of time and space contains the essential element of the integration of the three levels —outer, inner, and alternative. This system should thus be considered the supreme one.

[II]
MEASURES OF SPACE AND TIME

The explanation of measures has two parts: (1) an introduction, and (2) the main explanation.

[II.A]
Introduction

The subject is introduced in this way:

> **There are a variety of units for measuring space and time:**

[II.B]
Main Explanation

This section has two parts: (1) measures particular to the Wheel of Time, and (2) a supplementary discussion of measures used in the system of phenomenology.

[II.B.1]
Measures Particular to the Wheel of Time

Eight minute particles equals one fine particle;
A hair-tip, ketsé seed, louse, barley seed, and finger-width [are determined] in a similar manner.
Twenty-four [finger-widths equals one] cubit; four cubits equals one bow-length;
Two thousand [bow-lengths equals one] earshot; four of those equals a league.

The following measures are used to determine the spatial dimensions of the world and its inhabitants: Eight minute particles equals one fine particle. A hair-tip, ketsé seed,[54] louse, barley seed, and finger-width [are determined] in a similar manner; for all seven of these, eight of each of the previous measures, lined up side by side, equals the length of the subsequent one. Twenty-four finger-widths equals a cubit; four cubits equals one bow-length; two thousand bow-lengths, one earshot; and four earshots, one league. The league is used to measure the outer world.

[II.B.2]
Supplementary Discussion of Measurements Used in the System of Phenomenology

This section has two parts: (1) preamble, and (2) an extensive explanation.

[II.B.2.a]
Preamble

The phenomenology system presents units of form and time, and components of words.

Scholars of phenomenology describe the measures and the compositional elements of space and time in terms of units of form and time, and in terms of components of words. These are now explained as a supplementary topic.

[II.B.2.b]
Extensive Explanation

This section has three parts: (1) the units of form, (2) the units of time, and (3) the components of words.

[II.B.2.b.i]
Units of Form

Seven minute particles [equals] one fine particle;
Iron, water, rabbit, sheep, ox, and sun-ray particles
Louse egg, louse, barley seed, and finger-width are similarly determined.
Twenty-four finger-widths [equals] a cubit; four cubits, a bow-length;
Five hundred [bow-lengths], one earshot,
Or the measure to solitude; eight of those, a league.
The third-order thousand [world-system] is described and measured with these units.

These are the units of form:

Seven minute particles equals one fine particle.
Seven fine particles equals one iron particle.
Seven iron particles equals one water particle.
Seven water particles equals one rabbit particle.
Seven rabbit particles equals one sheep particle.
Seven sheep particles equals one ox particle.
Seven ox particles equals one sun-ray particle.
Seven sun-ray particles equals one louse egg.
Seven louse eggs equals one louse.
Seven lice equals one barley seed.
Seven barley seeds equals the width of the middle finger.
Twenty-four finger-widths equals one cubit.
Four cubits equals a bow-length.
Five hundred bow-lengths equals one earshot.
One earshot beyond a village is called solitude.
One half earshot nearer than that is called the outskirts.
Eight earshots equals one league, or four thousand bow-lengths.

Using the measure of a league, one can describe and measure [all form] including Meru, King of Mountains, up to the third-order thousand world-system.

[II.B.2.b.ii]
Units of Time

One sixty-fourth of a finger-snap
Is the smallest unit of time. One hundred and twenty [of these units]

Equals an instant. Sixty instants [equals] one moment.
Thirty [moments equals] a period; thirty periods, a solar day;
Thirty solar days, a month; and twelve months, a year.
Based on these units, the measurable and the immeasurable are calculated.

Sixty-four (or sixty, according to some) brief instants elapse during the snap of the fingers of a healthy individual. A single of these brief instants is the smallest unit of time. One hundred and twenty of these units equals one instant. Sixty instants equals one moment. Since there are nine hundred moments in a day, this is one nine-hundredth of a day. Thirty moments equals one period; thirty periods, one solar day; thirty solar days, one month; and twelve months, one year.

Time gradually elapses in the twelve continents (the four great and the eight smaller) as the function of the inner and outer aspects of the twelve experiential elements and of the twelve links of interdependent origination. The so-called twelve houses also move in stages.

Proficient [use of these units of measurement] permits calculation of time periods, lifespans of individuals, etc., of measurable durations (measured in hundreds, thousands, ten thousands, hundred thousands, and so on) and of that which is [considered to be] immeasurable (i.e., beyond ten to the sixtieth power).

[II.B.2.b.iii]
Components of Words

Individual letters are the components of words.
[Groups of words] form sentences.
If examined, [words] do not capture [the essence, but are] deceptive.

The [Sanskrit] vowel *a* and the consonant *ka* are examples of individual letters. A combination of two, three, or more of these letters forms a word. For example, the combination of *dha* and *i* is *dhi*, meaning intelligence, and the combination of three consonants [*b*, *d*, and *dh*] and two vowels is [the name] Buddha. A group of several words forms a sentence, *namo buddhāya* ("Homage to Buddha"), for example. Since a letter is the basic constituent of a word, a letter in itself does not convey meaning. A word conveys [the meaning of an] object; a term, the particularities of an object.

Upon closer examination, however, a group of words, whether many or few, does not capture the essence [of what is intended to be expressed by it]. It is simply a collection of individual letters. [To use some analogies,] what appears to be a coarse rope is [just] its strands; what appears to be a camel-hair tassel [is just its] individual filaments; and what appears to be a meadow [is just] individual blades of grass. Similarly, [words] are without any true objective status: they are like the reflection of the moon on water, or a mirage, which from the moment of their appearance have a deceptive nature.

Chapter IV
The Causes of Cyclic Life

The fourth chapter, an explanation of the conditions that create worlds and their inhabitants, has two parts: (1) the context, and (2) the main explanation.

[I]
CONTEXT

> **What causes create the world?**

These introductory words set the context for the main discussion.

[II]
MAIN EXPLANATION

The main explanation has two parts: (1) refuting non-Buddhist theories of creation, and (2) setting forth the Buddhist theories.

[II.A]
Refuting Non-Buddhist Theories of Creation

> **The erroneous theories of the non-Buddhists claim that [the world]**
> **Was created by Īśvara or the sage, or that it arose from the self or naturally.**

The scriptures of the believers in Īśvara[1] state:

> If Īśvara, like a potter [who makes his pots], had not created the manifold world,

> The earth would not exist, Mt. Meru would not be, and there would be no ocean.
> This array of sun, moon, and stars would not be an object of sight.
> Since they do exist, some say, "Īśvara is the creator of life."

This expresses the belief that Īśvara, like a potter, created these worlds where beings live. On the other hand, the Secretists who adhere to the finality of the Vedas,[2] contend that below all the worlds lives an individual—a great sage called Color of the Sun—who is the creator of the worlds. Others assert that everything arose from the self[3] or [non-manifest] principal.[4] Nihilists[5] claim that all worlds and beings have arisen naturally, without [depending on] causes. This is expressed in such words as these:

> Good lady, what learned [people] say
> Is misleading like the tracks of a wolf.
> Who created the pollen-bed of a lotus?
> Who designed the patterns on the peacock's [feathers]?
> Who sharpened the tip of the thorn?
> Everything arose naturally, without causes.

There are many erroneous theories [concerning the origin of the world] such as these, fabricated by the confused intellects of non-Buddhist sectarians who are proponents of nihilism or eternalism. [Those who follow] these theories, like blind persons trying to determine the topography of a land, do not reach correct conclusions, but stray far from the truth

[II.B]
Setting Forth the Buddhist Systems

This section has three parts: (1) a general presentation of the causes [that create cyclic life], (2) a detailed explanation of the causes that create the environment, and (3) a presentation of the general process of creation.

[II.B.1]
The Causes of Cyclic Life

This section has two parts: (1) creation caused by actions, and (2) the factor ensuring actions' results.

[II.B.1.a]
Creation Caused by Actions

> **It is taught in the scriptures that worlds and beings**
> **Are created by various actions influenced by subtle and proliferating [emotions].**

Who created worlds and beings? The scriptures of the excellent teachings of the Transcendent One state that they were not created intentionally by Īśvara or by any other creator. [Vasubandhu's *Treasury of Phenomenology*] states:

> The various worlds were produced by evolutionary actions.

Thus, the Buddha taught that all worlds and living beings were created by collective and personal evolutionary actions influenced by subtle and proliferating obscuring emotions.

[II.B.1.b]
The Factor Ensuring Actions' Results

> **The factor ensuring actions' results is said to be acquired or inevitable,**
> **The stream of mental consciousness, the fundamental consciousness,**
> **The mere individual, clear light, and so forth.**

Although an act ceases as soon as it has been done, it will inevitably produce its effect, even after a hundred eons have passed. What is the factor that makes inevitable the causal process through which cause and result are connected?

Some philosophers who have examined this subject assert that the supporting factor is something acquired or possessed. Others maintain that it is an inevitable phenomenon separate [from the cause or its result]. In either case, some sub-schools of the Analysts maintain that this supporting factor is substantially existent while others [maintain that it is] designatively existent. The Idealists assert that fundamental consciousness functions [as the support] upon which the instincts of evolutionary actions are imprinted, after which one experiences their ripening.

Those who postulate the six groups of consciousness[6] but not a fundamental consciousness state that [the support] is the continuum of mental consciousness, [itself only] a designation. Some Centrists assert that the supporting factor is designatively existent, [being the] designation of mere "I" or mere "person." However many similar philosophical views on this subject there are, all are simply reifications based on partial understanding; they do not reflect the truth. At this point, however, we will not refute or confirm any of these theses.

The Mantra perspective can be expressed in this way:

> A subtle, indestructible individual, the great self or person, who is radiant awareness co-existent with the six impure elements, is in every way the basis for the accumulation of actions.

There are two [kinds] of evolutionary action: that which results in shared perception and that which produces personal experience. The former creates the environmental world, and the latter, the inhabitants, sentient beings. The highest yoga tantra, when defining ground, path, and fruition, calls the environmental world "outer," the inhabiting beings "inner," and the ground for the manifestation of both environment and inhabitants—pristine wisdom which accords in quality with those two—"alternative." Both outer [environment] and inner [beings] are the pervaded elements; the alternative (pristine wisdom) is the pervading factor. Together, these are designated as the world-system. "And so forth" [in the root text] indicates that many different explanations of this subject, both general and detailed, have been expounded by Indian and Tibetan scholars.

[II.B.2]
The Causes of the Environment

This section has two parts: (1) the perspective of the Analysts and (2) the perspective of the Wheel of Time and other tantras.

[II.B.2.a]
The Perspective of the Analysts

> **The Analysts and Traditionists state that the environment is created from the wind at the peak [of existence] which remains from the time of destruction,**
> **Or from five types of seeds carried from other worlds.**

The stream [of phenomena] is undispersed and coheres through [the effect] of concordant actions.
Lasting form and time are deceptive impressions within naive minds;
It is taught that the exalted ones comprehend the cessation of particles and moments.

The Analyst and Traditionist Proclaimers, in addition to asserting that evolutionary actions cause the formation of the world, maintain that the cause of the first moment of the wind that creates the desire realm at [the outset] of the age of formation is the form realm wind located at the peak [of existence]. This wind is not destroyed during the previous age of destruction and has the power to [initiate] the production of various coarse results caused by [previous] actions.

Moreover, a discourse of the Buddha states:

> Winds come carrying seeds from other world-systems.

Based on that source, the environment is [said to be] created from five types of seeds: the seed of the root, the seed which opens, the seed of the seed, the seed of the tip, and the seed of the stalk.

To explain, the coarse world forms when many scattered, indivisible, subtle particles converge. The stream of phenomena, which gives the impression of lasting [over a period of time], remains undispersed by violent winds or other agents and coheres due to the effect of the concordant evolutionary actions of sentient beings. Lasting appearances—forms such as mountains [composed of] many subtle particles, and years [composed of] a sequence of moments—are gross deceptive impressions in the minds of the naive. However, the exalted ones are aware of the impermanence of moments and of subtle particles. As Tsunpa Pel Leg's *Seventy Particles*[7] states:

> A single hair in the palm of a hand
> Is not felt by anyone,
> But if it enters the eye,
> It causes great discomfort.
> The naive, who are like the palm of the hand,
> Do not understand conditioned phenomena as [a collection of] particles;
> But the exalted, who are like the eye,
> Understand this and develop disengagement.

[II.B.2.b]
The Perspective of the Tantra of the Wheel of Time

> **Most agree that in the formation [of the world] the mind is the agent, subtle particles and the moving and stationary winds are the objects acted upon,**
> **And the [winds' motions] are the means of creation.**

In order that the perspective of the Tantra of the Wheel of Time may be easily understood, we will explain it in detail employing the format of act, agent, and object acted upon. In the example of a potter who makes a pot, the [creation of the] pot is the act, the potter is the agent, and the clay is the object acted upon. The production process involving the belt, wheel, etc., is the means of creation. Since the act [the creation of the pot] and agent [the potter] are different in substance, the three-fold [format] of act, agent, and object acted upon, posited in relation to the cause and effect of material objects, is a valid one.

[As a second example,] when sense consciousness understands a blue appearance as blue, the understanding of blue as blue is the act. Sense consciousness to which blue appears is the agent. Blue is the object acted upon. The blue aspect [appearing] is the means in the process [of understanding blue]. In relation to consciousness understanding an object, the act and the agent are identical in substance. Therefore, [in this case,] the threefold [format] of act, agent, and object acted upon is a nominal one.

Of these two [examples], the former will be used here to explain how the physical world is formed. First, what is the agent that corresponds to the potter? Candrakīrti's[8] *Introduction to the Central Way*[9] states:

> The mind itself creates living beings
> And the great variety of worlds where they live.
> It is also taught that all forms of life are produced from evolutionary actions;
> But without the mind, there would be no action.

Thus, generally speaking [the agent that creates the world] is the minds of beings in general and in particular the minds of those beings who have performed concordant actions (such as those that impel them to be born in the same world-system). Principally, [the agent] is the radiant awareness nature of the mind of each being.

What is the means of creation that corresponds to [the production process employing] the [potter's] belt and so forth? The means of creation is described in the following way: from the mind's radiant awareness which is accompanied by the three [factors] of semen, blood, and energy-winds, the three inner lights[10] dawn. Following that, the eighty instinctive conceptions arise. These conceptions activate the instincts (that were created by previous virtuous and non-virtuous actions and that are imprinted on the mind) so that they approach the stage in which the form [of the world] manifests [as their result]. At this point, energy-winds that have a similarity with consciousness—which are only manifestations of the [instincts created by the] actions of beings—depart from one world-system and wander in order to form another world-system, moving into the space left empty after the dissolution of the previous world-system. The motions of these energy-winds are the means of creation [of the world]. This is analogous to the movement of a person's vital energy-wind which departs from the corpse after death and wanders until entering a womb in order to be reborn; the movement of this energy-wind is considered to be the means of creation of the body of a person.

What are the elements acted upon, corresponding to the clay? [These are twofold]: [First are] the subtle particles that remain scattered during the period when the world-system has been emptied [of manifest form]. These particles are not perceived by the limited eye [consciousness of an ordinary person] but appear to the eye [consciousness] of a yogi.[11] [Second are] the supports for these particles, the energy-winds that have a similarity with consciousness. These two elements are analogous to the internal phenomena acted upon during the fetal development of the human body—the semen and blood of the parents, and the ten energy-winds. The very subtle particles that remain scattered [after the destruction of a world-system] are termed emptied since they are merely a manifestation of mental instincts and not the object of sense perception.

Two action energy-winds, one mobile and one stationary, are referred to as "having a similarity with consciousness": one energy-wind wanders in order to create a new world when a previous world-system has been destroyed; the other energy-wind remains stationary and does not move elsewhere. They are said to have a similarity with consciousness not because they are of the nature of consciousness but because they display an attribute in common with consciousness, just as semen and blood are said to have attributes in common with the moon and sun.

What similarity do these energy-winds have with consciousness? Consciousness itself lacks color and shape, but due to its character of manifestation, consciousness exhibits various lights. Likewise, the nature of the two action energy-winds is that of space. Nevertheless, they manifest six lights, which cannot be perceived by the senses but are seen by the eye consciousness of the yogi. Therefore, the energy-winds have a similarity with consciousness [i.e., the lights].

These energy-winds manifest three principal lights (green, blue, and black) and other secondary ones. Ten energy-winds, such as the vital [energy-winds] and so forth, are produced from these lights. The ten energy-winds are classified into three [groups] according to their functions: holding energy-winds, churning energy-winds, and shaping energy-winds. Which of the ten energy-winds perform which functions? With regard to the microcosm [i.e., the human body], the chapter [of the *Wheel of Time Tantra*] "Ascertaining the Microcosm"[12] states:

> Oh Lord of Humanity,[13] the body is created through time in this way: The seeds that are present in the lotus [i.e., womb] are retained by that which holds [i.e., the energy-winds related to the element of earth] and then coalesce by [the action of the energy-winds related to the element of] water.
>
> After, the body is brought to maturation by [energy-winds related to the element of] fire, tastes, and tastes[14] being consumed. Its growth is caused by [the energy-winds related to the element of] wind.
>
> [The energy-winds related to the element of] space also provide room for growth.

This process, applied to the macrocosm [i.e., the universe], is explained as follows: The pervading and gift of the gods [energy-winds] (related to the water element) gather the subtle particles [that remain in space following the destruction of the previous world-system]; the *nāga* and wealth king [energy-winds] (related to the earth element) solidify this conglomerate of particles. These are the four holding winds.

The churning winds, the ascending and lizard [energy-winds] (related to the fire element), enhance the conglomeration of particles by their churning action. Following the churning and enhancement of the conglomeration of particles, the shaping energy-winds, the heat-accompanied and turtle [energy-winds] (related to the wind element), shape it while developing and placing it in various locations in space. The vital and downward-voiding [energy-winds] assist all these winds, as their nature is to facilitate [their functions].

Moreover, with respect to the microcosm, the human embryo develops from the semen and blood of the parents through the gelatin[15] and the oblong[16] stages to the fish [-shape][17] and later periods of fetal development.

With respect to the macrocosm, this corresponds to the motions of the most refined essences of the five elements [i.e., the particles] at the beginning stage of the formation of the world when the particular sizes and shapes of the wind and the other spherical foundations have not yet formed. First, during the period of space, the subtle particles, characterized by emptiness, remain scattered. Later, the moving and stationary vital winds (explained above) collide with the subtle particles and cause them to move and cohere. This is the period during which the most refined essence of wind is activated. Just as sparks are produced by striking stones, lightning is generated from the motion and collision of the subtle particles. This is the period during which the most refined essence of fire is set in motion. This produces water which appears like a fine drizzle. This is the period during which the most refined element of water is set in motion. The fine drizzle causes a rainbow to appear in space. This is the period during which the most refined essence of earth is set in motion.

These motions produce a great body of water. When the body of water is churned [by winds], its essence becomes the coarse elements. In the microcosm, this corresponds to the turtle-shape period[18] [of fetal development] during which the four limbs and the head start to emerge.

[Once the coarse elements are produced,] the shaping winds form Mount Meru, the continents and so forth. This corresponds to the pig-shape period[19] [of fetal development]. Gradually, the world's configuration forms in its entirety, from the wind sphere foundation up to Mt. Meru.

Thus, the power of the different energy-winds produces all the various sizes, shapes, and configurations that appear within our world-system. The distinct action energy-winds themselves are the result of the different manifestations of mind imprinted with instincts [derived from] evolutionary actions. These [different manifestations] are produced by the manifestation of the six lights that are coexistent with the six elements.

How the coarse world-system is formed from the six lights [is explained] in the *Glorious Tantra [of the Wheel of Time*[20]*]*, beginning with the statement:

> In the left branch is the white blaze.

The lights can be explained by using a format of [two sets of] seven pairs: The green light at the zenith and the blue light at the nadir, which are characterized by the radiant awareness of total emptiness,[21] produce two energy-winds, the vital and the downward-voiding. The black blaze in the east, characterized by approaching fullness,[22] produces the macrocosmic heat-accompanied and six other energy-winds. The red blaze in the south, characterized by increase,[23] produces the seven fires; these are the five wrathful planets—Fire of Time, Sun, Mars, Jupiter, and Saturn—plus Lightning and the Horse-faced Fire. The white blaze in the north, characterized by the dawning of inner light,[24] produces the seven waters: the five peaceful planets—Eclipser, Moon, Mercury, Venus, and Long Tail—plus the rain and the ocean. The yellow blaze in the west, characterized by coarseness, produces the seven earths: subtle earth, coarse earth, subtle minerals, coarse minerals, subtle stars, coarse stars, and rainbows. These are the two sets of seven pairs: the earths and winds of the west and east, and the fires and waters of the south and north. There is a single pair, space and pristine wisdom, at the zenith and at the nadir. The elements of this latter pair are the pervading factors and the former fourteen constitute the pervaded field.

As implied by this explanation, the shapes and the colors of the four sides of Mt. Meru and of the continents and so forth are created by the six lights.

In conclusion, in the formation of a world-system, the mind is the [productive] agent, the environment and inhabitants are the objects [created], and creation is accomplished by evolutionary actions. Most discourses and tantras agree with this presentation.

[II.B.3]
Presentation of the General Process of Creation

This section has two parts: (1) perspectives of the common systems and (2) the perspectives of exceptional systems.

[II.B.3.a]
The Perspectives of the Common Systems

This section has two parts: (1) the perspective of the Individualists' system of phenomenology[25] and (2) the perspective of the Universalists' system of phenomenology.[26]

[II.B.3.a.i]
The Perspective of the Individualists' System of Phenomenology

This section has two parts: (1) a general presentation and (2) a detailed explanation.

[II.B.3.a.i.A']
General Presentation

> **Six causes and four conditions produce conditioned phenomena;**
> **Five results are produced by these [causes].**
> **The Individualists' system of phenomenology follows these excellent explanations.**

Vasubandhu's *Treasury of Phenomenology*[27] states:

> Without causes and conditions,
> There is no production, no product, and no producer.

Various causes and conditions must interact for conditioned phenomena to arise. The scriptures elucidate six major causes and four conditions, as well as five results that they produce. The Individualists' system of phenomenology presents precise explanations based on these scriptures.

[II.B.3.a.i.B']
Detailed Explanation

This section has four parts: (1) the six causes, (2) the five results, (3) the general classes of resultant phenomena, and (4) the four conditions.

[II.B.3.a.i.B'.1']
The Six Causes

> **The productive cause of [a particular phenomenon] is that which is other than the conditioned phenomenon.**
> **Coemergent causes are [conditioned phenomena] that are causes and results of one another.**
> **Causes of the same outcome are preceding phenomena creating later similar phenomena.**
> **Concomitant causes are mind and mental events that share five aspects.**
> **Omnipresent causes are defiled phenomena.**
> **Developing causes are non-virtue and contaminated virtue.**

The *productive cause* of [a particular] conditioned phenomenon includes all things that are other than the conditioned phenomenon itself. When productive causes are divided into principal and secondary causes, the principal ones are effective productive causes. For example, the eye faculty and [visible] form are the [effective] productive causes that produce the eye consciousness. The eye faculty is the [sense]-base [effective] productive cause, and form is the objective [effective] productive cause. Food acts as the [effective] productive cause of the body because it has the ability to nourish the body. With respect to a seed, shoot, leaf, stalk, and so forth, the former is the [effective] productive cause of the latter in each case because each has the capacity to produce the latter. Secondary [i.e., ineffective] productive causes cannot produce [results], but are included in this category because they do not obstruct [the production of phenomena].

Coemergent causes are any conditioned phenomena that arise simultaneously and act as causes and results of one another. The four main elements [earth, water, fire, and air] are co-emergent causes of one another. Mental factors and [the primary] mind are mutual [co-emergent causes]. Similarly, the characteristics of conditioned phenomena, such as arising and so forth, and phenomena that possess [such] characteristics are mutual causes and results. Therefore, most conditioned phenomena can be considered as co-emergent causes, comparable to travellers who journey together and help one another on the journey.

Causes of the same outcome are preceding phenomena that produce later similar phenomena. For example, barley [is the cause of] similar barley; rice, the cause of rice. Similarly, the five virtuous aggregates act as the causes for the same outcome—virtuous aggregates; non-virtue and obscured neutral [phenomena] act as the causes for the same outcome—defiled [phenomena]; and non-obscured, neutral [phenomena] produce non-obscured, neutral [phenomena].

Concomitant causes denotes mind or mental factors that are concordant by virtue of sharing five factors—[sense-] base, objective object, aspect, time, and substance. The six consciousnesses, together with their respective supporting [sense faculties], are concomitant and identical at the moment [of engagement] of the sense faculties. Thus, they act as concomitant causes for one another and as co-emergent causes. [Concomitant causes] are like travellers who do everything identically—sharing food, drink, baths, bedding, etc.—while on a journey.

Omnipresent causes are the common [factors] relinquished [on the path of] seeing[28] that produce defiled [phenomena] as their result. *The Treasury of Phenomenology*'s presentation of the subtle and proliferating obscuring emotions uses the term *omnipresent* for the eleven subtle and proliferating [emotions].

A *developing cause* is non-virtue or contaminated virtue that has the ability to produce a developed result. [Developing causes] are like faultless seeds coming into contact with humidity. Neutral factors do not become developing causes; they are like rotten seeds. Even uncontaminated virtues are not [developing causes] because although they have potency, they do not bring about developed [results] since craving does not exist [at the stage of an exalted one]. They are like healthy seeds never exposed to humidity.

[II.B.3.a.i.B'.2']
The Five Results

> **Developed results arise after their causes, pertain to a continuum,**
> **And are unobscured and neutral.**
> **Results concordant with the causes are of a type similar to the same outcome and omnipresent [causes].**
> **Freedom results are cessations attained through appreciative discernment.**
> **Caused results are attainments through the power of the causes.**
> **Owned results [which are exclusively] conditioned phenomena arise from non-hindering phenomena.**

What is the nature of the five results? *Developed results* are produced by developing causes and arise subsequent to their causes. They pertain to the continuums of individuals, and are unobscured and neutral. Examples of developed results are higher existences [resulting] from virtue and lower existences [resulting] from non-virtue.

Results concordant with [their] causes are produced by either a cause of the same outcome or an omnipresent cause and are of a type concordant [to the cause]. Examples of results concordant with their causes are a short life [resulting] from killing and a long life [resulting] from giving up [killing].

Freedom results refers to cessations [of obscurations] achieved through the power of analytical discrimination. [A cessation is defined as] the attainment of the exhaustion [of obscurations] by eliminating the factors that are to be relinquished by means of appreciative discernment. The relinquishments [and] realizations of the four [types] of exalted ones[29] are examples of freedom results.

Results caused by persons, [also called] results caused by the actions of persons, denotes any results produced and acquired through the power of any cause [created by a person]—crops [produced] by farming, for instance.

Owned results are exclusively conditioned phenomena and arise from what is non-hindering. Such results arise from conditioned phenomena or things that are merely non-hindering [to their arising]. They do not [exist in] the past, but arise in the present and future. Examples are the owned results of virtue and non-virtue.

[II.B.3.a.i.B'.3']
General Classes of Results

> **It is asserted that [results] are all conditioned phenomena, as well as the attainment of freedom,**
> **And that the two unconditioned phenomena lack causes and results.**

The following citation provides a general definition of resultant phenomena:

> What are resultant phenomena? [They include] all conditioned phenomena and cessations attained through analytical discrimination.

In general, *result* refers to all conditioned phenomena, as well as analytical cessations or perfect peace, the freedom from obscuring emotions attained by applying the remedial path. Space and non-analytical cessations (both unconditioned phenomena) are considered to be without causes or results since no causal relations exist with respect to these. Being unproduced, no causes or conditions produced [them]; being timeless, they do not have the capacity to produce a result.

> **Developed [results] arise [from] the last [cause]; owned results from the first.**
> **Results concordant with the cause [from] the third and fifth; caused [results] from the second and fourth.**

What are the causes of the five results? Developed results arise from developing causes (the last mentioned in the section on causes) because developed results are the results of non-virtue or contaminated virtue.

Owned results are results of productive causes (the first of the six causes) because they are results that are possessed by an owner. Owned results are merely non-obscured, owned [phenomena]. Their [productive] causes, however, are not merely non-obscuring, but also produce results. For instance, the five consciousnesses, such as the eye-consciousness and so forth, are produced by the productive causes of the ten experiential elements. Similarly, the environmental world is produced by the productive causes of actions.

Results concordant with the causes arise from causes of the same outcome (the third) and omnipresent causes (the fifth) because they are similar to these causes.

Results caused by a person are produced by co-emergent causes (the second) and concomitant causes (the fourth). The acts or activity of a person are none other than the nature of that person, and the results are that same person. Likewise, the agents of these causes are the causes themselves, and the results are also [coemergent and concomitant causes]. If this is carefully analyzed, [it can be understood that] results caused by a person may also be produced by the same outcome, omnipresent, or productive causes.

[II.B.3.a.i.B'.4']
The Four Conditions

> **Except for the productive cause, the five [other] causes are causal conditions.**
> **Mind and mental factors producing results that arise immediately are immediate [conditions].**
> **Phenomena suitable to be objects of the six consciousnesses are objective conditions.**
> **Phenomena that do not obstruct arising are dominant conditions.**

Four conditions are explained in the scriptures. *Causal condition* refers to all of the [above-mentioned] causes with the exception of the productive cause: the co-emergent, concomitant, same outcome, omnipresent, and developing [causes]. These all act as productive conditions, assisting the production of their own respective results. Productive causes are not considered to be causal conditions because unconditioned phenomena are included within the category of productive causes. Thus, to include productive causes in this category would contradict the assertion that [only] conditioned phenomena are causal conditions.

Concomitant immediate conditions are the mind and mental factors that bring about their own results immediately. When the [previous mind or mental factors] cease, the new ones (of the same substance and not of another concordant type) arise instantly without being interrupted by similar [mind and mental factors] of a concordant type.

Objective conditions are conditioned and unconditioned phenomena that are suitable to be objects of the six consciousnesses (such as the eye [consciousness] and so forth). For example, the experiential element of form is the objective condition that is correlated with eye consciousness.

A *dominant condition* is any phenomenon that does not obstruct the arising of a conditioned phenomenon different from itself. The dominant condition and the productive mentioned above are mutually inclusive. More phenomena belong to this category of condition than to any other.

The arising, functioning, etc., [of conditions] can be learned from [Vasubandhu's] treatise.

What are the conditions that produce any specific phenomena? How many conditions are necessary? When and how do the different conditions function? How do the conditions [that produce] the elements and the evolutes of the elements function? An elaboration of these and other subjects would be endless. To fully understand [these subjects], one should refer to Vasubandhu's *Treasury of Phenomenology*. Since at the very least an understanding of the enumeration of causes and conditions and their definitions is indispensable, these have been presented here.

[II.B.3.a.ii]
The Universalists' System of Phenomenology

This section has three parts: an explanation of (1) causes, (2) conditions, and (3) results.

[II.B.3.a.ii.A']
The Causes

> **Productive causes which produce [a result]; assisting, co-emergent [causes];**
> **Augmenting or same outcome [causes]; concomitant causes, sharing four factors;**
> **Defiled omnipresent causes; developing causes of the body:**
> **All may be categorized as productive causes,**
> **Which the *Synthesis of Phenomenology* sets forth as twenty classes.**

The Universalists give names to causes, conditions, and results that are similar [to those of the Individualists]. However, the causes, conditions, and results are asserted in slightly different ways and therefore are explained separately here.

A cause is termed *productive* or *essential* when it has been definitely ascertained to be the producer of a particular result.

Phenomena that initially arise from the same [cause] and then continue to remain together while giving support to each other are called *co-emergent causes* or *accompanying causes*.[30] This is comparable to two siblings who are born from the same mother and then continue to live together while giving support to each other.

Co-emergent causes are of three types: external, internal, and both. The first refers to the four elements and evolutes of these elements. Each particle of the four elements has eight material particles [earth, water, fire, air, form, smell, taste, and touch]. Although the ceasing of the first moment of an earth particle and the arising of the second moment of a water particle occur simultaneously, a slight causal relationship exists between the former and the latter: they arise from the same productive cause and belong to the same conglomerate. An example in relation to an element evolute is the taste and form of cane sugar.

The second kind, [internal co-emergent causes,] refers to mind and mental factors. Mind and mental factors are co-emergent causes because they arise from the same cause, exist together, and are the cause and effect of one another.

The third, [co-emergent causes that are both internal and external,] are [phenomena] that are [only] designated as cause and effect, like the cause and effect [relationship] of ascribing a definition in relation to the object to be defined.

Causes of the same outcome or *augmenting causes* refers to virtue resulting in virtue, non-virtue resulting in non-virtue, or neutral [phenomena] resulting in neutral [phenomena]. They are increasing causes because they develop or increase [their results]. These are also called concordant causes since their [effects] are necessarily of the same state and same nature. For example, in order for a desire realm [being's] emotion of attachment to be a concordant cause, it must produce an emotion of the same state—that of the desire realm. It must not produce an emotion of the two higher realms. In this way, it would be of the same state. The emotions [produced] must not be of a dissimilar type, but of the same type—attachment produced as a result of attachment, for instance.

Concomitant causes are causes that are similar by virtue of sharing four common factors, or causes of concordant understanding. Both primary mind and accompanying mental factors have the same productive cause, the same objective object, the same continuum with respect to the object, and a single or identical aspect (i.e., perceptual pattern). For example, the eye consciousness arises from its substantial cause, the stimulation of the instincts present in the fundamental [consciousness]. According to a different explanation, it arises from the first moment of a similar type of consciousness. Likewise, mental factors, such as feeling, which accompany that [consciousness], arise from the [same] causes. The eye consciousness focuses on visual form; its objective condition and likewise [its correlated] mental factors, such as feeling, also focus on it. The object of experience of visual consciousness pertains to the person's [experiential] continuum; the object of experience of the mental factors such as feeling similarly pertain to that continuum. Eye consciousness has a perceptual pattern that perceives the aspect of form; mental factors, such as feeling, also have a perceptual pattern that perceives form. Therefore, both mind and mental factors are concomitant in that they share four common factors.

Omnipresent causes are emotions that produce emotions. [*Omnipresent*] indicates their functioning throughout the three realms. Since omnipresent causes interfere with beings' attainment of liberation, they are also called obstructive causes. The type, state, and other factors [of the results of omnipresent causes] are indefinite. For instance, anger may be the cause that produces desire or pride. Also, the result of the emotions of the desire realm [may] serve as the basis for the emotions of the two higher realms.

Developing causes are the causes that produce the body, i.e., its development [or result]. They are also called appropriating causes since their effect is to assume a physical form. [Developing causes consist of either] contaminated virtuous or non-virtuous [actions] which produce neutral results. For example, the body of a hell being is the result of non-virtuous developing causes. Although the experiences of the various sufferings of hell are impelled by non-virtue, the body, the basis [for the experiences of these sufferings], is definitely a neutral [result]. Similarly, contaminated virtuous actions impel [a rebirth as] a god, but the resultant body of a god is not virtuous in itself but solely a neutral phenomenon.

All these causes can be subsumed under productive causes alone. Since productive causes are causes that produce results, ineffective productive causes are not asserted in this system. Asaṅga's *Synthesis of Phenomenology* presents twenty distinct classifications of productive causes: causes for arising, [for example, the arising] of previously non-existant results; sustaining causes, [for example, sustaining] the body by eating food; supportive causes, like a container that holds water; causes for continuation, [for example, the continuation of] previously existant types [of phenomena]; causes for transformation, for instance, the change from childhood to adolescence; separating causes, [for instance, separation] from what was previously owned; transmuting causes, [for instance,] transmuting gold into statues of humans and gods; causes for proving, [for instance, proving] something as conditioned phenomena by reason of its having birth, abiding, and cessation; achieving causes, [for instance,] achieving the result by meditation on the path; propelling causes, [for instance,] projecting into another place and time; accomplishing causes which directly produce [their resultant] phenomena; disruptive causes; causes for the aging of any phenomena; causes for the abiding of what previously existed; causes for ascertainment, [for instance, that in a particular place] there is fire by the reason [that there is] smoke; causes for non-ascertainment, [for instance, that] there is fire by reason that there is no smoke; and other causes.

[II.B.3.a.ii.B']
The Conditions

> **Causal conditions are the five causes and the fundamental consciousness.**
> **The objective condition is the perceived object. The dominant condition is the support.**
> **The immediate condition is asserted in the third way.**
> **When four conditions are present, consciousness generates consciousness;**
> **When there are two or three, consciousness produces coarse objects.**

In this system, the five causes explained above—co-emergent, same outcome, concomitant, omnipresent, and developing—are considered to be *categorical causal conditions*. Not all the causes that fall into the five categories necessarily act as causal conditions. However, since causal conditions are included within all five categories, all five are considered as such. The Universalists' system of phenomenology also explains that the main substantial causal condition for all external and internal phenomena is the fundamental consciousness, or more specifically, the developed aspect of the fundamental consciousness. The five other causal conditions are in fact cooperative conditions [to the fundamental consciousness].

Objective conditions are objects perceived or objective objects. The five non-conceptual sense consciousnesses clearly perceive their respective objective conditions—the aspect of form, etc. These, therefore, are considered as the objects perceived by these consciousnesses. In the case of conceptual consciousness, the objective basis is merely the pattern of appearance or apprehension [of that conceptual consciousness].

Dominant conditions serve as supports for all phenomena, comparable to a container that holds water, preventing it from spilling out. The general dominant condition [for phenomena] is the fundamental consciousness, and the exclusive dominant conditions are the five sense faculties which provide the bases for the five sense consciousnesses. The dominant conditions for external appearances are the specific supports, locations, and bases of phenomena. The *Synthesis of Phenomenology*[31] lists nine types of dominant conditions:

> Support, propellent, co-emergence, object,
> Birth, location, experience of results [of actions],
> Mundane purity, and transcendent purity:
> All [act] as dominant conditions [for external appearances].

Both objective conditions and dominant conditions are included among productive causes.

The *immediately preceding condition* is asserted in three different ways. Teachers of the *[Treasury of] Phenomenology* maintain that the immediate condition has three characteristics: it is similar to its resultant phenomenon; it shares the same cause; and it immediately precedes [its result]. [Some] assert that the immediate condition provides the opportunity for any phenomenon to arise by not hindering it and serves as an aid to its [production]. [Others] assert that the immediate condition merely directs consciousness towards the object. The [Universalists'] system of phenomenology accepts the last of these three assertions.

When all four conditions [the causal condition, objective condition, dominant condition, and immediate condition] are present, consciousness generates [the subsequent] consciousness: the former eye consciousness produces the latter one, for example. When two or three of these conditions are present, consciousness produces the appearance of coarse objects, and coarse objects produce coarse objects. To explain, in order for consciousness to produce the appearance of coarse objects, two conditions are necessary: the causal conditions (i.e., instincts within the fundamental consciousness) and the co-emergent condition. An example of this is formative actions impelling [a being] to take rebirth. In order for coarse objects to produce coarse objects, two conditions are necessary. However, according to those who assert that the immediate condition is a previous similar type [of phenomenon], the immediate condition should also be present. In this case, three conditions are necessary [for coarse objects to produce coarse objects].

[II.B.3.a.ii.C']
Results

> **Freedom results are cessations without causes.**
> **Owned results pertain to external phenomena.**
> **Developed results pertain to the continuums of beings.**
> **Caused results [arise from] creating causes; results concordant with causes [arise] from same outcome [causes].**

Freedom results are cessations that have not been produced by causes. Analytical cessations are actual freedom results since they are superficial phenomena.

The truth of cessation that is the ultimate nature [of phenomena] is freedom itself and is a nominal [freedom] result. The ultimate sphere of reality is considered to be a nominal result because the intrinsic dimension of awakening, itself inseparable from the sphere of reality, is referred to as a result. In fact, the ultimate sphere of reality is not a true result because unconditioned phenomena cannot logically be described in terms of actual causes and results.

Owned results pertain to external objects. A non-analytic viewpoint accepts the existence of external objects: from that perspective, the environment and external form, sound, taste, smell, and touch are owned results. From a slightly analytical standpoint, the existence of external phenomena is not accepted. However, from that perspective, the aspect of consciousness appearing as places and the aspect of consciousness appearing as objects, etc., are considered as owned results.

Developed results pertain to the [experiential] continuums of sentient beings. Examples include the five appropriated aggregates integral to the body [when the existence of external objects is accepted] and the aspect of consciousness manifesting [as the five aggregates, when the existence of external objects is not accepted].

Caused results include all phenomena that arise from productive causes. Results concordant with their causes include all phenomena that arise from causes of the same outcome.

The main [causes, conditions, and results] have been explained above—this does not, however, constitute a definitive presentation of this subject.

Generally speaking, any cause that produces a phenomenon must fall into one of two categories of causes: defiled cause (i.e., the fundamental consciousness which possesses the instincts for cyclic life) or pure cause (the uncontaminated potential). The first—the defiled cause, the fundamental consciousness with all the types of instincts that are potentials for cyclic life—serves as the cause of everything that is defiled in the three realms of cyclic life.

The pure cause is the uncontaminated potential imprinted upon the fundamental consciousness. This cause, in Asaṅga's *Synthesis of Phenomenology,*[32] is called "the potential that arises from learning" which indicates that the nature of the [uncontaminated potential] is not merely a propensity developed by ordinary virtue (such as generosity and ethics) imprinted [on the fundamental consciousness]. Rather, its nature is an acquired propensity [that leads] one to comprehend the qualities of the Buddha's body, speech, and mind. In this system, the excellent teachings [of the Buddha] are the concordant cause for the reality dimension of awakening—the Buddha's mind. Therefore, the main [uncontaminated potential] is the propensity acquired from the study of these teachings and the consequent understanding of the profound secret aspects of Buddha's body, speech, and mind. This potential imprinted on the fundamental consciousness eventually becomes the cause for an individual's attainment of freedom. Because it leads to freedom, this potential is said to be uncontaminated. Not every sentient being necessarily possesses this uncontaminated potential.

The uncontaminated potential is also explained as either the cause present from birth or the cause that arises from education. The first is a developed aspect of the fundamental [consciousness] and the second is the causal aspect. For example, due to the development of the potential from learning in previous [lives], in this life one is born naturally endowed with superlative wisdom—wisdom present from birth. A great deal of learning in this life develops the [uncontaminated] potential; cultivation of this potential leads to superlative wisdom—wisdom arising from education.

These [explanations concerning contaminated and uncontaminated causes] supplement the discussion on results.

[II.B.3.b]
The Exceptional Systems

This section has two [parts]: (1) the ultimate view [concerning the origin of cyclic life] and (2) the origin of cyclic life according to the tradition of Radiant Great Perfection.

[II.B.3.b.i]
The Ultimate View [Concerning the Origin of Cyclic Life]

This section has three [parts]: (1) how the twelve links of interdependent origination deceive sentient beings, (2) the twelve links in relation to the eight consciousnesses, and (3) how cyclic life manifests from three instincts.

[II.B.3.b.i.A']
How the Twelve Links of Interdependent Origination Deceive Sentient Beings

This section has two parts: (1) a general presentation and (2) a detailed explanation.

[II.B.3.b.i.A'.1']
General Presentation

> **Although cyclic life and actions do not exist ultimately,**
> **Interdependent origination occurs superficially due to causes and conditions.**
> **Thus, the wheel of twelve links continually turns.**

A general overview of the causes and conditions that produce conditioned phenomena as asserted by the common spiritual ways has been presented above. The ultimate view of the exceptional [systems concerning the creation of cyclic life] is presented here.

The *Disclosure of the Awakening Mind*[33] by the exalted [Nāgārjuna] says:

> I maintain that just as sugar cane is sweet
> And the nature of fire is heat,
> The nature of all phenomena
> Is emptiness.

Cyclic life, evolutionary actions, and their results do not ultimately exist. [Their nature] is just emptiness, lacking true status. Nevertheless, [cyclic life, etc.,] have a superficial mode of appearance: various causes and conditions perpetuate the motion of the wheel of the twelve links of interdependent origination which turns around and around on the path of existence. As the Exalted One's [*Disclosure of the Awakening Mind*[34]] says:

> I assert that the process that unfolds
> From ignorance to old age and death—
> The twelve links of interdependent origination—
> Is similar to an illusion or to a dream.
> This wheel of twelve links
> Turns on the path of existence.

[II.B.3.b.i.A'.2']
Detailed Explanation

> **Adherence to a self is the root of cyclic life.**
> **Emotions produce actions and suffering.**
> **These lead to [the cycle of suffering] which manifests like [dreams during] sleep.**

Dharmakīrti's *Treatise on Valid Cognition*[35] states:

> When "I" exists, "other" is known.
> Self and other produce grasping and aversion.
> All faults arise
> In relation to these.

The root of cyclic life and of an individual's course of experience throughout it is the conception of "I." This "I" is the conceived object of the instinctive self-habit that apprehends "I" and "property." Self-habit and property-habit are the bases for all defiled views and emotions, such as desire. These generate formative actions that result [in rebirth]. These in turn lead to all the suffering of existence. Furthermore, the formations of actions and emotions cause the cycle of suffering to recur continually.

The cycle of suffering seems to be very real. However, if one examines it closely, one can see that it is only the magical display of emptiness. It appears although it is without reality, like the dream images seen when one is asleep [or] the hairs [seen] by a person with cataracts, etc. The Exalted One's [*Disclosure of the Awakening Mind*[36]] says:

> Empty phenomena produce empty phenomena.
> Agent, action, and experienced result
> Are superficial [reality].
> This, in brief, is what the Victorious One taught.

Further[37]:

> Emotions and evolutionary actions create
>   superficial reality;
> Actions are instigated by the mind.
> Mind is the sum of all instincts;
> Freedom from instinctual patterns is happiness.
> A happy mind is quietude itself;
> A quiet mind is not obscured.
> The unobscured [mind] knows reality;
> To know reality is to attain freedom.

In his first cycle of teachings, the Buddha taught that the root of cyclic life is self-habit, and that the cause of suffering and its origin is attachment. In the middle cycle, he taught that the root of cyclic life is the fabrication of grasping identifiable characteristics (i.e., habitual adherence to subject and object). In the last cycle, he taught that the root of cyclic life is fundamental consciousness itself.

The father tantras of the highest Secret Mantra [teach that] the bases for the origin of existence are the sets of the four emptinesses and the four elements. The mother tantras assert that cyclic life arises from the indestructible vital essence or mundane innate [bliss].

[II.B.3.b.i.B']
The Twelve Links in Relation to the Eight Consciousnesses

> **The beginningless nature of mind is empty, clear, [and] unobstructed,**
> **But its nature is not recognized.**
> **[The fundamental consciousness,] stirred by mental creations, produces dualistic appearances [and] the consciousnesses.**
> **Feeling develops from acceptance and rejection; discernment, from objectification-habit.**
> **[Discernment leads to] mental formations which are mental factors; habitual adherence creates form.**
> **With attachment and grasping as a link, the wheel of existence turns.**

This subject is a vast one if treated in detail. To further one's understanding of it, one should study the clear explanations given in such [texts] as the commentary on [Karmapa Rangjung Dorjé's] *Profound Inner Meaning* [called] the *Elucidation of the Profound Meaning* and the commentary on the *Showing of the Essence* called the *Elucidation of the Philosophy of Rangjung Dorjé*. What follows is simply a commentary on the words of the root verses written above.

The *Phenomenology Scripture*[38] states:

> The sphere [of reality] without commencement
> Is the source of all phenomena.
> Because the sphere of reality exists,
> Cyclic life and perfect peace exist.

The nature [of mind], being free of fabrications, is empty. Its character is unobscured clarity; its expression is unobstructedly manifest. This intrinsically pure nature of mind, existing from time without beginning, is the sphere of reality. It is transcendent reality without intrinsic objectivity.

The nature of mind is not recognized: Its unborn nature is conceived as self; its unimpeded radiance is conceived as other. Thus, the unobstructed creativity [of mind] appears as subject and object. Mental formations with regard to objects and mind agitate the fundamental consciousness like waves on water. The objective object and subjective consciousness, although not different, manifest as two and are apprehended as other and self.

[This dualistic apprehension] produces [the aggregate of consciousness], comprised of the six consciousnesses which apprehend objects as external. The increased manifestations of instincts create coarse deceptive appearances. These appear to the consciousnesses as pleasant, unpleasant, or neutral [objects], and as a consequence are regarded with acceptance, rejection, or indifference. In this way, the aggregate of feeling develops.

The aggregate of discernment is produced by the varying degrees of the objectification-habit with respect to objects perceived. Discrimination of the individual features of objects causes mental formations to occur with respect to them. These lead to the [aggregate] of formations constituted by the various mental factors. These mental formations stabilize instincts, which in turn produce habitual adherence to the nature of form, its characteristics, etc. The aggregate of form develops from this adherence.

The [five aggregates] have been presented here in their causal order. The *Treasury of Phenomenology* presents the [aggregates] in order of defilement or coarseness, beginning with [the coarsest,] the aggregate of form, and concluding with the most subtle. The *Treasury*[39] states:

> The order is [presented] in terms of coarseness or defilement.

Although their orders differ, the two presentations are not contradictory. [Once the five aggregates have formed,] desire and craving for an object, together with grasping to obtain the desired object, serve as the links that empower the formative actions to create existence. Consequently, one takes birth in a new life, [eventually experiencing aging and death]. In this way, the wheel of deception turns perpetually throughout cyclic life.

The wheel [of the twelve links] is set in motion because one's own nature is not recognized, just like the deception that occurs when a magical illusion is not recognized as a magical illusion or when a dream is not recognized as a dream.

[II.B.3.b.i.C']
How Cyclic Life Manifests from Three Instincts

In summation, three instincts imprinted on the fundamental consciousness

Cause three deceptive appearances — object, subject, and body.

To summarize what has been said above, three different mental instincts imprinted on the fundamental [consciousness] cause three different deceptive appearances: objects such as form; subjects, or consciousnesses that apprehend [objects]; and one's own body. These three appear but have no reality. Thus, like dust on a mirror, instincts obscure the mind's radiant awareness, and [beings] wander throughout cyclic life. Maitreya's *Scripture Ornament*[40] states:

> The three appear in three [aspects].

The meaning of this quotation is elucidated in the works of Drimé Özer (Longchenpa), Samantabhadra in person.

The environmental world, the five objects such as form,
The eight consciousnesses, and virtuous and negative actions [develop from objective instincts].
[Adherence to] the forms of the six [types of] beings, and the object, agent, and action
Generate object and subject, which in turn produce emotions.
[Emotions] create cyclic life without beginning or end.

The outer world and the five [types] of objects that find support in it—form, sound, smell, taste and touch—do not exist anywhere, externally or internally. Nonetheless, due to object-oriented instincts, objects appear to the mind as if they were externally existent. One adheres to them as [external] objects, and thus they become objects to be rejected or accepted. The constructive thought that the conceived object is external, expressed as "this is form," is the objective constructive thought.

The group of eight consciousnesses consists of the fundamental consciousness, defiled mind, and the six consciousnesses. Actions are instigated by these [eight] consciousnesses; these include virtuous (meritorious) and nonvirtuous (negative) ones. Instincts based on these actions remain in the mind just as ore and gold are found together. As the power of these subjective instincts increases, the eight consciousnesses apprehend their respective objects both conceptually and non-conceptually. This is the process of subjective constructive thought.

Because of body-oriented instincts, the six types of beings—the matrices for the arising of subject and object—adhere intensely to [their] individual forms and [their functions in terms of] object, agent, and action. Even while dreaming, they adhere to their bodies [as real]. Consequently, they experience pleasure and pain, and the strength of the three types of instincts increases, causing deceptive subjective and objective appearances to manifest. Rejection or acceptance of those [deceptive appearances] increases the power of obscuring emotions, leading to the accumulation of evolutionary actions. In this way, the beginningless and endless chain of cyclic life continuously recreates itself.

Instincts [created] from time without beginning produced our succession of past lives. Habituation to the stream of past lives has led us into the present life. Habituation to the experiences of this present life, such as dreams influenced by the [events] of the day, forms instincts [that will manifest as] objects, subjects, and bodies of future lives.

[II.B.3.b.i.D']
Supplementary Explanation: The Ending of Cyclic Life

When the course of interdependent origination is reversed
or its causes and conditions collapse from the inner core,
Deceptive [appearances] are exhausted and supreme
liberation is attained.

What causes aging and death, the main suffering of cyclic life? Examination reveals that aging and death arise from birth, which in turn arises from grasping, which is produced by attachment, and so on through the other links [of interdependent origination]. Analyzing this step by step, it can be understood that unawareness lies at the root of all these links. Applying the remedy that eliminates unawareness leads to cessation [liberation], by reversing the order of interdependent origination.

[Alternatively,] analytical discernment can be used to realize that the cause for wandering throughout cyclic life, i.e., self-habit, and its condition, instinctive unawareness, have no intrinsic reality. With this realization, the basis of deception collapses from its inner core. Deceptive appearances are exhausted within the sphere of reality, and liberation, supreme happiness, is attained.

Chapter V

The Primordial Purity of the Universe

[II.B.3.b.ii]

THE ORIGIN OF CYCLIC LIFE ACCORDING TO THE TRADITION OF RADIANT GREAT PERFECTION

This section has two parts: (1) the context, and (2) the main discussion.

[II.B.3.b.ii.A']

Context

> **The superior system of the Supreme Yoga is the culmination of all spiritual ways.**

The causes and conditions that produce deception [within cyclic life] and those that effect liberation from it will now be explained according to a system that surpasses the interpretations of common spiritual traditions. This brief presentation from the perspective of the Supreme Yoga, the culmination of the nine spiritual ways,[1] will lay the foundation [for understanding] the key points of the path and the result of this system.[2]

[II.B.3.b.ii.B']

Main Discussion

This section has four parts: (1) the fundamental nature of the ground of being, (2) how beings fail to recognize it, (3) the ever-presence of the ground of being [even] in the deceived state, and (4) a supplementary [explanation] of the abode of pristine wisdom and the ending of the deception [of apprehended] objects.

[II.B.3.b.ii.B'.1']
The Fundamental Nature of the Ground of Being

This section has three parts: (1) proof that the six grounds of being, as believed from partial perspectives, are mistaken, (2) proof that the fundamental nature of the ground is primordial purity, and (3) the eight ways the ground of being manifests.

[II.B.3.b.ii.B'.1'.a']
Proof that Six Grounds of Being, as Believed from Partial Perspectives, are Mistaken

Six [claims] concerning the fundamental nature of the original ground are mistaken.

What is the fundamental nature of the original, primordial ground of being, before buddhas appear by realizing it and before sentient beings appear by not realizing it? To answer this, the tradition of Great Perfection states that six claims concerning the ground based on the perspectives of persons who adhere to philosophical tenets are mistaken: the claim that [the ground] is (1) spontaneous; or (2) indeterminate; or (3) determinate; or (4) transmutable into anything; or (5) can be defined in any possible way; or (6) that it is manifold and multifaceted.

These six impressions of the ground are erroneous in that they are partial descriptions of the ground. The reasons for their erroneousness is as follows:

(1) The claim that [the ground of being] is spontaneous is mistaken because if both faults and qualities existed primordially in the ground, their presence would contradict primordial purity. Furthermore, such a ground would constitute an unsuitable basis for the practice of a path [to freedom], and even if practice were undertaken, freedom would be an unsuitable goal.

(2) The claim that [the ground] is indeterminate is mistaken because if the ground were indeterminate, it would become whatever it is intellectually designated to be, leading to the illogical conclusion that deception might be experienced even after freedom has been attained.

(3) The assertion that [the ground] is determinate is mistaken because [if this were the case], the ground would be unchange-

able, which implies that the stains of unawareness could never be purified.

(4) The assertion that [the ground] can change into anything whatsoever is mistaken because the ground would not be permanent; the result (freedom) could therefore turn again into a cause [of cyclic life].

(5) The assertion that [the ground] can be defined in any possible way is mistaken because if phenomena are infinite, the ground would also be infinite. [If this were the case,] one would have to assert the ground to be either permanent or terminated.

(6) The assertion that [the ground] is manifold is mistaken because such a ground would be unsuitable as the basis for authentic freedom, since a ground related to many thought constructs cannot be a primordially pure ground.

These six impressions, each in its own way, are erroneous in that they give one-sided views of the ground. Thus, they do not[3] provide adequate descriptions of the "ground of being," permitting only a partial comprehension of the fundamental nature of the ground.

[II.B.3.b.ii.B'.1'.b']

Proof that the Fundamental Nature of the Ground of Being is Primordial Purity

This section has two parts: (1) identification of the primordially pure nature [of the ground]; and (2) a precise explanation of the primordially pure character [of the ground].

[II.B.3.b.ii.B'.1'.b'.i']

Identification of the Primordially Pure Nature [of the Ground]

The correct [view is that the ground is] primordial purity, the common basis of both deception and freedom.

The primordial purity of the original ground is the domain of a practitioner of the path [of Great Perfection] who is free from the erroneous biases of conceiving [the ground] in various artificial ways and who has the correct [understanding] of the ground as primordial purity.

[The primordial purity of the ground] wholly transcends words, concepts, and formulations, and surpasses the limitations of existing or not existing.

The nature of the ground is primordially pure. Thus, the ground transcends the limitations of permanence or existence: it cannot be reduced to substantial or objectifiable characteristics. The character of the ground is spontaneous, and therefore the ground surpasses the limitation of non-existence or annihilation. It is radiant intrinsic awareness, the pure reality of emptiness itself, natural and primordial enlightenment, the immutable wisdom of the reality dimension of awakening. Existing neither as cyclic life nor perfect peace, it remains primordially empty. It is great self-existing wisdom, primordially present like space.

As [the nature of the ground] is primordial purity, isn't it illogical for sentient beings to be deceived into cyclic life? Since beings are intrinsically free, no real stains remain to be purified and no innate deception or freedom can be identified. However, beings are deceived into cyclic life because [freedom and deception], like the freedom and deception [experienced in a] dream, manifest as the simple play of intrinsic awareness, non-existent from the first moment they are experienced and therefore primordially pure.

If the character [of the ground] is spontaneous, wouldn't living beings be effortlessly liberated since the goal [i.e., enlightenment] is innate? Because [the ground] is spontaneous, the dimensions of awakening and the pristine wisdoms of the sphere [of reality] are complete in their pure nature from the very beginning. Nevertheless, an actualization [of the dimensions of awakening and of pristine wisdoms] in the primordial [ground] occurs [when beings], in a manner comparable to waking from sleep, become free from incidental stains.

When the [ground of being] arises as manifestation within its own nature, the ground serves as the basis for both freedom and deception and is therefore called the common ground. Because it serves as the basis for freedom, it is called the ground of freedom. Because it also serves as the basis for the deception of sentient beings, it is called the ground for deception. The ground's manifestation is of a single nature, but when distinguished in terms of [serving as the basis for] freedom, deception, [or both,] it is threefold.

Here, the word *primordial* (in "primordial purity") means "basic" or "fundamental" and is synonymous with "original," "from the beginning," "from the primordium," and so on.

[II.B.3.b.ii.B'.1'.b'.ii']
Precise Explanation of the Primordially Pure Character of the Ground

Two or three pristine wisdoms are inherent to the character [of the ground of being].

Two or three pristine wisdoms are inherent to the primordially pure character [of the ground of being].

Two exist in this way: Intrinsic awareness is devoid of substantiality and therefore indivisible from emptiness. Based on this indivisibility, the character comprises two pristine wisdoms: the pristine wisdom of the primordially pure nature, which is free of mentation, and the pristine wisdom of the spontaneous character, which is the original radiance glowing deep within. The *Sixth Expanse*[4] states:

> The nature [of the ground] is primordial purity;
> Its character is spontaneous accomplishment.

The nature aspect [of the ground] transcends the limitations of existing and not existing. The character aspect [of the ground] consists of the creative potential of the ground. The intrinsic indivisibility of these two is Great Perfection, free of limitations. The *Intrinsically Free Awareness*[5] states:

> [Great Perfection] is freedom from the stains of the four limits.

Three pristine wisdoms are inherent [to the ground of primordial purity], as stated in *Vajrasattva, Mirror of the Heart*[6]:

> Know that the ground has three attributes:
> Nature, character, and energy.

The reality dimension of awakening exists as the dimension of the originally pure nature and is therefore the basis for the arising of the three dimensions of awakening which are always inherently present in it. The reality dimension of awakening does not, however, have any diversified and objectifiable attributes, such as face and hands.

The character [of the ground] is clear [pristine wisdom], present as five lights. The three effulgences[7] (of these lights) are of original innate clarity; however, they do not exist as separate entities with particular colors.

The energy [of the ground] is present as intrinsic awareness of pristine wisdom: its quality of knowing manifests in various ways, clearly and unobstructedly, without a dualistic experience involving an observer and an observed object.

These pristine wisdoms (nature, character, and energy) are inherent to the primordially pure original ground of being simply as the creative potential of this ground, but they are not manifest. It is therefore consistent [to say] that two pristine wisdoms (that of the primordially pure nature and the spontaneous character) unfold at the time of enlightenment. The *Condensed Transcendent Wisdom Scripture*[8] states:

> Without pristine wisdom, there would be no qualities to develop, no awakening,
> And the oceans of the buddhas' virtues would not arise.

When intrinsic awareness dwells in the ground of being (i.e., is present as the inner sphere of reality), it is present at the beginning and the end[9] as an inner glow which is not manifest as dimensions of awakening and lights. When intrinsic awareness arises from the ground, it then manifests its intrinsic effulgent luminosity.

Intrinsic awareness dwelling in the heart is called intrinsic awareness dwelling in the temporary ground. However, in that case, intrinsic awareness has already arisen from the sphere of reality as cyclic life and has not yet reached the place of freedom; therefore, it is still considered to be the manifestation of the ground. To explain, immature intrinsic awareness[10] dwells, like an unhatched peacock, in the expanse of the self-radiant five lights, which is like the peacock's egg. When the manifestations of the path—the four visions—occur, intrinsic awareness arises like a rainbow in space. Once the material [body] is purified, intrinsic awareness is perfected and develops into the dimensions of awakening, like [the peacock] emerging from its egg. Consequently, the ground of the sphere of reality and the temporary ground differ in that the former does not have a visible luminous halo and the latter does.

[In summary,] the nature [of the ground] is the indivisibility of emptiness and clarity; its character is the indivisibility of clarity and emptiness; and its energy is the indivisibility of intrinsic awareness and emptiness. To use examples of its presence in us, the nature, a primordially pure pristine wisdom, is present like a clear sky; the character, a spontaneous pristine wisdom, is like a limpid ocean; and the energy, an all-pervasive pristine wisdom, is like an immaculate jewel.

[II.B.3.b.ii.B'.1'.c']
The Eight Ways the Ground of Being Manifests

The spontaneity of the ground manifests as eight gates.

The original ground of the primordially pure (inner) sphere of reality [is called] the youthful vase-body. When its seal breaks, the energy-wind of pristine wisdom is set in motion. The movement of the energy-wind of wisdom causes intrinsic awareness to emerge from the ground of being. This intrinsic awareness itself manifests as the eight gates of being's spontaneity. At that time, the manifestation of the primordially pure dimension of reality appears above, like a cloudless sky. The manifestation of the enjoyment dimension realms of clear light which pervades the expanse of space appears directly in front. From the creativity of intrinsic awareness, the great manifestation of the ground appears below. From the creativity of intrinsic awareness, the manifestation of the enjoyment dimension of awakening appears further below; and [around it] the realms of the natural manifest dimension of awakening appear in the cardinal and intermediate directions. Still further below, the countless realms that are personal perceptions of the six types of beings appear through the gate of cyclic life.

Everything arises naturally from the display of the eight gates of being's spontaneity and is therefore called the great simultaneous display of cyclic life and perfect peace. When inner clarity manifests as outer clarity [the display of cyclic life and perfect peace], the unceasing space of [this display's] nature is innate clarity; the manifestation of its character is the five lights, the primordial radiance; and the manifestation of its energy is the natural quality of openness, like a cloudless sky.

The eight gates of manifestation are as explained in the *Tantra of Great Beauty and Auspiciousness*[11]:

> Unceasing space is [the gate through which the ground of being] manifests as energy.
> Unceasing appearance is [the ground] manifesting as lights.
> Unceasing enjoyment is [the ground] manifesting as pristine wisdom.[12]
> Unceasing nature is [the ground] manifesting as dimensions of awakening.
> Unceasing view is [the ground] manifesting as non-duality.
> Unceasing method is [the ground] manifesting as freedom from limitations.
> The purity of pristine wisdom is the gate to perfection.
> Unceasing energy is [the gate] to impure [cyclic life].
> These [eight] are precious wish-fulfilling jewels.[13]

To elaborate, [the realms] of the enjoyment dimension of awakening appear from the creative dynamics of the nature [of the ground]. The natural realms of the manifest dimension of awakening appear from the creative dynamics of capabilities [that are the character of the ground]. The gate of cyclic life appears as a dream-like personal perception from the creativity of energy. Although the manifestations of the ground unfold in these ways, deception and freedom from deception have no reality with respect to the nature of the ground's manifestations. The gates of the ground's spontaneity are inherent to the manifestation of the ground: this is the factor that permits the perception of pure realms and impure deceptive appearances.

[The ground's manifestation] is the basis for freedom, while primordial purity is the place of freedom: this is a key distinction. In other words, if the nature of the manifestation of the ground is recognized, the manifestation serves as the condition for freedom, and is therefore considered the basis of freedom. If it is not recognized, the manifestation serves as the condition for deception and is therefore considered the basis of deception. For instance, a white conch shell can serve as a condition for the mistaken [cognition of it] as a yellow [conch shell]. [The ground's manifestation] is not actually deception, but it is regarded as such[14] when it serves as the condition for deception.

Liberation as the [primordial buddha] occurs in the following way: The instant the ground's manifestations arise, one does not apprehend them as something else but rather recognizes them as one's own inner radiance. Consequently, the movement [of constructive thoughts] ceases in itself: at the first instant [of movement], the recognition that the manifestations are inner radiance causes realization to dawn. This realization defines the difference [between liberation and deception].

Immediately thereafter, deception is dispelled and pristine wisdom unfolds. At this point, the ground fully develops into the result [i.e., awakening]. This is re-enlightenment, the realization of primordial enlightenment within one's own nature. When self-manifestations dissolve into primordial purity, the result is awakening within the ground of being itself before anything else manifests [from the ground]. [The personification of] this awakening is the enlightened guide known as Ever-Perfect.

[II.B.3.b.ii.B'.2']
How Beings Fail to Recognize the Ground of Being

This section has two parts: (1) a general presentation of the arising of deception, and (2) a detailed account of the formation of the body.

[II.B.3.b.ii.B'.2'.a']
General Presentation of the Arising of Deception

Three causes and four conditions [produce deception]: when the six cognitions arise,
The nature of the ground's manifestations is not realized; factors in groups of five [arise]
Based on subject and object. Through the course of the twelve links of interdependent origination, [the wheel] turns.

How does deception arise? [To give a brief overview,] due to the cause (the three unawarenesses) and the four conditions (the impure objective referent), consciousness mistakes the appearances [of the ground] through [dualistic] apprehensions of subject and object. When this occurs, the uninhibited functioning of the six [types of] grasping cognition causes the six emotions[15] to appear as dormant instincts which constrain intrinsic awareness. At this point, one becomes deceived with respect to the appearances of the six objects[16] by not recognizing that such appearances are of the nature [of intrinsic awareness of pristine wisdom], i.e., the basis for their manifestation.

As instincts intensify, various factors, such as the aggregates, sense objects, and so forth (each in groups of five), arise through [the dualistic apprehensions of] subject and object. The twelve links of interdependent origination unfold in their sequence and propel the turning of the dream-like cycle of lives.

To explain in detail, when [appearances] manifest from the ground, the creative dynamic of energy manifests naturally as cognition, which is the clarity and intrinsic awareness capable of analyzing objects. Through non-recognition of the nature [of appearances], three aspects of unawareness manifest in conjunction with appearances. The unawareness identical in nature [with intrinsic awareness],[17] the cause [for deception], is a failure to recognize that cognition is itself [intrinsic awareness]. Co-emergent unawareness is the simultaneous arising of cognition and a failure to recognize its actual nature. Conceptual unawareness is the apprehension of self-manifestations as something "other."

Further, four conditions contribute to deception: the causal condition is non-recognition of the manifestation of the ground as having arisen from itself; the objective condition is the manifestation [of the ground] as [outer] objects; the dominant condition is the apprehending of [objects] as "I" or "property"; and the immediate condition is the concomitance of these three conditions.

In summation, unawareness is the cause of deception, and the appearance of objects to cognition is the contributing condition.

Six obscurations are produced from the nature aspect of unawarenesses. The *[Tantra of] Self-Manifestation [of Awareness]*[18] states:

> Unawareness that is mind, as the root of cyclic life;
> Unawareness that becomes absorbed in the objective field that leads to deception;
> Unawareness-within-its-own-ground that is the basis of deception;
> Unawareness of constructive thought that is the grasping subject;
> Unawareness pursuing a path that is its own artificial creation;
> Unawareness of deludedness that is non-recognition;
> Owing to these six forms of unawareness, the [nature of the] self-manifestation is not seen.[19]

Unawareness causes the arising of six grasping cognitions: (1) mind and its movements; (2) consciousness knowing itself; (3) apprehension of objects; (4) ascertainment of objects; (5) distraction by objects; and (6) coarse emotions. All these are forms of intense grasping, and together they constitute the six obscurations.

These factors of deception propel beings through the course of the twelve links of interdependent origination. The interconnection between a twelve-year [cycle] and the twelve months [of a year] externally, and the twelve emotions internally, make possible the twelve experiential media.[20] Thus, the successive twelve links of interdependent origination evolve from the impure [factor of unawareness] in the following way.

When manifestations of the ground of being arise, the creativity of intrinsic awareness produces cognition which is co-emergent with non-recognition [of its own nature as the ground's manifestation]: this is "unawareness." The ensuing deceptions or "formative actions" lead to exploration of the object's basic appearance, which is "consciousness." Consciousness instigates the differentiations of objects by designations such as "this is an object," "this is an appearance," and so on. The nature of the object of designation is apprehended as "form." This constitutes the primary deception of existence: "name and form." Name and form give rise to the six senses, allowing cognitions to arise and develop in relation to the six types of objects. This leads to apprehension of objects, which is "contact" [between object, senses, and consciousness]. Contact leads to the experiences of attraction, aversion, or indifference, which is "feeling." This evolves into attachment to objects, which is "craving." Subsequently "grasping" arises, involving the grasper with the related act of grasping an object. The unfolding of unpredictable experiences related to various deceptive appearances is "becoming." As a result, one is born in the formless, form, or desire realms, which is "birth." The cycle continues through old age and sickness until death [i.e., the links of "aging" and "death"]. This progression repeats itself again and again. This is how the sequence of the twelve links of interdependent origination that causes cyclic life first arises from the manifestation of the ground.

[From one life to another,] one wanders through the various existences of cyclic life, following the successive links of interdependent origination. When the [manifestation of] reality[21] has passed [and before the intermediate state of existence arises], unawareness of the nature of [intrinsic awareness] generates formative actions for the next life. Consciousness seeks an embodied existence; after it enters a womb, name and form are developed through the phases of fetal development. The six senses develop, and the convergence of contributing factors [i.e., object, sense, and consciousness] creates contact. Then the feeling of pleasure or pain [is experienced], leading to craving for the experience [of feeling]. Grasping related to objects and the act of grasping are followed by intense grasping, [i.e., the entrance into a new life], which is "becoming." One is born from the womb and gradually experiences the transformations from youth to old age and finally death. All these links arise in dependence upon one another.

During the experience of cyclic life, the five objects (such as form) arise as a result of not recognizing the five lights as a self-manifestion and of apprehending these lights as [outer] objects. The five emotions arise because the nature of the five pristine wisdoms is not recognized. The five [aggregates] (such as body, mind, etc.), which are composite collections, arise from impurity [i.e., non-recognition] of the natural radiance of the reality [of the ground]. The five [mental phenomena] (such as the ever-searching mental cognition) arise from impurity [non-recognition] of the five energy-winds. The five conceptions of self (thought and memory conceived as the self; a multiplicity of objects conceived as the self; various currents of thoughts conceived as the self; the basic aspect of consciousness conceived as the self; and phenomena and discrimination of phenomena conceived as the self) arise because the movements [of constructive thoughts] do not cease in themselves.

In summation, the impure phenomena of cyclic life arise within ongoing intrinsic awareness, abide within intrinsic awareness, and are simply the play of intrinsic awareness. They have never existed outside intrinsic awareness, just as dreams never occur except in sleep. The various descriptions of cyclic life teach that [phenomena] are in fact empty forms, simply the magical play of vivid appearances that do not exist in reality.

[II.B.3.b.ii.B'.2'.b']
The Formation of the Body

This section has four parts: (1) a general presentation of the formation of the body in each of three realms; (2) the development of the body in the womb; (3) the relationship between superficial and ultimate [elements]; (4) and a statement concerning the presence of pervasive elements.

[II.B.3.b.ii.B'.2'.b'.i']
The Formation of the Body in Each of the Three Realms

> **Object, body, and mind arise from the three bases of deception.**
> **Mental, radiant, and material bodies develop in the three realms.**

The cause of deception is co-emergent unawareness, the failure to recognize that what arises from the ground of being is the self-manifestation [of intrinsic awareness] itself. The condition contributing [to deception] is unawareness of the imaginaries, apprehending as "other" [the appearances] that are [intrinsic awareness] manifesting to itself. The basis for deception is the manifestation of clear light, [which is also a] self-manifestation. In other words, three forms of deception—in relation to objects, body, and mind—arise due to [this cause, condition, and basis]. Since the nature [of the ground] is empty, it provides space, and thus reality becomes the basis for objective deception. The character of the ground—[clarity, manifesting as] the five lights—becomes the basis for deception with respect to the objective manifestations of the material body and external environment. Intrinsic awareness, creativity, and effulgence of energy are the bases for deception with respect to the mind.

The initial stage of deception within the three realms is the development of beings in the formless realm. Their mental bodies of contemplation, constituted of the four aggregates that are mere names,[22] serve as support for their mental continuums. Next appear beings of the form realm, for whom bodies of the radiant five lights serve as support for their mental continuums. Finally, beings of the desire realm appear, for whom material bodies of flesh and blood serve as support for their mental continuums.

[II.B.3.b.ii.B'.2'.b'.ii']
The Development of the Body in the Womb

> **Womb-birth: from the penetrating, scattering, and equalizing [properties of the] elements,**
> **The channels, syllables, energy-winds, and vital essences [form], and both the superficial and ultimate elements develop.**

For a being taking birth in a womb, the development of the adamantine body occurs as follows. The emotions cause the production of the elements of earth, water, fire, and wind. These elements perform the function of developing the body: through their three functions of penetrating, scattering, and equalizing, these four elements gather, distribute, and mix.

Initially, during the first week of embryonic development, the subtle channels of the four elements along with four seed-syllables form in the four directions. Subsequently, in the second and following weeks, the two pairs of small eyes—the physical eyes and the "eyes of the lamp"—form at the navel channel knot. The finest essences of flesh, blood, heat, and breath form in the four heart channels and reveal the sense-bases of the eight consciousnesses. The four channel wheels form gradually, each one having two eyes. On the three main channels which support the five sense faculties rest three seed-syllables which serve as supports for the three doors [body, speech, and mind] and the three poisons in the impure state, and as supports for the three dimensions of awakening in the pure state. On the five channel wheels rest the five seed syllables[23] of the heroes.[24] Four hundred and seventy-two subtle channels branch out from these [five channel wheels]. Then the main and secondary energy-winds, such as the three sets (outer, inner, and secret) of five energy-winds, form. [These energy-winds] are either the energy-winds of pristine wisdom or energy-winds of evolutionary actions. The superficial vital essence rests within the right channel; the ultimate vital essence rests within the left; and the natural vital essence rests within the central channel. Thus, the complete body forms through the developing process of the four ultimate and four superficial elements.

[II.B.3.b.ii.B'.2'.b'.iii']
The Relationship Between Superficial and Ultimate Elements

> **Through dependence on the former, the aggregates and so forth develop.**
> **The latter serve as the cause of the four lamps which reveal the four visions.**

[In the root verses above,] "former" refers to the four superficial elements which serve as the support for the development of the five aggregates. "And so forth" refers to pristine wisdom, since the elements act as the support for pristine wisdom. The development and formation of the aggregates is explained in the following way: The aggregate of form develops on the basis of flesh; discernment develops on the basis of blood; consciousness develops on the basis of heat; mental formations develop on the basis of inhalation; and feeling develops on the basis of exhalation.

Flesh is the basis from which the channels are produced. The channels are the basis from which energy-winds are produced. Energy-winds produce the energy-winds of both evolutionary actions and pristine wisdom. The energy-winds of evolutionary actions permeate cyclic life while [the energy-winds of] pristine wisdom permeate perfect peace.

Furthermore, blood leads to the production of lymph, which in turn produces the vital essences, which produce the five sense faculties, which themselves are the products of superficial elements. The causes of the five sense faculties are the five emotions, while myriad past, present, and future constructive thoughts cause both cyclic life and perfect peace. This completes the account of the development of the four superficial elements.

"The latter" refers to the four ultimate elements. These are based on the superficial elements and serve as the cause of the four lamps,[25] through which the pristine wisdoms of the four visions[26] manifest and are perceived. When the color white reaches full intensity, it serves as the cause for the "water-lamp of the far-sighted [eyes]," which arises from the water energy-wind channel. When red reaches full intensity, it serves as the cause for the "lamp of emptiness which is the sphere," which arises from the fire channel. When yellow reaches full intensity, it serves as the cause for the "lamp of the pure sphere [of intrinsic awareness]," which arises from the earth channel. When green reaches full intensity, it serves as the cause for the "lamp of self-existing wisdom," which arises from the path of the wind channel.

[The lamp of] self-existing wisdom produces intrinsic awareness. The [water-lamp of the] far-sighted [eyes] generates light; the [lamp of emptiness which is the] sphere produces the dimensions of awakening; [the lamp of the pure] sphere [of intrinsic awareness] produces pristine wisdoms. The water-lamp of the far-sighted [eyes] leads to the [vision of the] direct perception of reality. The lamp of emptiness which is the sphere leads to the vision of increasing contemplative experience. The lamp of the pure sphere [of intrinsic awareness] leads to the vision of reaching the limit of intrinsic awareness. The lamp of self-existing wisdom leads to the vision of the cessation [of phenomenal] reality.

The superficial channels, vital essence, and energy-winds of evolutionary actions result in evolutionary actions, in emotions, and in the increase and decrease of the four elements. The ultimate channels, vital essences, and the energy-winds of pristine wisdom cause the development of pristine wisdom (the cause), of the lights and colors (the conditions), and of the dimensions of awakening and pristine wisdoms (the result).

[II.B.3.b.ii.B'.2'.b'.iv']
The Presence of Pervasive Elements

> **Twenty-five elements generate the effulgence and creativity of pristine wisdom.**

The twenty-five elements that pervade the body (five sets of five) are all naturally complete in the body and generate the effulgence and creativity of pristine wisdom, etc. As the *Self-Manifestation* [*of Awareness*[27]] states:

> Five major elements are all present in one's body:
> Five kinds of energy-winds create the radiance of pristine wisdom.
> Five kinds of fire generate the creativity of pristine wisdom.
> Five kinds of earth create the nature of pristine wisdom.
> Five kinds of water create the object of pristine wisdom.
> Five kinds of space provide the abode of pristine wisdom.

This tantra provides an extensive explanation of these points.

The five earths are present [within the body] in this way: Ever-illuminating earth co-exists with intrinsic awareness; immutable and impenetrable earth co-exists with the lamps; precious earth, the source of everything, co-exists with the spheres; ever-limitless earth which displays appearances co-exists with both the sphere of reality and pristine wisdom. The earth of ultimate accomplishment co-exists with wisdom.

The five waters are present in this way: changeless water is present in all channels; the water of clear, pure tranquillity is present in every bone; water that increases qualities is present in the blood; water of non-attachment is present in the lymph; and water of perfect non-apprehension is present within the eyes.

The five fires are present in this way: the fire that pervades everything, internally and externally, is present in the lungs; the fire that illuminates everything, internally and externally, is present in the two eyes and the limbs; the fire that is uniform throughout everything is present between the skin and flesh; the fire that conceives of external and internal activities is present in the soles of the two feet; and fire that accomplishes external and internal activities is present in the palms of the two hands.

The five energy-winds are present in this way: life-sustaining energy-wind is present in the life channel; the energy-wind that produces luster and radiance is present between the eyebrows; the energy-wind that co-exists with fire is present in the abdomen; the energy-wind that pervades everything is present throughout the entire body; and the compassionless energy-wind of the evolutionary action of the eon is present between the heart and the heart membrane.

The five spaces are present in this way: all-pervading space is present, inseparable from actual intrinsic awareness; objectless, clear and pure space is present, inseparable from the five lights; unmixed pure space is present, inseparable from the pure sphere of reality; space that is symbolic of ultimate [reality, mind itself], is present, inseparable from pristine wisdom [expressed] as signs—the empty spheres; and liberative space of the pure realms is present, inseparable from all the manifestations of dimensions of awakening and pristine wisdoms.

Although comprehensive teachings exist concerning the location and function of the five energy-winds when each of them is divided into five, these are not included here.

[II.B.3.b.ii.B'.3']
Ever-Presence of the Ground in the Deceived State

> **Buddha-nature pervades all sentient beings.**
> **Its mode of appearance and mode of manifestation are taught in six sets of five.**

How is buddha-nature (the ground) pervasively present in the continuum of every sentient being in the state of deception? The *Vajrasattva, Mirror of the Heart Tantra*[28] says:

> Buddha-nature is present in all sentient beings throughout the universe, just as oil pervades sesame seeds.

The *Cluster of Jewels [Tantra]*[29] states:

> Oil is always naturally present
> In mustard and sesame seeds.
> Likewise, buddha-nature
> And its respective luminosity manifest
> In every sentient being who takes physical form.

Beyond the Limits of Sound Root Tantra[30] says:

> The pristine wisdom of intrinsic awareness is present
> in the body
> Like oil is present in the sesame seed.
> The luster and radiance of the body
> Are pervaded by the moisture of pristine wisdom.

The *Self-Manifestation [of Awareness] Tantra*[31] says:

> Authentic buddha-mind is present
> In the continuum of every sentient being
> As dimensions of awakening and pristine wisdoms.

These and other similar references accord with the discourses and tantras of the common [systems] that teach the definitive truth.

On this subject, Longchen Rabjam, [who is] Ever-Perfect [incarnate], using logical reasoning and scriptural references, refutes the viewpoints that buddha-nature [does not] possess the powers [of a buddha] and major and minor marks and signs [of awakening], and [refutes the viewpoints] that the scriptures that expound buddha-nature require interpretation.

Longchenpa gave [three] reasons why one should appreciate [the teaching on buddha-nature]: (1) If buddha-nature is not revealed by a spiritual friend, it cannot be recognized. Because it is discovered through reliance on an authentic master, one should appreciate [the teaching on buddha-nature]. (2) [Buddha-nature] is a difficult topic to understand, even for the bodhisattvas dwelling on the stages of awakening, not to mention egocentric people. Because it is an impenetrable secret known by enlightened beings only, one should appreciate [the teaching on the buddha-nature]. (3) Because one will clearly perceive buddha-nature if revealed by a qualified master, and because buddha-nature manifests naturally in the interval [between lives], one should appreciate [the teachings on buddha-nature]. Longchengpa taught this profound and secret subject [of buddha-nature] comprehensively. One should study his outstanding works in order to fully understand it.

This [completes] the general explanation on the ever-presence of the ground of being.

The special features [of the ground of being] will now be explained in detail. The modes of manifestation and appearance of the ground are taught in six sets of five: Primordially present in the pristine wisdom of the buddha-nature are five dimensions of awakening, five energy-winds of pristine wisdom awarenesses, five lights, five qualities of the [buddha] families, five pristine wisdom energy-winds, and five qualities of nature, character, and energy. Their primordial presence is indicated by impure manifestations: five emotions, five aggregates, five elements, five senses, five sense objects, and five natural qualities of the three doors. The *Garland of Pearls*[32] states:

> Five bodies, five pristine wisdoms,
> Five luminosities and their five colors,
> Five qualities, five energy-winds of pristine wisdom,
> Five natures, five characters,
> And five energies present in the [buddha-] nature
> Pervade all [beings].

To elaborate on this, the pristine wisdoms of intrinsic awareness present from the beginning as the five dimensions of awakening now manifest as the five aggregates.[33] The nature of intrinsic awareness and the sphere of reality manifesting as a spontaneous form is Buddha Illuminator (Vairocana). The unchanging [nature of intrinsic awareness] is Buddha Imperturbable (Akṣobhya). The treasury of precious qualities [of intrinsic awareness] is Buddha Source of Jewels (Ratnasaṃhava). The boundless light [of intrinsic awareness] is Buddha Measureless Light (Amitābha). Being primordial enlightenment, [the nature of intrinsic awareness] is Buddha Unfailing Accomplishment (Amoghasiddhi).

Likewise, the five pristine wisdoms are present from the beginning and now arise as the five emotions.[34] The dimensions of awakening, realms, and other phenomena naturally manifesting in the state of intrinsic awareness is mirror-like pristine wisdom. The equality of everything within intrinsic awareness is the pristine wisdom of equality. The distinct manifestations of the [dimensions of awakening and realms] is pristine wisdom of discernment. The [dimensions of awakening and the realms] being spontaneously present from the beginning is the pristine wisdom of accomplishing aims. That all are of a single flavor within reality is the pristine wisdom of the sphere of reality.

From the five lights arise five elements.[35] Intrinsic awareness being stainless is [present as] white light; intrinsic awareness being complete in all qualities is [present as] yellow light; intrinsic awareness being the union [of all qualities] is [present as] red light; intrinsic awareness being complete in everything without effort is [present as] green light; and intrinsic awareness being unchangeable is [present as] blue light. These [lights] in their pure aspect are the five consorts.

Five buddha families appear as the five sense faculties (which indicate their presence).[36] Pristine wisdom is inconceivably realized within the nature of the sphere of transcendent reality, and thus becomes indivisible from the sphere of reality. The inseparability of these two is the transcendent family. [Intrinsic awareness] being unchanging is the adamantine family. Its completeness in qualities is the jewel family. Its being unstained by evolutionary actions and emotions is the lotus family. Its being complete in the enlightened activity or magical play of intrinsic awareness is the action family.

Five energy-winds are related to the five sense objects. [Intrinsic awareness] reaching the warmth of pristine wisdom is the energy-wind that co-exists with fire. [Intrinsic awareness] serving as the basis for the arising of cyclic life [when its nature is not understood] and for perfect peace [when its nature is understood] is the life-sustaining energy-wind. [Intrinsic awareness] distinguishing various appearances is the energy-wind that separates the refined essence from the unrefined. [Intrinsic awareness] pervading everything, from cyclic life to perfect peace, is the pervasive energy-wind. At the time of actualizing intrinsic awareness, [intrinsic awareness] causing cyclic life to become the basis for freedom in the state of perfect peace is the energy-wind of evolutionary action devoid of compassion. These winds are not those related to the movements [of intrinsic awareness], but are designated [as energy-winds] with respect to the aspect [of intrinsic awareness] and are therefore winds of the intrinsic awareness of pristine wisdom.

Five qualities or five insights [are primordially present] and manifest as the groups of five natural qualities of the three gates. [Intrinsic awareness] discriminating the basis of the arising of cyclic life from the basis of the arising of perfect peace is "discriminating insight." [Intrinsic awareness] being one in ongoing awareness is "comprehensive insight." [Intrinsic awareness] not departing from intrinsic awareness is "pervading insight." [Intrinsic awareness'] presence at the time of actualizing intrinsic awareness is "presiding insight." As an alternative [to the latter], [intrinsic awareness that] cuts the life of both cyclic life and perfect peace is the "liberative insight." Since these insights are none other than intrinsic awareness, they are called self-existing pristine wisdom, because they are not forms of analytical discernment, but pertain instead to intrinsic awareness of pristine wisdom.

If these [six sets of elements] were not present in intrinsic awareness itself, which is the ground of being, they would not be present in the directly observable body and mind. If they were not present in these [body and mind], they would not be present as external objects appearing to the mind. If they were not present in intrinsic awareness, they would be like the reflection in a mirror of the face of a barren woman's son: his face cannot appear because the son has no face, and he has no face because he does not exist. What manifests as a phenomenon arises due to its presence in the body and mind, which [in turn] arises from being present in intrinsic awareness. This is comparable to Devadatta's having a head, therefore having a face which can appear in a mirror. Concerning this, the *Majestic Creative Energy of the Universe*[37] states:

> How things appear is my[38] being;
> How things arise is my reality;
> There is no phenomenon that is not me
> In the whole universe.

From the *Cluster of Jewels Tantra*[39]:

> All manifestations appear
> Just like a face in a mirror.

[II.B.3.b.ii.B'.4']
Supplementary Explanation of the Abode of Pristine Wisdom and the Ending of the Deception of [Apprehended] Objects

> **Intrinsic awareness is present in the center of the heart, based on the three palaces.**
> **The excellent vital essences abide in the four entrances of clear light.**
> **The two eyes are the doors for the manifestation of external clarity;**
> **[Depending on] objects and fulfilling crucial means, deception is ceased,**
> **And one effortlessly attains the original place of freedom.**

Buddha-mind (i.e., intrinsic awareness of pristine wisdom) is present mingling with the deceptive manifestation of the material body. The blessing of this presence—the pristine wisdom manifestation—arises in the following way: its actual dwelling place is the center of the glorious knot (Śrīvatsa) in the heart jewel; its effulgences are present in the blazing palace of the conch-shell (Bhenza), in the palace of the eyes that see, and in the palace of the channels that cause movement. *Beyond the Limits of Sound Tantra*[40] states:

> In the palace of the jewel of the heart
> Is a composite jewel of eight facets, the entrances;
> Five pristine wisdoms and five dimensions of awakening,
> Five energy-winds and five channels of consciousness:
> Everything has a fivefold character.

Further:

> Inside the head, heart, and channels,
> The reality of unfabricated purity is present.

Beyond the Limits of Sound Tantra and other scriptures explain this subject in detail.

The nature of intrinsic awareness is present as dimensions of awakening, like a statue in a vase. The character of intrinsic awareness is present as light, like a flame inside a vase. The energy of intrinsic awareness is present as light, like the rays of the sun. Four entrances which become four channels branch out from the clear light of the heart. The great golden crystal (*kati*) channel serves as the basis for the arising of the clear light vision. The white silk thread channel serves as the basis for apprehending external objects. The finely coiled channel serves as the basis for the self-arising [of intrinsic awareness]. The crystal tubular channel serves as the basis for the self-manifestation [of intrinsic awareness]. The emptiness channel of intrinsic freedom, which inserts itself into the heaven gate at the crown of the head, serves as the basis for the dimensions of the chains [of light].[41]

Together, these five inner channels are the luminosities of the five pristine wisdoms. Since they naturally serve as bases, they reveal and increase the four lamps. The spheres of clear light move through the four channels of light, and based on that, clear light is cultivated: in the excellent fundamental sphere of the great golden crystal channel, the embodiment of the three aspects (nature, character, and energy) is present and supported by the heart. In the excellent path vital sphere of the white silk thread channel, the four lamps, [principally] the water-lamp, is present in the right [side of the body]. In the peak sphere of excellence of the finely coiled channel, the various visions of increasing contemplative experience are present in the left side. In the crystal tubular channel, the basis for the vision of reaching the limit [of awareness] is present as the basis for manifestation of inner clarity. In the empty intrinsic-freedom channel, the dimensions of the indestructible chains of light are present.

The doors through which the visions of pristine wisdom pervade outwardly are the two eyes. In other words, from the right eye, both the lamp of the far-sighted [eyes] and the lamp of self-existing pristine wisdom manifest as the character of the visions; this is the pristine wisdom-means that understands the phenomenal [view]. From the left eye, both the lamp of emptiness which is the sphere and the lamp of the pure sphere [of awareness] manifest as the character of emptiness; this is the insight of pristine wisdom that understands the noumenal [view]. In the center [of the body], from the crown of the head aperture, the chains [of light] dimension of non-conceptual intrinsic awareness manifests as spheres [of light arranged] in tiers.

Based on what has been explained above, one trains in the crucial body postures,[42] ways of gazing,[43] and breathing techniques in relation to the targets of external and internal objects.[44] Practicing the yoga of luminous [absorption] as one's path, the deceptive appearances are ended [in the ground of being]. One effortlessly arrives at the secret jewel cave, the original place of freedom, primordial purity, and one is thereby liberated: this freedom arises from the natural [state] of reality.

Appendix

Outline of the Text

Introduction

I. The Title of the Root Verses
  A. The Title
  B. The Title's Meaning
    1. The Title's Literal Meaning
    2. The Five Essential Observations
    3. The Style of the Commentary, *The Infinite Ocean of Knowledge*
  C. Elimination of Doubts Concerning the Title
II. Expressions of Reverence
  A. Reverence to the Illustrious Spiritual Master
    1. Context
    2. The Meaning of the Words of Reverence
  B. Reverence to the Lord of Sages
  C. Praise and Supplication to the Lion of Speech
  D. Bowing to the Master and the Lineage
III. The Author's Resolve to Complete this Work
  A. Main Discussion
  B. Supplementary Discussion of the Four Components Necessary for Composing a Treatise

Overview of *The Infinite Ocean of Knowledge*

Chapter I

The Cosmology of the Universal Way

I. Causes and Conditions that Create the Realms of Existence

- A. Concise Presentation
- B. Extensive Explanation
  - 1. Relationships between Those to be Guided and the Enlightened Guides
  - 2. Particular Causes and Conditions

II. The Arrangement of the Realms

- A. Richly Adorned Realm
  - 1. A Description of Richly Adorned
  - 2. The Distinctive Features of the Realms within Richly Adorned
- B. The Flower-Filled World
  - 1. Overall Explanation
  - 2. Detailed Explanation
- C. Distinctive Features of Our Own World-System, Endurance
  - 1. Identification of Endurance
  - 2. The Supplementary Explanation

Chapter II

Our Universe according to the Individual and Universal Ways

I. The Preamble

II. Extensive Presentation

- A. The Age of the Initial Formation of our World-System
  - 1. The Environment
    - a. Main Explanation
      - i. The Origin of the Fortunate Age
      - ii. Arrangement of the Mountains and Continents
      - iii. The Meanings of the Names of the Continents
      - iv. The Three Miserable Realms and the Demi-gods' Realm
      - v. The Realm of the Gods
    - b. Supplementary Discussion of the Viewpoint of the Proclaimers and the Solitary Sages
  - 2. The Inhabitants, Sentient Beings
    - a. The Nature of Every Sentient Being
    - b. Manner of Diffusion
      - i. Concise Presentation
      - ii. Extensive Explanation

c. Happiness and Suffering
d. Categorization
B. The Interim Abiding of Our World-System
1. The Beings of Our World-System
2. The Land of Jambu
3. The Origin of the Wheel-Monarchs
4. Features of Life
C. The Ages of the Final Destruction and Vacuity of Our World-System
1. Main Discussion
a. The Emptying of the World-System of Inhabitants
b. Environment
2. Supplementary Discussion
a. Enumeration of Ages
b. Other Patterns of Destruction
c. Places That Are Not Destroyed

Chapter III

Space and Time in the Tantra of the Wheel of Time

I. Main Explanation
A. Space
1. The Source and Reason for this Description of Space and Time
2. Mount Meru and its Foundations
3. The Mountains and the Continents
4. The Twelve Lands of Evolutionary Action
5. The Small Land of Jambu and its Six Regions
6. The Types of Beings
7. The Celestial Sphere and Time-Conjunctions
B. Time
1. The Three Types of Days
2. Different Ways of Explaining the Four Eras
a. The Four Eras of the Buddha's Doctrine
b. The Four Eras of the Wheel-Holders
c. The Four Eras of Our World-System
d. The Four Eras of the Planets Entering Vacuity
C. A Conclusive Summary

II. Measures of Space and Time
  A. Introduction
  B. Main Explanation
    1. Measures Particular to the Wheel of Time
    2. Supplementary Discussion of Measurements Used in the System of Phenomenology
      a. Preamble
      b. Extensive Explanation
        i. Units of Form
        ii. Units of Time
        iii. Components of Words

Chapter IV

The Causes of Cyclic Life

I. Context
II. Main Explanation
  A. Refuting Non-Buddhist Theories of Creation
  B. Setting Forth the Buddhist Systems
    1. The Causes of Cyclic Life
      a. Creation Caused by Actions
      b. The Factor Ensuring Actions' Results
    2. The Causes of the Environment
      a. The Perspective of the Analysts
      b. The Perspective of the Tantra of the Wheel of Time
    3. Presentation of the General Process of Creation
      a. The Perspectives of the Common Systems
        i. The Perspective of the Individualists' System of Phenomenology
          A'. General Presentation
          B'. Detailed Explanation
            1'. The Six Causes
            2'. The Five Results
            3'. General Classes of Results
            4'. The Four Conditions
        ii. The Universalists' System of Phenomenology
          A'. The Causes
          B'. The Conditions
          C'. Results

- b. The Exceptional Systems
  - i. The Ultimate View [Concerning the Origin of Cyclic Life]
    - A'. How the Twelve Links of Interdependent Origination Deceive Sentient Beings
      - 1'. General Presentation
      - 2'. Detailed Explanation
    - B'. The Twelve Links in Relation to the Eight Consciousnesses
    - C'. How Cyclic Life Manifests from Three Instincts
    - D'. Supplementary Explanation: The Ending of Cyclic Life

Chapter V

The Primordial Purity of the Universe

- b. The Exceptional Systems (cont'd)
  - ii. The Origin of Cyclic Life according to the Tradition of Radiant Great Perfection
    - A'. Context
    - B'. Main Discussion
      - 1'. The Fundamental Nature of the Ground of Being
        - a'. Proof that Six Grounds of Being, as Believed from Partial Perspectives, are Mistaken
        - b'. Proof that the Fundamental Nature of the Ground of Being is Primordial Purity
          - i'. Identification of the Primordially Pure Nature [of the Ground]
          - ii'. Precise Explanation of the Primordially Pure Character of the Ground
        - c'. The Eight Ways the Ground of Being Manifests
      - 2'. How Beings Fail to Recognize the Ground of Being
        - a'. General Presentation of the Arising of Deception
        - b'. The Formation of the Body

Glossary of Technical Terms

An asterisk preceding a Sanskrit entry indicates reconstruction from the Tibetan.

English	Sanskrit	Tibetan
absorption	samāpatti	snyoms 'jug
accompanying cause		grogs kyi rgyu
action energy-wind	*karma-vāyu	las kyi rlung
aggregate	skandha	phung po
aggregate of consciousness	vijñāna-skandha	rnam shes kyi phung po
aggregate of discernment	samjñā-skandha	'du shes kyi phung po
aggregate of feeling	vedanā-skandha	tshor ba'i phung po
aggregate of form	rūpa-skandha	gzugs kyi phung po
aggregate of mental formations	saṃskāra-skandha	'du byed kyi phung po
Analyst	vaibhāṣika	bye brag tu smra ba
analytical cessation	pratisaṃkhyā-nirodha	so sor brtags pa'i 'gog pa
Annihilism	uccheda-dṛṣṭi	chad lta
Annihilist	uccheda-vādin	chad par smra ba
appreciative discernment, wisdom, insight	prajñā	shes rab
apprehended object	grahaṇīya	gzung bya
appropriating cause	*parigraha-hetu	yongs 'dzin gyi rgyu
aspect	ākāra	rnam pa
awakening	bodhi	byang chub
awakening mind, bodhicitta	bodhicitta	byang chub kyi sems

English	Sanskrit	Tibetan
barbarian	mleccha	kla klo
bodhisattva, awakening being	bodhisattva	byang chub sems dpa'
buddha-nature	buddha-garbha	sangs rgyas kyi snying po
causal condition	hetu-pratyaya	rgyu'i rkyen
cause	hetu	rgyu
cause of concordant understanding	sampratipatti-hetu	mthun par rtogs pa'i rgyu
cause of the same outcome	sabhāga-hetu	skal mnyam gyi rgyu
Centrism	Madhyamaka	dBu ma
Centrist	Mādhyamika	dBu ma pa
cessation	nirodha	'gog pa
character	svabhāva	rang bzhin
characteristic	lakṣaṇa	mtshan nyid
clear light, radiant awareness	prabhāsvara	'od gsal
co-emergent	sahaja	lhan cig skyes pa
co-emergent cause	sahabhū-hetu	lhan cig 'byung ba'i rgyu
co-emergent unawareness	*sahajāvidyā	lhan cig skyes pa'i ma rig pa
cognitive obscuration	jñeyāvaraṇa	shes bya'i sgrib pa
conceived object	abhiniveśya	zhen yul
conceptualization	parikalpita	kun brtags
concomitant	saṃprayukta	mtshungs ldan
concomitant cause	saṃprayukta-hetu	mtshungs ldan gyi rgyu
concomitant immediate condition	saṃprayukta samanantara-pratyaya	mtshungs pa de ma thag pa'i rkyen
concordant action	sādhāraṇa-karma	spyi mthun gyi las
condition	pratyaya	rkyen
conditioned phenomena	saṃskṛta-dharma	'dus byas kyi chos
contemplation	samādhi	ting nge 'dzin
continuum	saṃtāna	rgyud
creativity	kakṣya	rtsal

English	**Sanskrit**	**Tibetan**
cyclic life	saṃsāra	'khor ba
deception	bhrānta	'khrul pa
defiled mind	kliṣṭa-mana	nyon mongs pa can gyi yid
defiled views	dṛṣṭi-kleśa	lta ba nyon mongs can
definition	lakṣāṇa	mtshan nyid
designation	prajñapti	btags pa
designative existence	prajñapti-sat	btags yod
developed result	vipāka-phala	rnam smin gyi 'bras bu
developing cause	vipāka-hetu	rnam smin gyi rgyu
dimension of awakening pa'i sku	kāya	sku
discriminating wisdom	pratyavekṣaṇa-prajñā	so sor rtog pa'i shes rab
dominant condition	adhipati-pratyaya	bdag rkyen
effective productive cause	samartha-kāraṇa-hetu	byed rgyu nus ldan
eight material particles	aṣṭa-dravyaka	rdul rdzas brgyad
embodiment of complete liberation	vimukti-skandha	rnam par grol ba'i phung po
embodiment of contemplation	samādhi-skandha	ting nge 'dzin gyi phung po
embodiment of ethics	śilā-skandha	tshul khrims kyi phung po
embodiment of the vision of the pristine wisdom of complete liberation	vimukti-jñāna-darśana-skandha	rnam par grol ba'i ye shes mthong ba'i phung po
embodiment of wisdom	prajñā-skandha	shes rab kyi phung po
emotion	kleśa	nyon mongs
emptiness	śunyatā	stong pa nyid
energy	karuṇā	thugs rje
energy-wind	vāyu	rlung
enjoyment dimension of awakening	saṃbhoga-kāya	longs spyod rdzogs
environment and inhabitants	bhājana-sattva	snod bcud
eon, age	kalpa	bskal pa

English	Sanskrit	Tibetan
essential dimension of awakening	svabhāvika-kāya	ngo bo nyid sku
Eternalist	śāśvata-vādin	rtag par smra ba
ethical conduct, ethics	śila	tshul khrims
ever-perfect	samantabhadra	kun tu bzang po
evolutes of the elements	bhautika	'byung 'gyur
evolutionary action	karma	las
exalted	ārya	'phags pa
expanding cause	*upacaya-hetu	rgyas pa'i rgyu
experiential element	dhātu	khams
experiential medium	āyatana	skye mched
experiential teaching	adhigama-dharma	rtogs pa'i chos
external object	bāhyārtha	phyi don
fabrication	prapañca	spros pa
formative action	saṃskāra	'du byed
four elements	catvāri-bhūta	'byung ba bzhi
four visions		snang ba bzhi
freedom result	visaṃyoga-phala	bral pa'i 'bras bu
fundamental consciousness	ālaya-vijñāna	kun gzhi rnam shes
fundamental nature	*bhāva	gnas lugs
great perfection	mahāsaṃdhi	rdzogs chen
great thousand third-order thousand world-system	trisāhasra-mahā-sāhasra-loka-dhātu	stong gsum gyi stong chen po'i 'jig rten gyi khams
ground [of being]		gzhi
ground manifestation		gzhi snang
I	aham	nga
Idealist	vijñāna-vādin	sems tsam pa
immanent reality	tattva	de nyid, de kho na nyid
immature awareness		rig pa ma smin pa
incidental defilements	āgantuka-kleśa	glo bur gyi dri ma
indestructible reality	vajra	rdo rje
Indestructible Reality Way	vajrayāna	rdo rje theg pa

English	**Sanskrit**	**Tibetan**
Individual Way	hinayāna	theg pa dman pa
indivisible minute particle	parmāṇvabhāgi-pakṣa	rdul phran phyogs kyi cha med
ineffective creative cause	asamartha-kāraṇa-hetu	byed rgyu nus med
instinct	vāsanā	bag chags
instinctive self-habit	*sahajātma-grāha	bdag 'dzin lhan skyes
instincts of evolutionary actions	*karma-vāsanā	las kyi bag chags
interdependent arising	pratītya-samutpāda	rten cing 'brel bar 'byung ba
intrinsic awareness	vidyā	rigpa
intrinsic objectivity	svarūpa-siddha	rang gi ngo bos grub pa
lack of true status	asatya-siddha	bden par ma grub pa
lamp	pradīpa	sgron ma
lamp of emptiness which is the sphere		thig le'i stong pa'i sgron ma
lamp of self-existing wisdom		she rab rang byung gi sgron ma
lamp of the pure sphere of awareness		dbyings rnam par dag pa'i sgron ma
league	yojana	dpag tshad
learning	śruta	thos pa
level [of awakening]	bhūmi	sa
liberation	mokṣa, vikmokṣa	thar pa, rnam par thar pa
manifest dimension of awakening	nirmāṇa-kāya	sprul sku
meditative concentration	dhyāna	bsam gtan
meditative experience	anubhava	nyams
mental consciousness	manovijñāna	yid kyi rnam par shes pa
mental factor	caitta	sems byung
mental formation	saṃskāra	'du byed
mirror-like pristine wisdom	ādarśa-jñāna	me long lta bu'i ye shes
miserable existences	durgati	ngan 'gro
mutually inclusive	ekārtha	don gcig

English	Sanskrit	Tibetan
naive	bāla	byis pa
nature	bhāva	ngo bo
nature	svabhāva,	rang bzhin
neutral phenomenon	avyākṛta-dharma	lung ma bstan gyi chos
non-analytical cessation	apratisaṃkhyā-nirodha	so sor brtags min gyi 'gog pa
non-Buddhist	tīrthika	mu stegs pa
non-dual awareness	advya-jñāna	gnyis su med pa'i ye shes
non-obscured neutral [phenomena]	anivṛtāvyākṛta	ma bsgribs pa lung ma bstan
object defined, definiendium	lakṣya	mtshon bya
object of knowledge	jñeya	shes bya
objective condition	ālambana-pratyaya	dmigs pa'i rkyen
objective object	ālambana-viṣaya	dmigs pa'i yul
obscuration of emotions	kleśāvaraṇa	nyon mongs pa'i sgrib pa
obscuration to transition	*srotāvaraṇa	'pho ba'i sgrib pa
obscured neutral [phenomena]	āvaraṇāvyākṛta	bsgribs pa lung ma bstan
obstructive cause	antarāyika-hetu	bar du gcod pa'i rgyu
omnipresent cause	sarvatraga-hetu	kun 'gro'i rgyu
omniscience	sarva-jñāna	thams cad mkhyen pa
original		ye nas
owned result	adhipati-phala	bdag po'i 'bras bu
path	mārga	lam
path of accumulation	saṃbhāra-mārga	tshogs lam
path of learning	śaikṣa-mārga	slob pa'i lam
path of meditation	bhāvanā-mārga	sgom lam
path of no more learning	aśaikṣa-mārga	mi slob pa'i lam
path of preparation	prayoga-mārga	sbyor lam
path of seeing	darśana-mārga	mthong lam
perceptual-pattern	muṣṭi, grāha	'dzin stangs
perfect peace	nirvāṇa	mya ngan las 'das pa

English	**Sanskrit**	**Tibetan**
perfect peace without remainder	niravaśeṣa-nirvāṇa	lhag med myang 'das
perfection	pāramitā	pha rol tu phyin pa
personal liberation	prātimokṣa	so sor thar pa
phase of completion	saṃpanna-krama	rdzogs rim
phase of creation	utpatti-krama	bskyed rim
phenomena	dharma	chos
phenomenology	abhidharma	chos mngon pa
pioneer	ratha	shing rta
possession, acquired	prāpti	thob pa
potential [for awakening]	gotra	rigs
[primary] mind	citta	sems
primordial awareness	*adhijñāna	gdod ma'i ye shes
primordial purity		ka dag
principal	pradhāna	gtso bo
pristine wisdom	jñāna	ye shes
pristine wisdom dimension of awakening	jñāna-kāya	ye shes sku
pristine wisdom of discernment	pratyavekṣā-jñāna	so sor rtog pa'i ye shes
pristine wisdom of equality	samatā-jñāna	mnyam nyid kyi ye shes
pristine wisdom of accomplishing aims	kṛtyānuṣṭhāna-jñāna	bya ba grub pa'i ye shes
proclaimer	śrāvaka	nyan thos
productive cause	kāraṇa-hetu	byed rgyu
property	ātmīya	nga yi ba
radiance	*ojas	mdangs
reality	dharmatā	chos nyid
reality dimension of awakening	dharma-kāya	chos sku
realization	abhisamaya	mngon rtogs
reification	samāropa	sgro btags
superficial reality	saṃvṛti-satya	kun rdzob bden pa
result	phala	'bras bu

English	**Sanskrit**	**Tibetan**
result caused by the person	puruṣakāra-phala	skyes bus byed pa'i 'bras bu
result concordant with the cause	niṣyanda-phala	rgyu mthun gyi 'bras bu
sage	ṛṣi	drang srong
saint	arhat	dgra bcom pa
scriptural teaching	*āgama-dharma	lung gi chos
scripture, discourse	sūtra	mdo
Secret Mantra Way	guhya-mantrayāna	gsang sngags theg pa
self	ātman	bdag
self-existing wisdom	*svayaṃbhū-jñāna	rang byung ye shes
self-habit	ātma-grāha	bdag tu 'dzin pa
self-manifestation		rang snang
selflessness	anātmatā, nairātmya	bdag med pa
skillful means	upāya	thabs
solitary sage	pratyekabuddha	rang sangs rgyas, rang rgyal
sphere of reality	dharmadhātu	chos dbyings
spiritual way	yāna	theg pa
spontaneously accomplished, present	*sahaja-siddha	lhun grub
substance	dravya	rdzas
substantial cause	upādāna-kārana	nyer len gyi gyu
substantial existence	dravya-sat	rdzas su yod pa
subtle and proliferating	anuśaya	phra rgyas
subtle particle	paramāṇu	rdul phra mo
thing	bhāva	dngos po
three trainings	triśikṣā	bslab pa gsum
Traditionists	sautrāntika	mdo sde pa
transcendent one	tathāgata	de bzhin gshegs p
transcendent reality	tathatā	de bzhin nyid
treatise	śāstra	bstan bcos
truth of cessation	nirodha-satya	'gog bden
ultimate reality	paramārtha-satya	don dam pa'i bden pa

English	Sanskrit	Tibetan
unawareness, ignorance	avidyā	ma rig pa
unawareness identical in nature with the cause		rgyu bdag nyid gcig pa'i ma rig pa
unawareness of imaginaries		kun brtag pa'i ma rig pa
unborn nature		gshis skye med
understanding of the phenomenal	yāvata-jñāna	ji snyed pa mkhyen pa'i ye shes
understanding of the noumenal	yathāvadjñāna	ji lta ba mkhyen pa'i ye shes
Universal Way	mahāyāna	theg pa chen po
unwavering evolutionary action	āniñja-karma	mi gyo ba'i las
vision of direct perception of reality		chos nyid mngon sum gyi snang ba
vision of the cessation of [phenomenal] reality		chos nyid zad pa'i snang ba
vision of reaching the limit of awareness		rig pa tshad phebs kyi snang ba
vision of the increasing contemplative experience		nyams gon 'phel gyi snang ba
water lamp of the far-sighted [eyes]		rgyang zhags chu'i sgron ma
wisdom	prajñā	shes rab
world-system	lokadhātu	'jig rten
yoga of the innermost essence	atiyoga	shin tu rnal 'byor
youthful vase-body		gzhon nu bum sku

Glossary of Names

The following list is divided into three sections: Buddhas, Bodhisattvas and Deities; Persons; and Places. An asterisk preceding a Sanskrit name indicates reconstruction from the Tibetan.

BUDDHAS, BODHISATTVAS AND DEITIES

All-Seeing Guide (**Nātha Samantadarṣin, mGon po kun tu gzigs*)

Great Glacial Lake of Wisdom (*Kun tu zhal ye shes gang chen mtsho*)

Chief of the Gods (*Devendra, Lha'i dbang po*)

[Chiefs of the] Thirty-three [Groups of] Gods (*Trāyastriṃśadeva, Sum cu rtsa gsum kyi lha*):

- 1-8. Gods of wealth (*Vāsudeva, Nor lha*)
- 9-10. Two sons of the Aśvins (*Aśvinau, Tha skar*)
- 11-21. Eleven wrathful ones (*Rūdra, Drag po*)
- 22-33. Twelve suns (*Āditya, Nyi ma*)

Dawa Zangpo (*Sucandra, Zla ba bzang po*)

Delight in Stars (*Jyotirāma, sKar ma la dga' ba*)

Dharma Banner, Buddha (*Dharmadhvaja, Chos kyi rgyal mtshan*)

Dharma Radiance Fully Bloomed Flower Form, Buddha (**Dharma prabhā puṣpa, Chos kyi 'od zer me tog rab tu rgyas ba'i sku*)

Forceful Wheel-Holder, Kulika Raudracakrin (*Drag po 'khor lo can*)

Four Great Kings (*Caturmahārāja, rGyal chen bzhi*)

1. Defender of the Area (*Dhṛtarāṣṭra, Yul 'khor srung*)
2. Noble Birth (*Virūḍhaka, 'Phags skyes bu*)
3. Ugly Eyes (*Virūpākṣa, sPyan mi bzang*)
4. God of Wealth (*Vaiśravaṇa, rNam thos sras*)

Four Groups of the Great Kings (*Caturmahārāja kāyikā, rGyal chen ris bzhi*):

1. Vessel Bearers (*Karoṭapāṇi, gZhong thogs*)
2. Garland-Bearers (*Mālādhāra, Phreng thogs*)

3. Inebriates (*Sadāmatta, rTag myos*)
4. Four Great Kings (*Caturmahārāja, rGyal chen bzhi*)

Garland Necklace, demi-god (*Kaṇṭhābharaṇa, mGul phreng*)

Gentle Splendor (*Mañjuśrī, 'Jam dpal*)

Hidden Omnipresent One, Kulika (*Khyab 'jug sbas pa*)

Illuminator, Buddha (*Vairocana, rNam par snang mdzad*)

Imperturbable, Buddha (*Akṣobhya, Mi bskyod pa*)

Inspired, Buddha (*Roca, Mos pa*)

Īśvara (*dBang phyug*)

Invincible, lord (*Ajita, Ma pham pa*)

Joyful One (*Sugata, bDe bar gshegs pa*)

King Honored by Multitudes (*Rāja mahāsaṃmata, Mang pos bkur ba'i rgyal po*)

King of Wisdom Light, Buddha (**Jñānaprabhārāja, Ye shes 'od zer rgyal po*)

Lion, Buddha (*Siṃha, Seng ge*)

Lord of the Dead (*Yamarāja, rGyal po gshin rje*)

Measureless Light, Buddha (*Amitābha, 'Od dpag med*)

Measureless Life, Buddha (*Amitāyus, Tshe dpag med*)

Mighty Lord of the World (*Lokeśvara, 'Jig rten dbang phyug*)

Moon-like Intelligence, Buddha (*Candramati, Zla ba'i blo gros*)

Pure, The (*Brahmā, Tshangs pa*)

Radiant Fully Bloomed Lotus Form, Buddha (*'Od zer shin tu stug po padma rab tu rgyas pa'i sku*)

Rāhu, demi-god (*sGra can*)

Source of Jewels, Buddha (*Ratnasaṃbhava, Rin chen byung gnas*)

Sage of the Śākyas (*Śākyamuni, Shakya thub pa*)

Śakra (*brGya byin*)

Seer (*Dus dpog*)

Splendor of Excellence, Buddha (*Śrībhadra, bZang po'i dpal*)

Transcendent One (*Tathāgata, De bzhin gshegs pa*)

Unfailing Accomplishment, Buddha (*Amoghasiddhi, Don yod grub pa*)

Vajra Conqueror, Buddha (*Vajraprasphoṭaka, rDo rje rab 'joms*)

Wheel of Time, Buddha (*Kālacakra, Dus kyi 'khor lo*)

PERSONS

Candrakirti (*Zla ba grags pa*)

Devadatta (*Lhas byin*)

Dharmamitra (Dharma Friend, *Chos kyi bshes gnyen*)

Kapila (*Ser skya*)

Longchenpa (*Klong chen pa*)

Lotus-Born (*Padmākara, Pad ma 'byung gnas*)

Mikyö Dorjé (Unmoving Vajra, *Mi bskyod rdo rje*)

Sarvārthasiddha *(Don kun grub pa)*

Thumi Sambhota *(Thon mi Sambhota)*

Tsuglag Trengwa (*gTsug lag phreng ba*)

Tsunpa Pel Leg (*brTsun pa dpal legs*)

Vasubandhu (Wealthy Friend, *dByig gnyen*)

Vimalamitra (*Dri ma med pa'i bshes gnyen*)

PLACES

Cosmological Features

Activator, Realm (*'Pho byed*)

Bearing Wealth, Realm (*Vasudhāra, Nor 'dzin*)

Befriended, Realm (*gNyen ldan*)

Benefitting, Realm (*Phan byed*)

Blissful, Realm (*Sukhāvatī, bDe ba can*)

Canopus, star (*Agasti, Ri byi*)

Complete Joy, Realm (*Yongs su dga' ba*)

Covered, Realm (*Khebs ldan*)

Eight Cold Hells (*Aṣṭaśītanaraka, Grang dmyal brgyad*):
1. Blistering (*Arbuda, Chu bur can*)
2. Blisters Bursting (*Nirarbuda, Chu bur rdol ba can*)
3. Teeth Chattering (*Aṭaṭa, So tham tham pa*)
4. Moaning with Cold (*Hahava, A chu zer ba*)
5. Wailing with Cold (*Huhuva, Kyi hud zer ba*)
6. Splitting Like a Blue Lotus (*Utpala, Utpala ltar gas pa*)
7. Splitting Like a Lotus (*Padma, Padma ltar gas pa*)
8. Splitting Widely Like a Great Lotus (*Mahāpadma, Padma ltar cher gas pa*)

Eight Hells according to the Kālacakra Tantra:

1. Pebbles (*gSeg ma*)
2. Sand (*Bye ma*)
3. Swamp (*'Dam chu*)
4. Smoke (*Du ba*)
5. Fire (*Me*)
6. Great Darkness (*Mun pa che*)
7. Great Wailing (*Ngu 'bod che*)
8. Vajra Flame Hell (*rDo rje me lce*)

Eight Hot Hells (*Aṣṭa-uṣṇa-naraka, Tsha ba'i dmyal ba brgyad*):

1. Ceaseless Torture (*Avīci, mNar med*)
2. Extreme Heat (*Pratāpana, Rab tu tsha ba*)
3. Heat (*Tāpana, Tsha ba*)
4. Loud Shrieking (*Mahāraurava, Ngu 'bod chen po*)
5. Shrieking (*Rāurava, Ngu 'bod*)
6. Crushing (*Saṃghāta, 'Dus 'joms*)
7. Black Lines (*Kālasūtra, Thig nag*)
8. Reviving (*Saṃjīva, Yang sros*)

Eight Islands (*Aṣṭa-antara-dvīpa, Gling phran brgyad*):

1. Body (*Deha, Lus*)
2. Majestic Body (*Videha, Lus 'phags*)
3. Tail-Fan (*Cāmara, rNga yab*)
4. Other Tail-Fan (*Avara-cāmara, rNga yab zhan*)
5. Crafty (*Śāthā, gYo ldan*)
6. Treading the Perfect Path (*Uttara-mantriṇa, Lam mchog 'dro*)
7. Unpleasant Sound (*Kuru, sGra mi snyan*)
8. Moon of Unpleasant Sound (*Kaurava, sGra mi snyan gyi zla*)

Endurance, World-System (*Sahā-lokadhātu, Mi mjed kyi 'jig rten gyi khams*)

Faultless Light, Realm (**Vimalaprabhā, Dri med 'od*)

Fine Land, Realm (**Bhūmibhadra, Sa bzang*)

Flower-Filled World (*Kusuma-tala-garbha-alaṃkāra-kṣetra, gZhi dang snying po me tog gis brgyan pa*)

Four Absorptions of the Formless Realm (*Cātvari-ārūpyasamāpatti, gZugs med snyoms 'jug bzhi*):

1. Absorption of Infinite Space (*Ākāṣānantyāyatana, Nam mkha' mtha' yas kyi skye mched*)
2. Absorption of Infinite Consciousness (*Vijñānānantyāyatana, rNam shes mtha' yas kyi skye mched*)
3. Absorption of Nothing Whatever (*Ākiṃcanyāyatana, Ci yang med pa'i skye mched*)
4. Absorption of Neither Discernment nor No Discernment (*Naivasaṃjñā-nāsaṃjñāyatana, 'Du shes med 'du shes med min gyi skye mched*)

Four Continents (*Caturdvīpa, gLing bzhi*):

1. Majestic Body (*Videha, Lu 'phags po*)
2. Land of Jambu (*Jambudvīpa, 'Dzam bu gling*)
3. Bountiful Cow (*Godānīya, Ba lang spyod*)
4. Unpleasant Sound (*Kuru, sGra mi snyan*)

Four Neighboring Hells (*Pratyekanaraka, Nye 'khor ba'i dmyal ba*):

1. Pit of Live Embers (*Kukūla, Me ma mur*)
2. Swamp of Filth (*Kuṇapa, Ro myags 'dam*)
3. Road of Razor Blades (*Kṣuramārga, sPu gri'i lam*), Forest with Leaves Like Swords (*Asipattravana, Ral gri'i lo ma*), Forest of Iron Spikes (*Ayaḥśālmalīvana, Shal ma li'i nags*),
4. River Without Ford (*Nadī-vaitaraṇī, Chu bo rab med*)

Four Parks :

1. Park of Various Chariots (*Cāitrarathavana, Shing rta sna tshogs kyi tshal*)
2. Park of Armoury (*Pāruṣyaka, rTsub 'gyur gyi tshal*)
3. Park of Various Activities (*Miśrakavana, 'Dres pa'i tshal*)
4. Park of Delights (*Nandanavana, dGa' ba'i tshal*)

Infinite Links, Realm (*Rab 'byams mtshams sbyor*)

Infinite of Continuums, Realm (*Rab 'byams rgyud*)

Joyful, Realm (*dGa' ba*)

Lion Inhabited, Realm (*Seng ge yod pa*)

Lovely, City (*Sudarśana, lTa na sdug*)

Lyra, constellation (*Abhijit, Byi bzhin*)

Mount Meru (Supreme Mountain, *Ri rab*)

Not Great, Realm (*Avṛha, Mi che ba*)

Oceanic Infinity, Realm (*Rab 'byams rgya mtsho*)

Oceanic World-System (*'jig rten gyi khams rgya mtsho*)

Pole-star (*Ḍriḍha, brTan pa*)

Pure Cluster, Realm (*rDul dral yang dag bsags*)

Resounding Melody, Realm (*dByangs sgrogs*)

Resplendent Lotus, Realm (*Padma'i dpal*)

Richly Adorned, Realm (*Ganavyūha, sTug po bkod pa*)

Saffron Banner, Realm (*Ngur smrig gi rgyal mtshan*)

Seven Golden Mountain Ranges (*gSer gyi ri bdun*):

1. Yoke (*Yugandhara, gNya' shing 'dzin*)
2. Plough (*Īśādhara, gShol mda' 'dzin*)
3. Forest of Acacia Trees (*Khadiraka, Seng ldeng can*)
4. Pleasing (*Sudarśana, lTa na sdug*)

5. Horse Ear (*Aśvakarṇa, rTa rna*)
6. Bent (*Vinataka, rNam 'dud*)
7. Rim (*Nimindhara, Mu khyud 'dzin*)

Seventeen Form Realm Heavens (*gZugs khams gnas rigs bcu bdun*):

1. Group of the Pure (*Brahmakāyika, Tshangs ris*)
2. Priests of Brahma (*Brahmapurohita, Tshangs pa'i mdun na 'don*)
3. Great Pure Ones (*Mahābrahmāṇa, Tshangs chen*)
4. Dim Light (*Parīttābhā, 'Od chung*)
5. Measureless Light (*Apramāṇābhā, Tshad med 'od*)
6. Clear Light (*Ābhāsvara, 'Od gsal*)
7. Lesser Virtue (*Parīttaśubha, dGe chung*)
8. Limitless Virtue (*Apramāṇaśubha, Tshad med dge*)
9. Flourishing Virtue (*Śubhakṛtsna, dGe rgyas*)
10. Cloudless (*Anabhraka, sPrin med*)
11. Merit-Born (*Puṇyaprasava, bSod nams skyes*)
12. Great Result (*Vṛhatphala, 'Bras bu che*)
13. Not Greater (*Avṛha , Mi che ba*)
14. Without Distress (*Atapas, Mi gdung ba*)
15. Manifest Richness (*Sudṛśa, Gya nom snang ba*)
16. Good Vision (*Sudarśana, Shin tu mthong ba*)
17. Unsurpassed (*Akaniṣṭha, 'Og min*)

Six Desire Realm Heavens, (*'Dod lha rigs drug*)

1. Four Groups of the Great Kings (*Caturmahārāja-kāyikā, rGyal chen ris bzhi*)
2. The Thirty-three (*Trāyastriṃśa, Sum cu rtsa gsum*)
3. Free From Conflict (*Yāma, 'Thab bral*)
4. Joyful (*Tuṣita, dGa' ldan*)
5. Enjoying Creations (*Nirmāṇarati, 'Phrul dga'*)
6. Mastery Over Others' Creations (*Paranirmita-vaśavarttina, gZhan 'phrul dbang byed*)

Stainless, Realm (*rDul bsal*)

Surpassing, Realm (*Chag pa*)

Ten Planets:

1. Sun (*Āditya, Nyi ma*)
2. Moon (*Soma, Zla ba*)
3. Mars (*Aṇgāraka, Mig dmar*)
4. Mercury (*Budha, Lhag pa*)
5. Jupiter (*Bṛhaspati, Phur bu*)
6. Venus (*Śukra, Pa sangs*)
7. Saturn (*Śanaiścara, sPen pa*)
8. Long Tail of Smoke, (*Ketu, Du ba 'jug ring*)
9. Seizer (*Rāhu, sGra gcan*)
10. Fire of Time (*Kālāgni, Dus me*)

Thumb-Size, Realm (*Aṇguṣṭha, mThe bo can*)

Truly Joyous, Realm (*Abhirati, mNgon dga'*)

Twenty-eight Constellations (*Aṣṭāviṃśati-nakṣatrāṇi, rGyu skar nyi shu rtsa brgyad*)

1. Beta Arietis (*Aśvinī, Tha skar*)
2. 35 Arietis (*Bharaṇī, Bra nye*)
3. Eta Tauri (*Kṛittikā, sMin drug*)
4. Aldebaran (*Rohiṇī, sNar ma*)
5. Lambda Orionis (*Mṛgaśirā, mGo*)
6. Alpha Orionis (*Ārdrā, Lag*)
7. Beta Geminorum (*Punarvasu, Nabs so*)
8. Delta Cancri (*Puṣyā, rGyal*)
9. Alpha Hydroe (*Āśleṣā, sKag*)
10. Regulus (*Maghā, mChu*)
11. Delta Leonis (*Pūrvaphālgunī, Gre*)
12. Beta Leonis (*Uttaraphālgunī, dBo sbo*)
13. Delta Corvi (*Hastā, Me bzhi*)
14. Spica Verginis (*Citrā, Nag pa*)
15. Arcturus (*Svātī, Sa ri*)
16. Alpha Libroe (*Viśākhā, Sa ga*)
17. Delta Scorpio (*Anurādhā, Lha mtshams*)
18. Antares (*Jyeṣṭhā, sNron*)
19. Lambda Scorpii (*Mūlā, sNrubs*)
20. Delta Sagittari (*Pūrvāṣādhā, Chu stod*)
21. Sigma Sagittari (*Uttarāṣāḍhā, Chu smad*)
22. Alpha Aquiloe (*Sravaṇa, Gro bzhin* or *Gro zhun*. Adding to this *Abhijit, Byi bzhin*, makes 28 constellations.)
23. Lambda Aquarius (*Śatabhiṣaj, Mon gre*)
24. Betha Delphinum (*Dhaniṣthā, Mon gru*)
25. Alpha Pegasi (*Pūrvabhadrapadā, Khrums stod*)
26. Gama Pegasi (*Uttarabhadrapadā, Khrums smad*)
27. Zeta Piscum (*Revatī, Nam gru*)

Unbearable, Realm (*Duṣprasaha, bZod dka'*)

Unsurpassed, Realm (*Akaniṣṭhā, 'Og min*)

Variously Appeared, Realm (*Kun song*)

Variously Emerged, Realm (*Vibhūta, rNam 'byung*)

Well Formed, Realm (*rNam bsags*)

Well Protected, Realm (*Shin tu srung*)

India

Campāka

Kothan (*Kaṃsadeśa, Li yul*)

Kormo Jig (*'Khor mo 'jig*)

Magadhā
Rājagṛha (King's residence, *rGyal po'i khab*)
Sāketa (*gNas bcas*)
Seat of Enlightenment (*Vajrāsana, rDo rje gdan*)
Śrāvastī (*gNyan yod*)
Vaiśālī (Spacious, *Yangs pa can*)
Vikramaśīla (*rNam gnon ngang tshul)*
Vulture's Peak (*Gṛdhrakūṭa, Bya rgod phung po*)

Abbreviations

DAM — *Disclosure of the Awakening Mind,* Dg.T. rGyud 'bum, vol. Ngi, ff. 38-42 (Toh. 1800)

Dg.K. — Degé Kangyur (sDe dge bKa 'gyur): Degé edition of the Tibetan canonical collection of sūtras and tantras

Dg.T. — Degé Tengyur (sDe dge bsTan 'gyur): Degé edition of the Tibetan canonical collection of commentarial treatises

FOS — *Flower Ornament Scripture,* Dg.K. phal chen, vols. Ka, Kha, Ga, A (Toh. 44)

GKT — *Great King of Tantras issued from the Sacred Primordial Buddha, The Glorious Wheel of Time,* Dg.K. rGyud 'bum, vol. Ka, ff. 22-128 (Toh. 362)

GMS — *Great Mindfulness Scripture*: Dg.K. mDo sde, vols. Ya, Ra, La, Sha (Toh. 287)

NG — *The Hundred Thousand Tantras of the Ancient Tradition* (*rNying ma rgyud 'bum*). 36 vols. Thimpu: Jamyang Khyentse Rinpoche, 1973.

NST — *The Nyingma School of Tibetan Buddhism, Its Fundamentals and History,* Translated by Gyurme Dorje with the collaboration of Matthew Kapstein. 2 vols. Boston: Wisdom, 1991

SMA — *Tantra of Self-Manifestation of Awareness, NG* vol. Tha, ff. 1-167

Syn. — *Synthesis of Phenomenology,* Dg.T. Sems tsam, vol. Ri (Toh. 4049)

Toh. — *A Complete Catalogue of the Tibetan Buddhist Canons,* edited by Ui, Suzuki, Kanakura, and Tada. Sendai, Japan: Tohoku University, 1934.

TOP — *Treasury of Phenomenology,* Dg.T. mNgon pa, vol. Ku, ff. 1-25 (Toh. 4089)

YTD — Commentary to 'Jig-med Gling-pa's *Yon tan rin po che'i mdzod,* by KhenpoYonten Gyatso, vol. Hung (vol. 40 of the *rNying ma bka' ma rgyas pa*)

f., ff.	folio(s) (Tibetan book)
p., pp.	page(s)
vol., vols.	volume(s)

Notes

Translators' Introduction

1. *Phyogs med ris med kyi bstan pa la 'dun shing dge sbyong gi gzugs brnyan 'chang ba blo gros mtha' yas kyi sde'i byung ba brjod pa nor bu sna tshogs mdog can* (reproduced from a xylographic print from the Pelpung [dPal-spungs] blocks by Kandro, Tibetan Khampa Industrial Society, P.O. Bir, Dist. Kangra, H.P. India, 1973). This autobiography was completed after Kongtrul's death by one of his students, the learned monk Trashi Chöpel (bKra-shis Chos-'phel). The details of the life of Kongtrul as presented here are based on this autobiography.

2. Milarepa (Mi-la-ras-pa, Cotton-clad Mila), the eleventh-century yogi and poet, disciple of Marpa the Translator, the forefather of the Kagyu order of Tibetan Buddhism.

3. Khyung-po rNal-'byor (Yogi of the Khyung Clan), born 1086. Initially a Bön scholar, he later embraced the Dzog-chen system. He traveled to Nepal and India several times, where he studied with 150 masters, including the Pamtingpa (Pham thing pa) brothers; Vajrāsana; Maitrīpa; the ḍākinī Sukhasiddhī, a disciple of Virūpā; and Niguma, Nāropa's sister. He introduced to Tibet the Six Yogas of Niguma, the Six-Armed Mahākāla, and numerous other tantras, and also initiated the Shang-pa Kagyu lineage. It is said that he had 80,000 disciples and lived to the age of 150.

4. Dusum Kyenpa (Dus-gsum mKhyen-pa) (1110-1193) was a recognized embodiment of many previous Indian and Tibetan masters. Famous for his miraculous powers and knowledge, he founded the monastery of Tsurbu (mTshur-phu), the main seat of the incarnations who followed him.

5. *Tertön (gTer-ston)*, "treasure discoverers," were masters who discovered texts, relics, or transmissions of teachings concealed by Guru Padmasambhava.

6. The raven symbolizes the guardians of the Buddha's doctrine.

7. Menri (sMan-ri), the main seat of the Bön in Tsang (gTsang) (western Tibet).

8. Degé (sDe-dge), a region in eastern Tibet, was the location of the Degé kings' fortress and Pel Lhundrup Tengichödra (dPal lhun-grub steng-gi chos-drwa), a monastery founded in 1448 by the great mystic Tangtong Gyelpo (Thang-stong rGyal-po) (1385-1509).

9. *Ma-bu dgra-grogs*, the two cycles of five elemental energies or movements that regulate transformations in the outer world, climate, etc., and in human physiology. Each elemental energy is associated with the element that most closely represents its function and nature, and takes its name from this element: wood, fire, earth, metal, and water.

The creative cycle is one of generation, like the relation between a mother and son: water generates wood, wood creates fire, fire develops earth, earth yields metal, and metal dissolves to become water. The control cycle is one of subjugation: wood is suppressed by metal, fire extinguished by water, earth penetrated by wood, metal melted by fire, and water obstructed by earth. These relationships are used in astrological calculations to prognosticate and advise people regarding both the present and the future.

10. *Mirror of Poetry* (Skt. *Kāvyādarśa*; Tib. *sNyan-ngag me-long)*, by Daṇḍin (Dg.T. Toh. 4301). Once a widely used manual of poetic composition, this work is viewed by modern Tibetan poets as an impediment to spontaneous and communicative poetry.

11. *Cāndrapa, Kalāpa*, and *Sarasvatī*: the three Sanskrit grammars that were famous in Tibet. The first was written by Candragomin as a summary of the *Pāṇini* grammar; the second, by Saptavarman; and the third, by the brahmin Anubhuti, who was inspired by the goddess Sarasvatī.

12. *Mañjuśrīnāmasaṃgīti* (*Chanting the Names of Mañjuśrī*) (Dg.K. Toh. 360) was one of the first tantras to emerge in India and a source of later commentaries. See Bibliography for translation by Alex Wayman.

13. Two collections of texts primarily concerned with the three inner tantras of the Nyingma school, contained in nine and thirty-three volumes, respectively. *Kama (bka'-ma)* is the collection of canonical teachings. *Terma (gter-ma)* refers to treasure teachings, i.e., the texts, relics, and the transmissions of teachings concealed by Guru Padmasambhava and his consort Yeshé Tsogyel (Ye-shes mTsho-rgyal).

14. Śākyaśrī (1127-1225), the Indian scholar attached to Vikramaśīla Monastery, who in 1144 arrived in Tibet at the invitation of the translator Kropu (Khro-phu).

15. Kongpo (Kong-po), a southeastern region of Tibet, south of the Nyong River and close to the power place of Pemakö (Padma-bkod).

16. Vairocana of Pagor (Pa-gor), one of the foremost disciples of Guru Padmasambhava and a famous translator. He traveled widely in India, where he received the three series of Dzog-chen teachings. Back in Tibet, he preached to King Trisong De'utsen (Khri-srong-lde'u-btsan) and his court the highly esoteric doctrine that he had obtained. Those who were jealous of him had him exiled to eastern Tibet. Vairocana moved to Gyalrong (rGyal-rong), where

he taught extensively until he was called back to central Tibet, where he played a key role as a teacher.

17. Jamyang Kyentsé Wangpo ('Jam-dbyangs mKhyen-brtse'i dBang-po) (1820-1892) was born in Degé, studied at the Nyingma monastery of Mindroling (sMin-grol-gling) and in several Sakya institutions, and became one of the most complete spiritual masters of the nineteenth century.

18. Āryadeva (third century) was the foremost propagator of Nāgārjuna's Centrist philosophy.

19. Tāranātha (1575-1634), whose real name was Kunga Nyingpo (Kun-dga' sNying-po), was born into a family of translators. He was a disciple of the Indian siddha Buddhagupta and became a brilliant scholar, translator, and historian of the Jonang school. He wrote numerous works on history as well as works of a tantric nature, such as manuals on the Kālacakra Tantra. He translated or revised about ninety of the works contained in the Tibetan commentarial canon (bsTan-'gyur). He also was instrumental in transmitting numerous tantric teachings and lineages. Tāranātha died in Mongolia, where he had been asked to visit. Although the Jonang school was suppressed after Tāranātha's death by the government of the fifth Dalai Lama, his influence remains strong in every area of Tibetan Buddhism.

20. Orgyen Terdag Lingpa (O-rgyan gTer-bdag Gling-pa) (1617-1682) was both disciple and teacher of the fifth Dalai Lama. His work was essential to the transmissions of the Nyingma tradition. In 1676 he founded Mindroling Monastery in central Tibet, which was renowned as a center of learning.

21. These accounts are to be found in *'Du shes gsum ldan spong ba pa'i gzugs brnyan padma gar gyi dbang phyug phrin las 'gros 'dul rtsal gyi rtogs pa brjod pa'i dum bu smrig rgyu'i bdud rtsi,* a text written by Kongtrul himself describing his previous incarnations. See note 1 above.

22. In a later age/ There will come a great hero/Called Lodrö the Guide,/A teacher of the five sciences.

23. Lumé Tsultrim Sherab (Klu-mes Tshul-khrims Shes-rab), a significant figure in the preservation of the Vinaya transmission in Tibet after the persecution of the Buddhist doctrine by Langdarma (Glang Dar-ma).

24. Sumpa Kenpo (Sum-pa mKhan-po Ye-shes dPal-'byor) (1704-1788), born in Amdo, was a famous Tibetan author who wrote on subjects such as medicine, astrology, history, and Buddhism.

25. Atiśa was an Indian saint who in 1042 came to Tibet at the invitation of Lhalama Yeshé Ö (lHa-bla-ma Ye-shes-'od) and by the order of Tārā, his tutelary deity. When Nagtso the Translator invited the saint to Tibet, the abbot of Vikramaśila made him promise to lead Atiśa back after three years. When three years later they were approaching Nepal, however, they heard that the road was blocked, so Dromtön ('Brom-ston), who would be Atiśa's successor, asked the master to visit central Tibet. Atiśa did so, greatly benefiting Tibetan Buddhism. He did not return to India, and he died at Nyetang (sNye-thang) in 1054.

26. Śāntideva was an eighth-century Indian master who was famous for his attainments and for preaching the *Bodhisattva's Way of Life* (*Bodhicaryāvatāra*).

27. Candragomin. Without studying with anyone, this Indian scholar acquired knowledge of grammar, logic, and other subjects. Later, when he received tantric instructions and meditated, he had a vision of Tārā and Avalokiteśvara and attained spiritual realization. Although he was a layman, Candragomin became one of the most learned and accomplished masters in India. It is said that he composed 432 works.

28. Vajrakīlāya (rDo-rje Phur-ba) is a tantric deity whose practice is popular in the Nyingma, Sakya, and Kagyu sects.

29. Tsedrup Namchag Dorjé (Tshe-sgrub gNam-lcags rDo-rje), which belongs to the Rainbow Cycle of Teachings (*'Ja' tshon chos skor*).

30. The Direct Leap (*thod-rgal*) is the final phase of Dzog-chen practice in which the inner light manifests outwardly.

31. Vārāhī (rDo-rje Phag-mo) is a female tantric deity and the consort of Cakrasaṃvara.

32. Lama Gongdu (Bla-ma dGongs-sdus).

33. Dromtön ('Brom-ston) was the chief disciple of the Indian sage Atiśa and the founder of the Kadampa tradition, from which the Gelug school of Tibetan Buddhism grew.

34. This refers to Avalokiteśvara, the deity who symbolizes compassion and love.

35. Marpa the Translator (1012-1097) was the father of the Kagyu tradition and a disciple of the Indian siddha Nāropa.

36. Mipam Gyatso (Mi-pham rGya-mtsho), a major contributor to the Nyingma renaissance of the nineteenth century in eastern Tibet. He was an extraordinary scholar who wrote more than thirty volumes on subjects such as medicine, poetry, painting, philosophy, and tantra.

37. mKhan-po gZhan-dga'.

38. Adzom Drugpa (A-Dzom 'Brug-pa) was a disciple of the first Kyentsé and teacher to the second. A visionary and treasure discoverer, he had a mystic encounter with Jigmé Lingpa ('Jigs-med Gling-pa) when he was thirty and became a key master in the transmission of the *Klong-chen snying-thig*.

39. Peltrul Rinpoché (dPal-sprul) (1808-1897) was an erudite, compassionate scholar and an accomplished master of the Dzog-chen system. A highly respected figure, his writings, example, and life story continue to inspire modern spiritual seekers.

40. Butön (Bu-ston), a compiler of the Tibetan canon, excluded the tantras of the Nyingma because he believed there was reason to doubt their authenticity.

41. Cool Grove (Skt. Śītavana, Tib. bSil-ba'i tshal) was a place in India that was sacred to Mahākāla and had previously been a cremation ground.

42. Drugpa ('Brug-pa) Rinpoché, the ninth Gyelwang Drugchen (rGyal-dbang 'Brug-chen), Jigmé Mingyur Wang-gyel ('Jigs-med Mi-'gyur dbang-rgyal) (1823-1883), was the head of the Drugpa Kagyu ('Brug-pa bKa-'brgyud) school and a close associate of the fourteenth Karmapa.

43. Shedra (dBang-phyug rGyal-po bShad-grwa), the prime minister (*sde-srid*) at the time of the twelfth Dalai Lama.

44. The monastery in Tsang founded in 1446 by Gendun Drup (dGe-'dun Grub), the first Dalai Lama, and the seat of the various incarnations of the Penchen Lama, starting with Jé Lozang Chögyen (rJe Blo-bzang Chos-rgyan).

45. Nyarong (Nyag-rong), a region of eastern Tibet located south of Degé.

46. The Tibetan army, headed by the minister Pulungpa (Phu-lung-pa), was sent by the prime minister Shedra (bShad-grwa) at the request of the people who lived in the regions attacked by Gönpo Namgyel (mGon-po rNam-rgyal). The fighting lasted two years, and at the end, Gönpo Namgyel and his supporters were burned to death in their fortress.

47. Dongkam Trulku (gDong-sprul mKhas-mchog Ngag-dbang Dam-chos rGya-mtsho). Kongtrul later entrusted him (along with others) with the transmission of his teachings.

48. Tsongkapa (Tsong-kha-pa) (1357-1419) was a scholar and saint who founded the new Kadampa, or Gadenpa (dGa'-ldan-pa) school, named from the Gaden (dGa'-ldan) Monastery, which Tsongkapa himself founded.

49. Longchenpa (Klong-chen-pa) (1308-1363) was the most important master in the Dzog-chen system after Guru Padmasambhava. A great adept, philosopher, and writer, he became the systematizer of the Dzog-chen system. He was the author of 263 works, the most important being the *Seven Treasures*.

50. Earth Treasures (*sa-gter*) are rediscovered teachings that are usually in the form of scrolls. They are called "Earth" Treasures because the symbolic script of these scrolls is the tool that awakens the recollection of the teaching in the mind of the treasure discoverer. Mind Treasures (*dgongs-gter*) are those that emerge in the conscious mind of the discoverers, who are realized disciples of Guru Padmasambhava or others.

51. Nyangrel Nyimé Özer (Nyang-ral Nyi-ma'i 'Od-zer) (1124-1192) was, along with Guru Chökyi Wangchug (Guru Chos-kyi-dbang-phyug) (1212-1270), the first *tertön* to appear in Tibet. These two are known as the sun and the moon, and the treasures that they discovered are known as Upper and Lower Treasures (*gter-kha gong-'og*).

52. Rigdzin Gödem (Rig-'dzin rGod-ldem) (1337-1409), the third of the great treasure discoverers. The *terma* he discovered and later edited are known as the Northern Treasures (*byang-gter*).

53. Pure Vision (*dag-snang*) teachings are transmitted from the state of realization of Guru Rinpoché and concealed in the nature of the mind of a realized disciple, and later awakened in his or her pure vision.

54. The modern edition consists of three volumes in book form accompanied by the commentary. It was edited by Dorjé Gyelpo (rDo-rje rGyal-po) and Tubten Nyima (Thub-bstan Nyi-ma). It was printed first in 1982 and again in Beijing in 1985 by Mi rigs dpe skrun khang.

55. The Pelpung edition is a three-volume xylograph printed at Pelpung Tubten Chökorling (dPal-spungs Thub-bstan Chos-'khor-gling). For this translation we have consulted two editions: the Beijing edition and the Pelpung edition.

56. For the contents of each chapter and section, see "Overview" section.

57. For an exhaustive treatment of this tantra, see Nāropa, *Iniziazione Kālacakra*. Edited by Raniero Gnoli and Giacomella Orofino. Milan: Edition Adelphi, 1994.

Prologue

1. Gentle Splendor (Mañjuśrī, 'Jam-dpal): Depicted as a sixteen-year-old youth (Kumāra) to represent purity and unobstructed intellect, in the Universal Way he is a tenth-stage bodhisattva identified with transcendent wisdom, while in the tantras he is a buddha who awakened countless ages ago. Often he is seen to be the triad of son, father, and mother of the Victorious Ones.

It is customary for a Buddhist author to begin a work of this genre with words of reverence to Mañjuśrī.

2. Highest doctrine (*sad-dharma, dam pa'i chos)*: the doctrine of the Buddha. The Sanskrit word *dharma* is derived from the verbal root *dhṛ* meaning "to hold" — the Buddha's doctrine being "a bearer of true and incontrovertible meaning."

The doctrine is "highest" *(sat)* because it is the teaching of the "Highest One" (the Buddha). As alternative interpretations, *sat* denotes "supreme" (among all other doctrines), or denotes the virtuous (high) persons for whom the doctrine is intended (Bu-ston's *The Jewelry of Scripture*, trans. E. Obermiller, p. 21).

3. *Rigs brgya khyab bdag*: an appellation of Vajradhara (rDo-rje 'chang). "Families" refers to families of buddhas.

4. *Jina, rGyal ba*: an appellation of the Buddha.

5. Threefold greatness (*chen po gsum*): greatness in compassion, greatness in realization, and greatness in relinquishment.

6. Padmākara, (Lotus-Born, Pad-ma 'Byung-gnas).

7. Two understandings (*mkhyen gnyis*): the understandings of the noumenal (*ji lta ba)* and of the phenomenal (*ji snyed pa*).

8. A reference to the verses of *The Encompassment of All Knowledge*.

9. The victorious ones and their heirs (*jina-putra, rgyal ba sras bcas*): the buddhas and bodhisattvas.

10. The two objectives (*don gnyis*) are to benefit oneself (*rang don*) and to benefit others (*gzhan don*). The first is realized through the attainment of the reality dimension of awakening, i.e., the omniscient mind of a buddha. The second is realized through the attainment of the enjoyment dimension of awakening and the manifest dimension of awakening.

Introduction

1. The four canonical languages: Sanskrit (*saṃskṛt, legs sbyar*), Prākrit (*rang bzhin*), Apabhraṃśa (*zur chag*), and Piśāci (*sha za*).

2. The three trainings (*triśikṣa, bslab pa gsum*): the training relating to ethics, to meditation, and to wisdom.

3. At this point in the text Kongtrul writes, "The three sixth case particles do not appear here because the Sanskrit is condensed." This refers to "*yāna,*" "*ratna,*" and "*sudeśika*" in the Sanskrit title, which are not declined. In the Tibetan title, the equivalent words end in sixth case or "connecting" particles, i.e., "*theg pa'i,*" "*rin po che'i,*" and "*legs par ston pa'i.*"

4. The three systems or spiritual ways (*triyāna, theg pa gsum*) found within the Indo-Tibetan Buddhist tradition: the Individual Way, the Universal Way, and the Way of Indestructible Reality or Secret Mantra.

The nine systems or spiritual ways (*theg pa dgu*) refers to a classification of the teachings of the above three systems particular to the Tibetan Nyingma (ancient) tradition: the Individual Way is divided into two paths—that of the proclaimers and the solitary sages; the Universal Way (also called the Bodhisattva Way) constitutes a single path; the Way of Indestructible Reality is divided into the six paths of Kriyāyoga, Caryāyoga, Yoga, Mahāyoga, Anuyoga, and Atiyoga.

5. Treatise (*śāstra, bstan bcos*). The Sanskrit word *śāstra* is derived from *śasti,* "to rule over, overcome," and *trāyate,* "to save or protect oneself." This etymology is found in the sentence, "It has the qualities... miserable forms of life."

6. Asaṅga's *Yogacaryābhūmi* enumerates nine kinds of treatises, six flawed and three valid. The six flawed treatises are the following: senseless, mistaken, overemphasizing learning, emphasizing sophists' debates, misleading, and encouraging cruelty. The three valid treatises are meaningful, conducive to the realization of awakening, and conducive to the elimination of all sufferings of cyclic life.

7. The three kinds of wisdom (*shes rab gsum*): the wisdoms resulting from study, reflection, and meditation.

8. Vikramaśila Monastery (rNam gnon ngang tshul): founded by King Dharmapāla (770-810), it was an ancient monastic university second only to Nālandā. Although its actual site remains uncertain, it probably lay somwhere near what is now the border between Bengal and Bihar.

9. The path of the perfections (*pāramitāmārga, pha rol (tu) phyin pa'i lam*): the path of the bodhisattva in which six perfections are cultivated—generosity, ethics, patience, effort, meditation, and wisdom—with the addition of the perfections of skill in means, vow, power, and pristine wisdom.

10. Secret Mantra (*guhya-mantra, gsang sngags*) or Way of Indestructible Reality (*vajrayāna, rdo rje theg pa*): both terms refer to the Buddhist "Way of Transformation," also known as tantra.

11. *dPal ldan* (*śrīmāṃ*): lit. "glory-possessing."

12. *Great King of Tantras of the Sacred Primordial Buddha, the Glorious Wheel of Time*: Dg.K. rGyud ' bum, vol. Ka, f. 113a1-2 (Toh. 362).

13. The three disciplines (*trisaṃvara, sdom pa gsum*): the vows accepted as the bases of training in the three spiritual ways—the Individual, Universal, and Indestructible Reality Way.

14. Contemplation (*samādhi, ting nge 'dzin*): a total mental equanimity in a state of concentration. When *ting nge 'dzin* indicates mind-training in general (as in the three trainings, the six perfections, etc.), it will be translated as "meditation."

15. Two kinds of selflessness (*dvinairātmya, bdag med gnyis*): non-self of a person (*pudgalanairātmya, gang zag gi bdag med*) and non-self of an object (*dharmanairātmya, chos kyi bdag med*).

16. The sage who developed the philosophical system of the Sāṃkhya school.

17. Perfect peace without remainder (*niravaśeṣa nirvāṇa, lhag med myang 'das*). Four types of perfect peace are generally presented in the Buddhist scriptures: perfect peace without remainder; perfect peace with remainder (**sāśesānirvāṇa, lhag bcas myang 'das*); dynamic perfect peace (*apratiṣṭhita nirvāṇa, mi gnas pa'i myang 'das*); and natural perfect peace (*prakṛti nirvāṇa, rang bzhin gyi myang 'das*).

Perfect peace with and without remainder are explained in different ways depending on the philosophical approach. In the Individualists' philosophies, the former is the perfect peace in the mind of a saintly one (*arhat*) who is still endowed with his body (i.e., the remainder). The latter is the perfect peace in the mind of a saintly one who has passed away, relinquishing his body, and is thus without the remainder of the body. In the higher Universalists' philosophies, "remainder" denotes the constructive thought of intrinsic existence: when a bodhisattva becomes free of that constructive thought, he or she is said to have attained perfect peace without remainder. This is confirmed in Nāgārjuna's *Jewel Garland (Ratnāvalī)*: "The disappearance of all constructive thoughts of existence and non-existence...."

Dynamic perfect peace is that of a Buddha, so-called because it is not bound either by the limitation of cyclic life or by the limitation of the inactivity of peace.

Natural perfect peace refers to emptiness. Because all phenomena are free of true existence, their nature is said to be natural perfect peace. As Śāntideva's *Guide to the Bodhisattva's Way of Life* states: "Beings are by nature in perfect peace."

18. The four pristine wisdoms (*catvārijñāna, ye shes bzhi*): the mirror-like pristine wisdom (*ādarśajñāna, me long lta bu'i ye shes*), the pristine wisdom of discernment (*pratyavekṣaṇajñāna, so sor rtog pa'i ye shes*), the pristine wisdom of equality (*samatājñāna, mnyam nyid kyi ye shes*), the pristine wisdom of accomplishing aims (*kṛtyānuṣṭhānajñāna, bya ba grub pa'i ye shes*).

19. Age of conflict (*kaliyuga, rtsod ldan gyi dus*): the present world-age, the last and most degenerate of the ages mentioned in classical Indian cosmology.

20. The proclaimers (*śrāvaka, nyan thos*), along with the solitary sages (*pratyekabuddha, rang sangs rgyas*), are adherents of the Individual Way. Proclaimers are so called because they listen to (*nyan*) the doctrine, practice it, and then cause others to hear (*thos par byed pa*), in this case not what they have heard but what they have achieved. Alternatively, proclaimers are so called because upon hearing (*thos*) about buddhahood or its path, they proclaim (*sgrogs*) it to others without practicing it themselves.

21. This reverence presents the three trainings in the traditional order of the proclaimers: ethics, meditation, and wisdom.

22. The commentary, *The Infinite Ocean of Knowledge*, presents the three trainings in the order of the Buddha's Way (Universal Way): ethics, wisdom, and meditation.

23. The three ways to develop the mind of awakening: to resolve to lead all beings to enlightenment (the king-like mind of awakening); to resolve to accompany beings to enlightenment (ferryman-like); and to resolve to follow beings to enlightenment (shepherd-like).

24. See note 9 above.

25. Bodhisattva (awakening being, *byang chub sems dpa'*): one who has developed the authentic wish to attain enlightenment for the sake of all beings.

26. The faults of attachment (*chags*) and impediment (*thogs*): the obscurations of emotions (*kleśāvaraṇa, nyon sgrib*) and of knowables (*jñeyāvaraṇa, shes sgrib*).

27. *Transition* refers to an inconceivably subtle transition (*'pho ba*) between the final point of the tenth stage of the bodhisattva and the eleventh stage, the state of a fully enlightened buddha. What hampers this transition is the most subtle of all obscurations, which is the last remaining imprint (*bag chags*), itself related to the three appearances (*sgang gsum: dkar lam, dmar lam, nag lam*).

28. The four dimensions of awakening (*kāya, sku*): the reality dimension of awakening (*dharmakāya, chos sku*); the enjoyment dimension of awakening (*saṃbhogakāya, longs spyod rdzogs pa'i sku*); the manifest dimension of awakening (*nirmāṇakāya, sprul pa'i sku*); and the essential dimension of awakening (*svabhāvakāya, ngo bo nyid kyi sku*).

29. Three Jewels (*triratna, dkon mchog gsum*): the enlightened guide (the Buddha); his doctrine (the Dharma); and the followers of his doctrine (the Saṅgha).

30. Minor texts (*gzhung lugs*): works that expound minor sciences as opposed to the "inner knowledge" of Buddhist teaching.

31. Dg. K. Sems tsam, vol. Shri, f. 30b3 (Toh. 4061).

Chapter I
Cosmology of the Universal Way

1. Unawareness (*avidyā, ma rig pa*): in this context, ignorance of the fundamental nature of things, i.e., emptiness. Generally, two types of unawareness are explained—unawareness with respect to immanent reality, i.e., emptiness *(de kho na nyid la rmongs pa'i ma rig pa)* (the root of cyclic life), and unawareness of the causal relatedness of evolutionary actions and their results *(las 'bras la rmongs pa'i ma rig pa)*.

2. Sphere of reality (*dharmadhātu, chos kyi dbyings):* the fundamental nature of all phenomena, i.e., emptiness.

3. The three realms (*tridhātu, khams gsum*) of cyclic life: the desire realm, the form realm, and the formless or immaterial realm.

4. The four great miracles (*cho 'phrul chen po bzhi*): the blessings, empowerment, activity, and meditative concentration of the Buddha.

5. Joyful one (*sugata, bde bar gshegs pa*): lit. "one who has attained bliss," an epithet of the buddhas.

6. Transcendent one (*tathāgata, de bzhin gshegs pa):* lit. "thus gone" or "thus come" ("thus" denoting the state of awareness of reality), an epithet of the buddhas.

7. *Flower Ornament Scripture* (*FOS*): Dg.K. Phal chen, vol. Ka, f. 92a1-5 (Toh. 44). See also Cleary's translation, *The Flower Ornament Scripture: The Avataṃsaka Sūtra* (Boulder and London: Shambhala, 1984), vol. I, pp.174 and 185.

8. Unsurpassed (Akaniṣṭha, 'Og min): According to the master Ānandagarbha, this realm is called Unsurpassed because the enjoyment dimension of the Buddha Vairocana abides there as the king of the "unsurpassed deities," i.e., the bodhisattvas on the tenth stage of awakening.

Scholars hold three different views concerning the nature of the realm Unsurpassed: (1) that it is the highest of the pure heavens, (2) that it is included within the pure heavens, but above the ordinary Unsurpassed, and the abode of only tenth-stage bodhisattvas, (3) that it is a realm not included within the pure heavens. Kongtrul states that Unsurpassed is not to be considered as any particular place, but transcends all world-systems.

9. The famous *Prayer for Excellence*, otherwise known as *The Vows of Samantabhadra*, is found at the end of the *Entering the Realm of Reality* (*Gaṇḍavyūha*) section of the *Flower Ornament Scripture* (*Avataṃsaka Sūtra*). It was spoken by Samantabhadra to the bodhisattva Sudhana. For centuries, it has served as a source of great inspiration to followers of the Universal Way. Dg.K. Phal chen, vol. A, f. 360a7 (Toh. 44) (cf. Cleary tr. vol. III, p.391, lines 1-4).

10. *FOS*: Dg.K. vol. Ka, f. 93a3-5 (cf. Cleary tr. vol. I, p.187, l.9).

11. *FOS*: Dg.K. vol. Ka, f. 94a6-b1 (cf. Cleary tr. vol. I, pp.248-249).

12. Delightful (Abhirati, mNgon dga'): the buddha realm of the buddha Imperturbable *(*Akṣobhya*)*, situated in the eastern direction.

13. Blissful (Sukhāvatī, bDe ba can): the buddha realm of the buddha Measureless Light (Amitābha), situated in the West.

14. Thumb-size (Aṅguṣṭha, mThe bo can): here beings live only ten years and are in height no taller than a thumb. They are presided over by the buddha Delight in Stars (Jyotīrāma) whose height is one cubit and seven fingers.

15. *FOS*: Dg.K. vol. Ka, f. 144a6 (cf. Cleary tr. vol. I, p.249).

16. *FOS*: Dg.K. vol. Ka, f. 143b3 (cf. Cleary tr. vol. I, p.247).

17. *FOS*: Dg.K. vol. Ka, f. 144b1 (cf. Cleary tr. vol. I, p.250, l.1).

18. *FOS*: Dg.K. vol. Ka, f. 144b6 (cf. Cleary tr. vol. I, p.250, verse 8).

19. *FOS*: Dg.K. vol. Ka, f. 144b6 (cf. Cleary tr. vol. I, p.251 verse 1).

20. *FOS*: Dg.K. vol. Ka, ff. 144b6-145a1 (cf. Cleary tr. vol. I, p.251, verse 1).

21. *FOS*: Dg.K. vol. Ka, f. 145a1-2 (cf. Cleary tr. vol. I, p.251, verse 5).

22. Third-order thousand world-system (*trisāhasra-mahāsāhasra-loka-dhātu, stong gsum gyi stong chen po*). A description of its magnitude is presented in the following section, "The Flower-Filled World."

23. Literally, "The Realm Whose Foundation and Center Are Adorned with Flowers" (*Kusumatalagarbhālaṃkārakṣetra, gZhi dang snying po me tog gis brgyan pa*).

24. The four continents, Mount Meru, the outer rim, and the configuration of wind are all features described in detail in the next chapter.

25. Teachers of phenomenology (*abhidharmika, chos mngon pa ba*): scholars of the *Abhidharmakośa (Treasury of Phenomenology)* of Vasubandhu.

26. Powerful ones (*maheśvara, dbang phyug chen po*): the bodhisattvas who dwell on the tenth stage of awakening.

27. Dg.K. Shes phyin, vol. Nga, f. 103b3-4 (Toh. 3796).

28. From *The Treatise on the Transcendent Wisdom Pith Instructions, Commentary on the Ornament of Realization* (*Abhisamayālaṃkārakārikā-prajñā-pāramitopadeśa-śāstraṭīkā-prasphuṭapadā, Shes rab phar phyin man ngag gi bstan bcos mngon rtogs rgyan gyi 'grel pa*). Dg. T. Shes phyin, vol. Nga, ff. 1-110 (Toh. 3796).

Chapter II
Our Universe according to the Individual and Universal Ways

1. The age of formation (*vivartakalpa, chags pa'i bskal pa*); the age of abiding (*vivartāsthayikalpa, gnas pa'i bskal pa*); the age of destruction (*saṃvartakalpa, 'jig pa'i bskal pa*); the age of vacuity (*saṃvartasthāyikalpa, stong pa'i bskal pa*).

2. Solitary sage, (*pratyekabuddha, rang sangs rgyas*): a saint of the Individual Way who attains liberation without relying on a teacher in that lifetime.

3. Purifying realms: the spiritual influence that a bodhisattva has over a whole "realm of beings" when he or she is cultivating the ten perfections.

4. Ten directions (*daśadiga, phyogs bcu*): the four cardinal and the four intermediate directions, the zenith, and the nadir.

5. Pure domains (*brahmakāyika, tshangs ris*): the five highest heavens within the fourth level of meditative concentration of the formless realm.

6. Lit. "disc" (*maṇḍala, dkyil 'khor*).

7. League (*yojana, dpag tshad*). The *yojana* is an ancient Indian measure of distance. The length of the *yojana* differs in the systems of the Wheel of Time Tantra and *The Treasury of Phenomenology.* In both cases we have translated *yojana* as "league." In the system of phenomenology, a *yojana* is 16,000 cubits; in the Wheel of Time system it is 32,000 cubits. Taking eighteen inches as the equivalent of a cubit—the unit of length based on the length of the forearm from the elbow to the tip of the middle finger—a *yojana* in the Wheel of Time would be nine miles, or 14.8 km, and a *yojana* in the phenomenology system would be 4.5 miles, or 7.4 km.

8. *Nāga* (*klu*): creatures classified as animals or demi-gods that live beneath the surface of the earth and in water. They generally exist in the form of snakes, but some can assume human form. They are believed to be the guardians of treasures hidden under the earth. When provoked they can cause various maladies.

9. Siṃhala (Sing ga la) (Sri Lanka), Suvarṇadvīpa (gSer gling) (*Sumatra) , Tāmradvīpa (Zangs gling) (*Java), Tokarling (Tho dkar gling) (*Tukhara), Kamboja (Kam po dzi) (Cambodia). The *Brāhmaṇa Vyāsa Scripture*, however, enumerates the following sixteen states (Mahājanapadas): Aṅga, Magadha, Kośala (Yul dge ba can), Kāśī (Varanasi), Vṛji, Malla, Pundra, Sreg pa, Kama, Avantī (Srung byed), Kuru, Pañcāla (lNga len), Matsya (Bad sa), Śūrasena (dPal sde), Yavana, and Kamboja, which were regions within ancient India. (The asterisk indicates unattested identification). For a discussion of these sixteen, see *Constitution of the Buddhist Sangha* by Kanai Lal Hazra (Delhi: B.R. Publishing, 1988), p.1.

10. Bodhgaya, in the modern-day Indian state of Bihar.

11. Snowy Mountain Range (Himavān, Gangs chen).

12. Fragrant Mountain Range (Gandhamādana, Ri bo sPos ngad ldan pa).

13. Cool (Anavatapta, Ma dros pa): presumably Lake Manasarovar, located near the sacred mountain of Kailash in southern Tibet.

14. Wheel-monarch (*cakravartin, 'khor los sgyur ba'i rgyal po*).

15. Ganges, Indus, Oxus, and Tarim, respectively.

16. The *jambu* tree is presumed by some to be the rose-apple tree (*Eugenia jambolana*). However, legend says that only one *jambu* tree exists, which is not visible to ordinary persons but only to enlightened beings.

17. Cannibal demons (*rākṣasa, srin po*), lit. "to be guarded against": generally considered as ogre-like evil creatures. According to some, they may also be benevolent semi-divine beings.

18. Starving spirits (*preta, yi dwags*).

19. Desire realm (*kāmadhātu, 'dod khams*): the worlds of hell beings, animals, starving spirits, humans, demi-gods, and desire gods, where beings experience coarse emotions and are preoccupied with sensual pleasures.

20. Śakra (brGya-byin) also known as Indra (dBang-po), an important god in the Hindu pantheon. In the Buddhist scriptures he is the chief of the gods as well as a protector of the Buddhist Doctrine.

21. *Great Mindfulness Scripture* (*GMS*): Dg.K. mDo sde, vol. Ra, f. 109b4-110a1 (Toh. 287).

22. Armoniga (or Armonig) (*pāṇḍū kambala śila tala, a mo ni ka [ar mo nig], lta bu'i rdo leb*): a flat stone resembling a white blanket.

23. The four insignia of the Buddhist teaching, i.e., the four tenets that characterize the Buddhist philosophy (*catvāri ḍṛṣtinamittamudrā, lta ba bkar btags kyi phyag rgya bzhi*): all conditioned phenomena are impermanent (*sarvasaṃskārānityatā, 'du byas thams cad mi rtag pa*); defiled phenomena are suffering (*sarvasāsravaduḥkhatā, zag bcas thams cas sdug bsngal ba*); phenomena are empty and selfless (*sarvadharmaśunyāsvāmika, chos thams cad stong zhing bdag med pa*); and nirvāṇa is peace (*nirvāṇaśānta, mya ngan las ' das pa zhi ba*).

24. The Sanskrit word *yakṣa* seems to be derived from *yakṣ* which means "to be quick, speed on"; the Tibetan word, however, is *gnod sbyin*, "bringer of harm." *Yakṣas* are semi-divine beings, generally considered to be benevolent; however, they are occasionally classed among malignant spirits. According to *The Treasury of Phenomenology*, the secretive (*guyhaka*) *yakṣas* who dwell on the top of Mount Meru prevent the playful gods and goddesses from falling off the side of the mountain.

25. Miraculous mode of birth (*upapādukaja, brdzus skyes*): an instantaneous mode of birth through which gods and hell beings are born. Miraculous birth, birth from a womb, from an egg, and from moisture and heat constitute the four modes of birth (*catvāri-yonidvāra, skye sgo bzhi*).

26. Invincible (Ajita, Ma-pham-pa): another name for Maitreya, the next Buddha to appear in the sequence of the one thousand buddhas of the Fortunate Age.

27. Form Realm (*rūpadhātu, gzugs khams*): a divine state of existence where physical suffering and mental unrest are absent and where gods dwell in contemplation without experiencing the arising of emotions.

28. Brahmā (Tshangs-pa): the creator of the universe in Hinduism; in Buddhism, rather than being a single god, Brahmā refers to a type of god who has obtained an elevated status in the universe. Thus, for Buddhists, Brahmās are as numerous as the universes that exist.

29. Evolutionary action is generally divided into three types: virtuous, non-virtuous, and unwavering (*aniñjanakarma, mi gyo ba'i las*). Unwavering evolutionary action is called "unwavering" because the cause, unmoving

contemplation, leads to a developed result only within the same level of existence.

30. Exalted ones (*ārya, 'phags pa*): those who have perceived the truth. This includes individuals on levels of realization from the path of seeing to final enlightenment.

31. The pure stages (*viśuddhibhūmi, dag pa'i sa*): the eighth, ninth, and tenth stages of awakening. They are called pure because the bodhisattvas who have reached those stages have completely purified pride.

32. "Saintly" denotes the attainment of arhatship (*arhat*, lit. "worthy of veneration"), most frequently translated into Tibetan as *dgra bcom pa*, "one who has defeated the enemy" (of the four demons—the emotions, the psychophysical constituents, death, and the sensual pleasures). Here, the term refers specifically to proclaimers who have attained this level. The *arhat* has become free of attachment, aggression, and other mental impurities and has reached the "healthiest" state; it is therefore appropriate to call him or her a saintly one (from the Latin *sanus*, meaning "clean," "pure," or "healthy").

33. Rhinoceros-like solitary sages *(khaḍgaviṣāṇakalpa-pratyekabuddha, bse ru lta bu'i rang rgyal*): Like the unicorn rhinoceros that lives alone in the forest apart from the company of other animals of its kind, the solitary sages attain their own awakening in solitude without relying on a teacher and in a world where there are no buddhas.

34. Non-Buddhists (*tīrthika, mu stegs pa*), lit. "forders to the end": a term used, often pejoratively, by Buddhists to refer to adherents of Indian philosophical systems or religions, mainly to the Sāṃkhyas (Enumerators), Brāhamaṇas (Followers of Brahmā), Vedāntins (Adherents to the Finality of the Vedas), Mīmāṃsakas (Analyzers), Jainas (Followers of the Jinas), Śaivas (Followers of Śiva) and Lokāyata or "materialists," etc., who do not take the Triple Jewels as their refuge and do not accept the four insignia of the Buddhist philosophy.

35 Fundamental consciousness (*ālayavijñāna, kun gzhi rnam shes*): a type of consciousness asserted mainly in the Idealist trend in Buddhist philosophy as the repository of predispositions and the source of the phenomenal world.

36. Absorption or meditative absorption, lit."arising and development" (*āyatana, skye mched*).

37. *FOS:* Dg.K. vol. Kha, f. 303a1.

38. The earlier translations (*snga 'gyur*): the translations of Sanskrit Buddhist texts into Tibetan done prior to the translator Rinchen Zangpo (958-1055), during the first period of propagation of Buddhism in Tibet and mainly during the reign of the Tibetan King Trisong De'utsen (Khri-srong-lde'u-btsan).

39. Reading *kham gyi zas* for *khams kyi zas*. Coarse food: food with taste, odor, and tangibility that needs to be swallowed.

40. *Reunion of Father and Son Scripture*: Dg.K. dKon brtsegs, vol. Nga, f. 61b6 (Toh.60).

41. *Marvellous Life of the Buddha Scripture*: Dg.K. mDo sde, vol. Kha, f. 88a2-3 (Toh.95).

42. The intermediate state: the period between death and the next life.

43. The five evil acts that bring immediate results (*pañcānantarya, mtshams med lnga*), lit. "without limit" (*mtshams med*): murder of one's father, one's mother, an arhat; creation of discord within the community of ordained persons; and intentionally causing the Buddha to bleed. They are called "immediately ripening" because the person who has committed such acts is reborn in hell as soon as he or she dies without going through the intermediate existence between death and rebirth.

44. Intermediate age (*antarakalpa, bar bskal*): the individual ages, eighty of which make up the four long ages, which compose a cosmic age.

45. One "ear-shot" (*krośa, rgyang grags*): two thousand cubits.

46. Evolutionary action (*karma, las*): physical, verbal, and mental actions and the cumulative force of these actions which remains in the individual and later evolves to determine future experience.

47. Long decline (*apakarṣa, ya thog ring mo*).

48. Long rise (*utkarṣa, ma thog ring mo*).

49. Inspired (Roca, Mos-pa): the last of the one thousand buddhas of the Fortunate Age.

50. *GMS:* Dg.K. vol. Ra, f.6b3-5.

51. Seat of enlightenment (*vajrāsana, rdo rje'i gdan*): also referred to as the heart of enlightenment (*bodhimaṇḍa, rdo rje snying po*), the place where the Buddha attained enlightenment.

52. Natural laws of existence (*srid pa'i chos nyid*): refers to the laws of nature, for example that water flows downward, that fire burns, etc., or the inconceivable natures, or the actual natures of things.

53. Śāli rice (*śāli*): possibly *Oryza saliva*, a kind of wild rice.

54. The five degenerations (*paṇcakaṣāyā, snyigs ma lnga)*: degeneration in terms of lifespan (*āyukaṣāya, tshe'i snyigs ma*), views *(dṛṣṭikaṣāya, lta ba'i snyigs ma),* emotions (*kleśakaṣāya, nyon mongs pa'i snyigs ma*), beings (*sattvakaṣāya, sems can gyi snyigs ma*), and time (*kalpakaṣāya, dus kyi snyigs ma*).

55. The four eras: the era of completeness (*kṛtayuga, rdzogs ldan gyi bskal pa*); the era of three-quarters (*tretāyuga, gsum ldan*); the era of two-quarters (*dvāparayuga, gnyis ldan*); the era of conflict (*kaliyuga, rtsod ldan*).

56. The four classes (*catvārivarṇā, rigs bzhi*): royalty (*kṣatriya, rgyal rigs*), brahmins (*brāhmaṇa, bram ze'i rigs*), merchants (*vaiśya, rje'u rigs*), and the menial class (*śūdra, dmangs rigs*).

57. Rājagṛha (rGyal po'i khab): a ancient city in Bihar which was an important center of Buddhism. The King Bimbisāra reigned there at the time of the Buddha and became his patron. It was here that the Buddha converted Śāriputra and Maudgalyāyana, his two chief disciples, and gave sermons.

58. Suckle Me (*Māndhāta, Nga las nu*): the name he received at birth because the queens, anxious to nurse him, all said: "Suckle me."

59. Golden wheel-monarch (*suvarṇa-cakravartirāja*), silver wheel-monarch (*rūpya-cakravartirāja*); copper wheel-monarch (*tāmra-cakravartirāja*); iron wheel-monarch (*ayaś-cakravartirāja*).

60. The thirty-two characteristic marks and eighty minor signs of a great being (*mahāpuruṣa-lakṣaṇānuvyañjana, skye bu chen po'i mtshan dpe*), such as the crown protuberance, a golden skin complexion, etc.

61. *GMS:* Dg.K. vol. Ya, ff. 102a4-104a1.

62. *Discussion on the Scripture of Transcendent Wisdom in Eight Thousand Lines*: Dg.K. Shes phyin, vol. Cha, f. 110b3 (Toh. 3791).

63. Dg.K. mDo sde, vol. Za, f. 43a4 (Toh. 247).

64. Ounce (*pala, srang*): originally an ancient Indian unit of weight equalling roughly forty grams, subsequently used in Tibet.

65. "Isolation" refers to the state of meditative concentration. For a detailed discussion, see Asaṅga's *Proclaimer's Levels (Śrāvakabhūmi)*, Dg.T. Sems tsam, vol. Dzi, ff. 168a-169b (Toh. 4036).

66. Dg.K. mDo sde, vol. Ya, ff. 5b3-7a2 (Toh. 268).

67. Blissful (Sukhāvatī, bDe ba can): the pure land of Buddha Amitābha.

68. Vulture's Peak (Gṛdhrakūṭa, Bya rgod phung po'i ri): the highest hill surrounding Rājagṛha. A place Buddha favored for his sermons belonging to the second turning of the Wheel of Dharma, which expound the lack of intrinsic existence of all phenomena.

Chapter III

Space and Time in the Tantra of the Wheel of Time

1. The *Tantra of the Wheel of Time* (*Kālacakra-tantra, Dus kyi 'khor lo'i rgyud*) According to Butön Rinpoche, the Kālacakra Tantra was taught by the Buddha at Śrī Dhānyakaṭaka (Amaravati, Guntur District, in Andhra Pradesh, South India) in the year of his enlightenment to Sucandra, the King of Śambhala. Another version says that the Buddha taught this tantra in the year of his passing away into perfect peace at the age of eighty. It became widespread in India around the 966 C.E. and was introduced into Tibet in 1026.

Kālacakra means "Wheel of Time." "Time" refers to immutable bliss, and "wheel" to the special emptiness that this tantra teaches, the emptiness of material particles. Thus, *Kālacakra* means "union of immutable bliss and emptiness."

This multi-level teaching comprising descriptions of the universe, human body, and elaborated tantric techniques is linked to the mythical land of Śambhala where this tantra flourished.

2. The original tantra of Kālacakra (said to be in 12,000 verses) was never translated into Tibetan, with the exception of a part entitled *The Rite of Initiation (dBang mdor bstan)* (Dg.K. rGyud 'bum, vol. Ka, ff. 14a-21a [Toh. 361]). However, some of its passages are quoted in related texts extant in the Tibetan language. What is referred to today as the Kālacakra Tantra is a condensed form (*laghutantra, bsdus rgyud*) known as the *Great King of Tantras Issued from the Sacred Primordial Buddha, The Glorious Wheel of Time (Paramādibuddhod-dhṛta-śrīkālacakra-nāma-tantrarāja, mChog gi dang po'i sangs rgyas las phyung ba rgyud kyi rgyal po dpal dus kyi 'khor lo*) (Dg.K. rGyud 'bum, vol. Ka, ff. 22a-128 [Toh. 362]) in five chapters and one thousand and forty-seven verses. This was composed by Mañjuśrīyaśas ('Jam-dpal Grags-pa), the eighth king of Śambhala, and the first to be called "one who bears the lineage" (*kulika, rigs ldan*). It is said that Mañjuśrīyaśas was prophesied in the original tantra as the one who would write a condensed form of this tantra.

3. Adamantine body, "vajra body" (*vajra-kāya, rdo rje lus):* the human body and particularly the internal channels and wheels of channels with energies and vital essences.

4. Maṇḍala (circle, *dkyil 'khor*) here refers to the mystic palace and its setting where the Buddha Wheel of Time resides as the central figure surrounded by a number of deities.

5. Wheel of Time (Kālacakra, Dus-kyi-'khor-lo) here refers to the deity Kālacakra, the central figure of the Wheel of Time Tantra.

6. The four branches of familiarization and accomplishment: four stages of meditation practice in the Vajrayāna: familiarization (*āsevita, bsnyen pa*), close familiarization (*upāsevita, nye bar bsnyen pa*), accomplishment (*pratipatti, sgrub pa*), and great accomplishment (*mahāpratipatti, sgrub pa chen po*).

7. The four indestructible states (*vajra*) of body, speech, mind, and pristine wisdom.

8. The four states: ordinary waking consciousness, deep sleep, dream, and sexual union.

9. Kuśa grass (*Poa cynosuroides*): a sacred grass used at certain rites of initiation and other religious ceremonies.

10. Centaur, literally "man or what?" (*kiṃnara, mi'am ci*), here refers to a place; however, its name presumably comes from its inhabitants, mythical beings with a horse head and human body (or vice versa). They became celebrated as celestial musicians, along with the *gandharvas.*

11. The mountain is presumably called by this name because of the presence of the mandara tree or coral tree (*Erythrina indica*), which has scarlet flowers.

12. Vessel (*droṇa, bre*): a wooden vessel or bucket used as a measure of weight in ancient India. This mountain range apparently resembles the shape of this vessel.

13. Three attributes or qualities (*guṇa, yon tan*): motility (*rajas, rdul*), darkness (*tamas, mun pa*), and lightness (*sattva, snying stobs*). A concept prevalent

in and borrowed from the ancient Sāṃkya philosophy according to which these qualities are the three constituents of *prakṛti* (universal or primal substance) and evolve into all the various categories of existence. *The Wheel of Time Tantra* correlates these with the three poisons — attachment, ignorance, and hatred — as well as other elements.

14. Magadhā refers here to a city; however, Magadhā was once an ancient kingdom and is now a district within the north-central Indian state of Bihar. Many of the major events of early Buddhist history, including the enlightenment of Buddha at the "seat of awakening" (rDo rje gdan), now called Bodhgaya, took place within this kingdom.

15. Adamantine contemplation (*vajropamasamādhi, rdo rje lta bu'i ting nge 'dzin*): the final contemplation of a bodhisattva dwelling on the tenth level at the end of which the full awakening of a buddha is attained.

16. Vaiśālī (Yangs pa can): the ancient capital of the Licchavi republic. On the ancient location, 70 km from Patna, now lies the modern town of Basarh, Mazaffarpur District in Tirhut, Bihar, India. At one time the city was an important Buddhist center; one hundred years after Buddha's death the Second Council took place there.

17. Srāvastī (mNyan yod): the ancient city founded by King Śrāvasta in the second quarter of the first millenium B.C.E. It later became the capital of the northwestern kingdom of Kosala, ruled by King Prasenajit, one of Buddha's patrons. Anāthapiṇḍika, a wealthy merchant of this town, built a residence for Buddha known as the Jetavana, which became a favorite dwelling of the Buddha. In this place, the Enlightened One spent twenty-three rainy season retreats and he delivered a number of discourses on the Universal Way. Near the ancient site is present-day Sāheṭh-Māheṭh, on the borders of the Gonda and Bahraich districts of Uttar Pradesh, fifty-eight miles north of Ayodhyā.

18. 'Khor mo 'jig: unidentified.

19. Sāketa (gNas bcas): also called Ayodhā; in ancient times the capital of the kingdom of Kosala.

20. Campāka was once the capital of Aṅga, a region covering a vast area of the delta of the Ganges including parts of modern-day West Bengal and Bangladesh. Identified as the modern Bhagalpur.

21. Mighty Lord of the World (Lokeśvara, 'Jig-rten dBang-phyug): Another name for Loving Eyes (Avalokiteśvara), the bodhisattva symbolizing compassion, and the patron deity of Tibet.

22. Khotan (Kaṃsadeśa, Li yul): An ancient city-state in Central Asia, lying beyond the Karakorum Range. Once an important center of Buddhist learning, it was part of the early centuries C.E. Kushāna empire that extended from the northern plains of India up to the oases of the Takla Makan desert. The city has been buried for centuries under the sand near the village known as Yotkan. See David Snellgrove's *Indo-Tibetan Buddhism* (Boston: Shambhala, 1987).

23. Vaiśravaṇa (rNam-thos-sras): the God of Wealth.

24. Stūpa (*caitya, mchod rten*): a dome-like Buddhist monument crowned with sun and moon on concentric rings, sometimes enshrining relics of a saint, but often of symbolic value.

25. Chieftain (*kulika, rigs ldan*): the general name for the kings of Śambhala. The name means "one who bears the lineage." The first to receive this name was the eighth king of Śambhala, Mañjuśrīyaśas ('Jam-dpal grags-pa), after he was empowered by the deities of the adamantine (*vajra*) family. *The Wheel of Time Tantra* mentions twenty-five chieftains; the twenty-first, Aniruddha (*Ma 'gags pa*), who is reigning at present, ascended the throne in 1927.

26. Kālapa: "composed of aspects." In the context of the Wheel of Time, "aspect" refers to pristine wisdom.

27. The celestial sphere (*go la*) is a word that Tibetan translators left in Sanskrit. The word is derived from the combination of the first syllable of *guru*, meaning heavy, and the first syllable of *loghama*, meaning light. "Heavy" denotes its ability to support the heavens; "light," its ability to move.

28. Dg.K. rGyud 'bum, vol. Na (Toh. 543).

29. Capricorn, lit. "sea monster" (*makara, chu srin*): A mythical creature, probably an idealized synthesis of different sea creatures that Indian sailors or fisherman met on their journeys. In depictions the lower part of its body is that of a dolphin and its head has a long snout and horns. Here, we have taken the liberty of translating *chu srin* as "Capricorn" because the symbol of Capricorn is a creature whose lower body resembles that of a dolphin.

30. Astrological language for the following enumeration: sky of six empty spheres indicates six zeros; *nāga*, the number eight; and eyes, two: reading backwards, this gives twenty-eight million.

31. The planets move faster than the constellations, giving the impression that they are positioned above the stars.

32. The house where the influence of the sun is greatest.

33. The house where the influence of the moon is greatest.

34. Long Tail of Smoke (Ketu, mJug ring), Eclipser (Rāhu, sGra gcan), Fire of Time (Kālāgni, Dus me). In Indian mythology, Rāhu is a demon who is believed to cause eclipses by seizing the sun and moon. He is said to have a dragon's tail. Legend says that when the gods had churned the ocean for the nectar of immortality, he disguised himself as one of them and drank a portion. The sun and moon revealed the fraud to Viṣṇu, who cut off Eclipser's head, which thereupon became fixed in the stellar sphere. Having become immortal through drinking the nectar, [he] has ever since wreaked vengeance on the sun and moon by occasionally swallowing them.

Sakuntala Devi writes: "Rāhu and Ketu play an important role in the Indian Astrology. However, it must be mentioned here that Rāhu and Ketu are not exactly planets, though for the purpose of prediction, in view of their obvious effects on human affairs, are considered as such in Indian Astrology. They are in fact the Ascending and Descending nodes of the moon, the places where the moon in its orbit cuts the celestial equator. The nodes are called the tail and the head of the dragon." (*Astrology For You* [Delhi: Oriental Paperback, 1983]).

35. *Ghaṭikā (chu tshod).*

36. Movement (*'pho ba*): a cycle of breaths. A great movement of breath (*'pho chen*) is made of five cycles of small breath movements (*'pho chung*), each constituted by 360 breaths, to a total of 1,800 breaths.

37. Lunar day (*tshe zhag*), solar day (*nyin zhag*), and house day (*khyim zhag*).

38. Dg.T. mNgon pa, vol. Ku, f. 155b2-3 (Toh. 4090). The three seasons have four months each.

39. Dg.K. rGyud 'bum, vol. Ka, f. 64b7 (Toh. 370).

40. This is because the sun is regular in its movement.

41. *Tantra of the Wheel of Time*, Dg.K. rGyud 'bum, vol. Ka, f. 39b2 (Toh. 362).

42. Wheel-holder (*cakrin, 'khor lo can*).

43. The division [of the Buddha's teachings] concerned with ethics (*vinaya, 'dul ba*).

44. There are four defeating acts (*pham pa*) for a full-fledged monk. The first is the breaking of the vow of celibacy; the second, the vow prohibiting stealing; the third, the vow prohibiting murder; and the fourth, the vow prohibiting false claim to spiritual attainments.

45. *Commentary to Large, Medium, and Small Transcendent Wisdom Scriptures*, Dg.K. Shes phyin, vol. Pha, f. 208a2 (Toh. 3808): "The duration of the sacred doctrine of the Transcendent One is 5,000 years" *(de bzhin gshegs pa'i dam pa'i chos gnas pa'i dus ni lo lnga stong ngo).*

46. *The Concise Tantra* (*bsDus pa'i rgyud*): *The Great King of Tantras Issued from the Sacred Primordial Buddha, The Glorious Wheel of Time*. Dg.K. rGyud 'bum, vol. Ka, f. 38a6 (Toh. 362). The full sentence quoted reads, "Outer time is definitely classified just as the Protector of the World [taught]."

47. Hidden Omnipresent One (Khyab-'jug sbas-pa) was the seventh chieftain of Śambhala.

48. Forceful Wheel-Holder (Raudracakrin, Drag-po 'khor-lo-can) is the twenty-fifth chieftain of Śambhala and the last specifically mentioned in *The Tantra of the Wheel of Time*. He will ascend the throne in the year 2327.

49. Barbarians (*mleccha, kla klo*). The term *mleccha* was originally used to refer to uncultured people who did not speak Sanskrit, i.e., non-Aryans.

In this work, "barbarian" denotes those who practice cruel rites as a form of religion and deny the existence of the Three Jewels. "Barbarian" comprises a variety of religious systems found in different parts of the world whose spiritual practices do not lead to fortunate rebirths.

50. The four traditional divisions of the ancient Indian army: infantry, cavalry, charioteers, and elephant-mounted soldiers.

51. *Tantra of the Wheel of Time*, Dg.K. rGyud 'bum, vol. Ka, f. 31b4-6 (Toh. 362).

52. This citation indicates the time measure of the four eras in terms of human years. The first four lines respectively indicate 1,628,000, 1,296,000, 864,000, and 432,000 years. For a detailed discussion, see the *Stainless Commentary to the Kālacakra Tantra*, Dg.K. rGyud 'bum, vol. Tha, f. 238a3-6 (Toh. 1347).

53. In Tibetan language, the seven days of the week are named after the sun, and moon, and the five planets, as in the Western system.

54. Ketsé seed (*rājikā, Sinapis ramosa*): about one-third the size of a mustard seed.

Chapter IV
The Causes of Cyclic Life

1. Īśvara (*dBang phyug*): a general name for God in Hinduism.

2. The Secretists (Guhyakas): adherents to the finality of the Vedas (*rig bye mtha' gsang ba pa*). An ancient Indian school of philosophy.

3. Self (*ātman, bdag*): in this context, presumably identical with Brahmā, who is asserted by some Hindu schools to be the creator.

4. Principal (*pradhāna, gtso bo*): equivalent to the primordial substance (*prakṛti, rang bzhin*) asserted by the Sāṃkhyas (Enumerators) to be the cause of environments and animate beings. The Sāṃkhya is an ancient Indian philosophical school whose followers assert that all phenomena are included within twenty-five categories. They adhere to the view of permanence and follow the doctrine of the sage Kapila. The school has a theistic and non-theistic branch. The theistic Sāṃkhya assert that the world and inhabitants are produced through mutual dependence by Īśvara, the Lord, and the primordial substance.

5. Nihilists (*ucchedavādin, chad par smra ba*). In this context, the Indian school of the Cārvākas (Hedonists) is implied. The Cārvākas are followers of the god Bṛhaspati and of Juktopchenpa ('Jug stobs can pa), a student of the sage Lokacakṣu. They believe only in what can be perceived directly and deny moral laws.

6. The five sense consciousnesses and mental consciousness.

7. Text unidentified.

8. Candrakīrti (Zla-ba Grags-pa) was born in Samanta, south India, in the sixth century. Studying under Bhāvaviveka and Buddhapālita's disciple Kamalabuddhi, he mastered the knowledge of all Buddhist teachings. Later, he moved to Nālandā Monastery in central India and became the abbot and

master of all scholars there. He was the real inheritor of Nāgārjuna's Centrist philosophy and had a visionary relation to Mañjuśrī. He had the power to move freely through walls and the eloquence to defeat numberless opponent philosophers. He is famous as the composer of *Lucid Exposition* and *Luminous Lamp*, which are compared to the sun and moon in illuminating the sūtras and the tantras respectively. Legend says that he returned to the South where he extensively propagated the Buddha's doctrine and then remained in seclusion practicing the Secret Mantra.

9. Dg.T. dBu ma, vol. Ha, f. 208b2 (Toh. 3861).

10. The dawning of the inner light (*āloka, snang ba*), the increase of the inner light (*ālokābhāsa, mched pa*), and the inner light approaching fullness (*upalabdha, nyer thob*). In this context, the inner lights occur in the reverse order of their natural sequence at the time of death.

11. The eye consciousness of a yogi refers to the sense perception of an exalted one.

12. Dg.K. rGyud 'bum, vol. Ka, nang le, f. 40b2-3 (Toh. 362).

13. Lord of Humanity refers to King Dawa Zangpo (Sucandra, Zla-ba bZangpo) to whom *The Wheel of Time Tantra* was taught by the Buddha.

14. The first "tastes" means six times; the second "taste" means taste eaten up, i.e., time passing.

15. *Kalala, nur nur po.*

16. *Arbuda, mer mer po.*

17. *Nya'i gnas skabs.*

18. *Rus sbal gyi gnas skabs.*

19. *Phag pa'i gnas skabs.*

20. *GKT*: f.22a3.

21. Radiant awareness of total emptiness (*thams cad stong pa 'od gsal*): the macrocosm light corresponding in the microcosm to the radiant awareness that naturally appears at the culmination of the death process of an individual; if radiant awareness is recognized, whatever binds the individual to existence is dissipated in the radiant awareness of emptiness.

22. [Light] approaching fullness (*upalabdha, nyer thob*): the macrocosm light corresponding in the microcosm to the experience of black light immediately preceding the radiant awareness of death.

23. Increase [of light] (*ālokābhāsa, mched pa*): the macrocosm light corresponding in the microcosm to the red light experienced during the death process when a part of instinctive constructive thoughts dissolves.

24. Dawning of inner light (*āloka, snang ba*): the macrocosm light corresponding in the microcosm to the white light, the first of the four experienced in the process of death when the sense perceptions have subsided and instinctive constructive thoughts start to dissolve. As this refers to a process of creation, the order of the lights is reversed.

25. Individualists' system of phenomenology (*mngon par 'og ma'i lugs*): *Abhidharmakośa [The Treasury of Phenomenology]* of Vasubandhu.

26. Universalists' system of phenomenology (*mngon par gong ma'i lugs*): *Abhidharmasamuccaya [The Synthesis of Phenomenology]* of Asaṅga.

27. *TOP:* Dg.T. mNgon pa, vol. Khu, f. 5b6 (Toh. 4089).

28. The path of seeing (*darśanamārga, mthong lam*): one of the five paths of inner realization — the path of accumulation, path of preparation, path of seeing, path of meditation, and path of no-more-learning, i.e., liberation. The path of seeing is attained when the individual achieves the initial non-conceptual insight into the ultimate nature, i.e., emptiness of all phenomena, and thus sees the truth. The common relinquishments of the path of seeing (*thun mong gi mthong spang bya*) refers to constructed disturbing emotions and gross cognitive obscurations.

29. Four types of exalted ones (*catvāri-ārya, 'phags pa bzhi*): four types of individuals who have perceived the truth — the exalted proclaimer, exalted solitary sage, exalted bodhisattva, and exalted buddha.

30. The alternative (second) name of the causes given in this section correspond to the terms used in Vasubandhu's *Treasury of Phenomenology*, the former being the terms used in Asaṅga's *Synthesis of Phenomenology*.

31. *Synthesis of Phenomenology* (abbreviated hereafter as *Syn.*): Dg.T. Sems tsam, vol. Ri, ff. 68a1-2 (Toh. 4049) (fragmented citation).

32. Although Kongtrul mentions the *Synthesis of Phenomenology* at this point, it is in another work, the *Compendium of the Universal Way* (*Mahāyānasaṃgraha, Theg chen bsdus pa*), that Asaṅga discusses this subject at length.

33. *Disclosure of the Awakening Mind* (abbreviated hereafter as *DAM*): Dg.T. rGyud 'bum, vol. Ngi, ff. 38-42 (Toh. 1800).

34. *DAM:* f. 40b3-4.

35. Dg.T. Tshad ma, vol. Ce, f. 116a1-2 (Toh. 4210).

36. *DAM:* f. 40b5-6.

37. *DAM:* f. 41a1-2.

38. Original text no longer exists but is quoted in Dg.T. Theg bsdus, f. 3a7 (Toh. 4048).

39. *TOP:* f. 2b6.

40. Dg.T. Sems tsam, vol. Phi, f. 14b6 (Toh. 4020).

Chapter V
The Primordial Purity of the Universe

1. See Kongtrul's Introduction, n. 4.

2. The key points of the path and result of the Supreme Yoga are explained in latter sections of *The Infinite Ocean of Knowledge*.

3. For a detailed explanation of the various assertions concerning the nature of the ground, see Kenpo Yönten Gyatso's commentary on Jigmé Lingpa's *Yonten Dzö* (*Yon tan rin po che'i mdzod*) (*YTD*), vol. Hung, ff. 530-538 (vol. 40 of the *rNying ma bka' ma rgyas pa*).

4. *Kun tu bzang po klong drug*: one of the Seventeen Tantras of the Pith Instruction Section (*man ngag sde*) of the Great Perfection (*rDzogs chen rgyud bcu bdun*) in the collection of *The Hundred Thousand Tantras of the Ancient Tradition (rNying ma rgyud 'bum)* (*NG*), vol. Tha, f.324b7.

5. *NG* vol. Tha, f. 181a7.

6. *NG* vol. Tha, f. 288b3-4.

7. Three radiances (*gdangs gsum*) reflect the nature, character, and energy of the ground of being.

8. *Condensed Transcendent Wisdom Scripture (Ārya-prajñāpāramitā-sañcayagāthā, 'Phags pa shes rab kyi pha rol tu phyin pa sdud pa tshigs su bcad pa)* found in *Collection of Scriptures and Dhāraṇī (gZungs bsdus/mDo sngags gsung rab rgya mtsho'i snying po sdud pa)* (two volumes; Dharamsala, 1976), vol. sMad cha, f.8a5.

9. In the system of the Great Perfection, the beginning and end refers to the time when the nature of reality manifests spontaneously during the final stage of the death process. That stage is the end in relation to the manifestations of the previous life and the beginning with respect to the manifestations of the future life.

10. Immature intrinsic awareness (*ma smin pa'i rig pa*): the intrinsic awareness that has arisen from the ground but exists like a seed; it is uncertain whether it will serve for freedom or for deception.

11. *NG* vol. Tha, f. 336b7-337a1.

12. It is as the radiance of this awareness that the pure realms of the enjoyment dimension of awakening appear. For a detailed explanation of the Eight Gates of Being's Spontaneity, see *YTD*, ff. 551-552.

13. These eight are distinguished as six ways of manifesting and two gates — one to awakening, one to deception.

14. The ground manifestation is compared to camphor, which acts as a remedy for the "hot" illnesses and a poison for the "cold" illnesses.

15. Six emotions: unawareness (*avidyā, ma rig pa*), desire (*rāga,'dod chags*), hatred (*pratigha, khong khro*), ignorance (*moha, gti mug*), pride (*māna, nga rgyal)*, and jealousy (*īrṣyā, phrag dog*).

16. Six objects (of the mental consciousness): form (*rūpa, gzugs*), sound (*śabda, sgra)*, smell (*gandha, dri*), taste (*rasa, ro*), texture (*sparśa, reg bya*), and phenomena (*dharma, chos*).

17. This is explained in other commentaries (*mDzod bdun* and *YTD*) as follows: When the manifestation of the ground arises, not to recognize it to be a display of one's own intrinsic awareness and to apprehend it as "something else" is unawareness. This unawareness is not present in the primordial

ground and is therefore nothing more than a non-existent, transitory veil. This veil, which triggers deception, is simply an effulgence of intrinsic awareness which obscures intrinsic awareness itself, like the clouds which are formed by the heat of the sun and obscure the sun that created them. Because unawareness proceeds from intrinsic awareness and in its actual nature is not different from intrinsic awareness, one speaks of "unawareness which is of an identical nature [with intrinsic awareness]" (*bdag nyid gcig pa'i ma rig pa*).

18. *SMA*: *NG* vol. Tha, ff. 100b3-4 and 101a3.

19. For a detailed explanation of these verses, see *YTD*, f. 575.

20. Twelve experiential media (*dvādaśāytanāni, skye mched bcu gnyis*): the six objects and the corresponding six sense organs.

21. The manifestation of reality: the final stage in the death process at which the radiant awareness manifests.

22. Reading *ming gzhi* as *ming bzhi*. This refers to the four aggregates that are "mere names" (that is, without coarse form): the aggregates of feeling, discernment, mental formations, and consciousness. These are the only aggregates that beings of the formless realm possess.

23. The four syllables: *kham, sum, ram, yam.*

24. Heroes (*ḍaka, dpa' bo*).

25. See *NST*, p.338.

26. See *NST*, p.339.

27. *SMA:* f. 29a7-29b1.

28. *NG* vol. Tha, f. 271b6-7.

29. *NG* vol. Ta, f. 242b2.

30. *NG* vol. Tha, f. 230b4-5.

31. *NG* vol. Tha, f. 49a1-2.

32. *NG* vol. Ta, f. 275b6-7.

33. The aggregate of form manifests as Vairocana; the aggregate of feeling manifests as Ratnasaṃbhava; the aggregate of discernment manifests as Amitābha; the aggregate of mental formations manifests as Amoghasiddhi; and the aggregate of consciousness manifests as Akṣobya.

34. Ignorance manifests as the pristine wisdom of the sphere of reality (*dharma-dhātujñāna, chos dbyings ye shes*); hatred manifests as mirror-like pristine wisdom (*ādarśajñāna, me long lta bu'i ye shes*); pride manifests as the pristine wisdom of equality (*samatājñāna, mnyam nyid ye shes*); attachment manifests as the pristine wisdom of discernment (*pratyavekṣājñāna, so sor rtogs ye shes*); and jealousy manifests as the pristine wisdom of accomplishing aims (*kṛtyānuṣṭhānajñāna, bya sgrub ye shes*).

35. The element of space manifests as blue light; water manifests as white light; earth manifests as yellow light; fire manifests as red light, and air mani-

fests as green light. In their purified aspects, the elements become the five consorts of the dhyani buddhas. Earth manifests as Locanā (sPyan-ma), water as Māmakī, fire as Pāṇḍarā (Gos-dkar-mo), air as Tārā (sGrol-ma), and space as Dhātviśvarī (dByings-kyi-dbang-phyug-ma).

36. The eye sense manifests as the adamantine (*vajra, rdo rje*) family; the ear sense manifests as the action (*karma, las*) family; the nose sense manifests as the lotus (*padma*) family; the tongue sense manifests as the jewel (*ratna, rin chen*) family, and the body sense manifests as the transcendent (*tathāgata, de bzhin gshegs pa*) family.

37. *Majestic Creative Energy of the Universe* (*Kun byed rgyal po*): the main tantra of the Mind Section (*sems sde*) of the Great Perfection (in *NG* vol. Ka, f.11a3-5).

38. The "I" speaking in the *Majestic Creative Energy of the Universe* is awareness or Ever-Perfect (Samantabhadra).

39. *NG* vol. Ta, f. 242a3.

40. *NG* vol. Tha, ff. 230b7-231a1.

41. Indestructible chains of light (*rdo rje lu gu rgyud*): awareness as expanse of reality manifesting in the form of spheres of light.

42. Refers to three postures (*'dug stang gsum*): the watchful and dignified posture of a lion, the bent-forward posture of a resting elephant, and the crouching posture of a sage, related respectively to the reality, enjoyment and manifest dimensions of awakening.

43. Refers to three gazes (*lta stang gsum*): gazing upward, gazing sideways, and gazing downward, related respectively to the reality, enjoyment, and manifest dimensions of awakening.

44. This alludes to the practices in the Direct Leap (*thod rgal*) practice of Great Perfection. See *NST*, p. 338.

Bibliography of Works Cited

Scriptures

Beyond the Limits of Sound Root Tantra
sGra thal 'gyur rtsa ba'i rgyud
NG vol. Tha, ff. 193-265

Blossomed Wisdom Scripture
Niṣṭhāgata-bhagavajjñana-vaipūlyasūtra
bCom ldan 'das kyi ye shes rgyas pa'i mdo
Dg.K. mDo sde, vol. Ga, ff. 1-275 (Toh. 99)

Brāhmaṇa Vyhāsa Scripture
gNas 'jog pa'i mdo
Dg.K. mDo sde, vol. Sa, ff. 263-268 (Toh. 333)

Cluster of Jewels Tantra
Nor bu phra bkod pa'i rgyud
NG vol. Ta, ff. 234-262

Condensed Transcendent Wisdom Scripture
Ārya-prajñāpāramitā-sañcayagāthā
'Phags pa shes rab kyi pha rol tu phyin pa sdud pa tshigs su bcad pa
In: *Collection of Scriptures and Dharani (gZungs bsdus/ mDo sngags gsung rab rgya mtsho'i snying po sdud pa)*, two vols. Dharamsala: 1976. Vol. sMad cha, ff. 1-30

Descent into Laṅka Scripture
Laṅkāvatārasūtra
Lang kar gshegs pa'i mdo
Dg.K. mDo sde, vol. Ca, ff. 56-191 (Toh. 107)
Translated by D.T. Suzuki, *The Laṅkāvatāra Sūtra* (London: Routledge, 1932)

Flower Ornament Scripture (FOS)
Buddha-avataṃsaka-nāma-mahāvaipūlyasūtra
Sangs rgyas phal po che zhes bya ba shin tu rgyas pa chen po'i mdo
Dg.K. Phal chen, vol. Ka, Kha, Ga, A (Toh. 44)
Trans. from Chinese by Thomas Cleary, *The Flower Ornament Scripture*, 3 vols. (Boulder: Shambhala, 1984, 1986, 1987)

Fundamental Tantra of Mañjuśrī
Mañjuśrīmūlatantra
'Jam dpal gyi rtsa ba'i rgyud
Dg.K. rGyud 'bum, vol. Na, ff. 105-351 (Toh. 543)

Garland of Pearls Tantra
Mu tig rin po che'i phreng ba'i rgyud
NG vol. Ta, ff. 234-289

Glorious Tantra (see *Great King of Tantras Issued from the Sacred Primordial Buddha, the Glorious Wheel of Time*)

Great Array: The Tantra of Supreme Wish-Fulfillment
bKod pa chen po yid bzhin mchog gi rgyud
NG

Great King of Tantras Issued from the Sacred Primordial Buddha, the Glorious Wheel of Time (GKT)
Paramādibuddhoddhṛta-śrīkālacakra-tantrarājā
mChog gi dang po'i sangs rgyas las phyung ba rgyud kyi rgyal po dpal dus kyi 'khor lo
Dg.K. rGyud 'bum, vol. Ka, ff. 22-128 (Toh. 362)

Great Mindfulness Scripture (*GMS*)
Saddharmasmṛityupasthāna
Dam pa'i chos dran pa nye bar gzhag pa
Dg.K. mDo sde, vol. Ya, Ra, La, Sha (Toh. 287)

Inconceivable King Scripture
Acintyarājasūtra
bSam gyis mi khyab pa'i rgyal po'i mdo
Dg.K. mDo sde, vol. Ya, ff. 5-7 (Toh. 268)

Inconceivable Secrets of the Transcendent Ones Scripture
Tathāgatācintyaguhya-nirdeśa-sūtra
De bzhin gshegs pa'i gsang ba bsam gyis mi khyab pa bstan pa'i mdo
Dg.K. dKon brtsegs, vol. Ka, ff. 100-203 (Toh. 47)

Intrinsically Free Awareness Tantra
Rig pa rang grol ba'i rgyud
NG vol. Tha, ff. 167-193

Majestic Creative Energy of the Universe
Kun byed rgyal po
NG vol. Ka, ff. 1-110

Marvellous Life of the Buddha Scripture
Lalitavistarasūtra
rGya cher rol pa'i mdo
Dg.K. mDo sde, vol. Kha, ff. 1-216 (Toh. 95)
Translated from French by Gwendolyn Bays, *The Voice of Buddha: The Beauty of Compassion*. Berkeley: Dharma Publishing, 1983

Phenomenology Scripture
Abhidharmasūtra
Chos mngon pa'i mdo
unidentified

Pure Golden Light Scripture
Suvarṇaprabhāsottama-sūtrendrarājasūtra
gSer 'od dam pa mdo sde'i dbang po'i rgyal po'i mdo
Dg.K. rGyud 'bum, vol. Pa, ff. 151-273 (Toh. 556)

Questions of Gaganaganja Scripture
Gaganagañja-paripṛcchāsūtra
Nam mkha' mdzod kyis zhus pa'i mdo
Dg.K. mDo sde, vol. Pa, ff. 243-330 (Toh. 148)

Reunion of Father and Son Scripture
Pitāputra-samāgamanasūtra
Yab dang sras mjal ba'i mdo
Dg.K. dKon brtsegs, vol. Nga, ff. 1-168 (Toh. 60)

Scripture Revealing Dharma and its Meaning
Dharmārtha-vibhaṅgasūtra
Chos dang don rnam par 'byed pa'i mdo
Dg.K. mDo sde, vol. Za, ff. 42-46 (Toh. 247)

Sixth Expanse Tantra
Kun tu bzang po klong drug pa'i rgyud
NG vol. Tha, ff. 305-335

Tantra of Great Beauty and Auspiciousness
bKra shis mdzes ldan chen po'i rgyud
NG vol. Tha, ff. 335-343

Tantra of Self-Manifestation [of Awareness] (*SMA*)
Rig pa rang shar chen po'i rgyud
NG vol. Tha, ff. 1-167

Transcendent Wisdom in One Hundred Thousand Lines
Śatasāhasrikā-prajñāpāramitā
Shes rab kyi pha rol tu phyin pa stong phrag brgya pa
Dg.K. Shes phyin, vol. Ka through vol. A (Toh. 8)

Vajra Daka
Śrī-vajraḍāka-mahātantrarāja
rGyud kyi rgyal po chen po dpal rdo rje mkha' 'gro
Dg.K. rGyud 'bum, vol. Ka, ff. 1-125 (Toh. 370)

Vajrasattva, Mirror of the Heart Tantra
rDo rje sems dpa'i snying gi me long gi rgyud
NG vol. Tha, ff. 265-291

White Lotus of Compassion Scripture
Karuṇāpuṇḍarīkasūtra
sNying rje pad ma dkar po'i mdo
Dg.K. mDo sde, vol. Cha, ff. 129-297 (Toh. 112)

Treatises

Asaṅga

Compendium of Determinations

Viniścayasaṃgraha/Nirṇayasaṃgraha

rNam par gtan la dbab pa bsdu ba

Dg.T. Sems tsam, vol. Shi, ff. 1-289 (Toh. 4038)

Compendium of Enumerations

Paryāyasaṃgraha

rNam grangs bsdu ba

Dg.T. Sems tsam, vol. Hi, ff. 22-47 (Toh. 4041)

Compendium of Explanations

Vivaraṇasaṃgraha

rNam par bshad pa bsdu ba

Dg.T. Sems tsam, vol. Hi, ff. 47-68 (Toh. 4042)

Compendium of Facts

Vastusaṃgraha

gZhi bsdu ba

Dg.T. Sems tsam, vol. Zi, ff. 127-335 (Toh. 4039)

Compendium of the Universal Way

Mahāyānasaṃgraha

Theg pa chen po bsdus pa

Dg.K. Sems tsam, vol. Ri, ff. 1-43 (Toh. 4048)

Facts of the Stages

Bhūmivastu/Yogācārabhūmi

Sa'i dngos gzhi/rNal 'byor spyod pa'i sa

Dg.T. Sems tsam, vol. Tshi, Dzi, Wi (Toh. 4035-37)

Includes *Bāhubhūmika*, *Śrāvakabhūmi*, and *Bodhisattvabhūmi*

Synthesis of Phenomenology (Syn)

Abhidharmasamuccaya

Chos mngon pa kun las btus pa

Dg.T. Sems tsam, vol. Ri, ff. 44-120 (Toh. 4049)

Translated from Sanskrit, Tibetan, and Chinese by Walpola Rahula, *Le Compendium de la Super-Doctrine d'Asaṅga* (Paris: École Française d'Extrême-Orient, 1980)

Candrakīrti

Introduction to the Central Way

Madhyamakāvatāra

dBu ma la 'jug pa

Dg.T. dBu ma, vol. Ha, ff. 201-219 (Toh. 3861)

Daṃṣṭrāsena

Commentary to the Large, Medium and Small Transcendent Wisdom Scriptures

Śatasāhasrikā-pañcaviṃśatisāhasrikā-aṣṭādaśasāhasrikā-prajñā-pāramitā-bṛhaṭṭikā

'Phags pa shes rab kyi pha rol tu phyin pa 'bum pa dang nyi khri lnga

stong pa dang khri brgyad stong pa'i rgya cher bshad pa
Dg.K. Shes phyin, vol. Pha, ff. 1-292 (Toh. 3808)

Dharmakīrti
Treatise on Valid Cognition
Pramāṇavārttika
Tshad ma rnam 'grel
Dg.T. Tshad ma, vol. Ce, ff. 94-151 (Toh. 4210)

Dharmamitra
Treatise on the Transcendent Wisdom Pith Instructions, Commentary on the Ornament of Realizations
Abhisamayālaṃkārakārikā-prajñāpāramitopadeśa-śāstraṭīkā-prasphuṭapadā
Shes rab kyi pha rol tu phyin pa'i man ngag gi bstan bcos mngon rtogs rgyan gyi tshig le'ur byas pa'i 'grel bshad tshig rab tu gsal ba
Dg.T. Shes phyin, vol. Nga, ff. 1-110 (Toh. 3796)

Haribhadra
Discussion on the Scripture of Transcendent Wisdom in Eight Thousand Lines
Aṣṭasāhasrikā-prajñāpāramitāvyākhyā-abhisamayālaṁkārāloka
Shes rab kyi pha rol tu phyin pa brgyad stong pa'i bshad pa mngon par rtogs pa'i rgyan gyi snang ba
Dg.T. Shes phyin, vol. Cha, ff. 1-341 (Toh. 3791)

Maitreya
Scripture Ornament/Ornament of the Scriptures of the Universal Way
Mahāyānasūtrālaṁkāra
Theg pa chen po'i mdo sde'i rgyan
Dg.T. Sems tsam, vol. Phi, ff. 1-39 (Toh. 4020)

Nāgārjuna
Disclosure of the Awakening Mind (*DAM*)
Bodhicittavivaraṇa
Byang chub sems kyi 'grel pa
Dg.T. rGyud, vol. Ngi, ff. 38-42 (Toh. 1800)

Puṇḍarika
Stainless Commentary to the Kālacakra Tantra
Vimalaprabhā-nāma-mūlatantrānusāriṇī-dvādaśāsahasrikā-laghukālacakratantrarāja-ṭīkā
bDus pa'i rgyud kyi rgyal po dus kyi 'khor lo'i 'grel bshad rtsa ba'i rgyud kyi rjes su 'jug pa stong phrag bcu gnyis pa dri ma med pa'i 'od ces bya ba
Dg.K. rGyud, vol. Tha, ff. 107-277 and vol. Da, ff. 1-297 (Toh. 1347)

Purṇavardhana
Commentary to the Treasury of Phenomenology
Abhidharmakośaṭīkā-lakṣanānusāriṇī
Chos mngon pa'i mdzod kyi 'grel bshad mtshan nyid kyi rjes su 'brang ba
Dg.T. mNgon pa, vol. Cu, ff. 1-347 and vol. Chu, ff. 1-322 (Toh. 4093)

Śāntipa
Supreme Essence Commentary on the Transcendent Wisdom in Eight Thousand Lines
Aṣṭasāhasrikāprajñāpāramitā-pañjikāsārottamā
Shes rab kyi pha rol tu phyin pa brgyad stong pa'i dka' 'grel snying po mchog
Dg.T. Shes phyin, vol. Tha, ff. 1-230 (Toh. 3803)

Subhūticandra
Wish-Fulfilling Scripture
Amarakoṣaṭīkākāmadhenu
'Chi ba med pa'i mdzod kyi rgya cher 'grel pa 'dod 'jo'i ba mo
Dg.T. sGra mdo, vol. Se, ff. 244-318 (Toh. 4300)

Vasubandhu
Commentary to the Treasury of Phenomenology
Abhidharmakośabhāṣya
Chos mngon pa'i mdzod kyi bshad pa
Dg.T. mNgon pa, vol. Ku, ff. 26-258 (Toh. 4090)

Principles of Elucidation
Vyākhyāyukti
rNam par bshad pa'i rigs pa
Dg.T. Sems tsam, vol. Shi, ff. 29-134 (Toh. 4061)

Treasury of Phenomenology (*TOP*)
Abhidharmakośakārikā
Chos mngon pa'i mdzod kyi tshig le'ur byas pa
Dg.T. mNgon pa, vol. Ku, ff. 1-25 (Toh. 4089)

Tibetan Works

Kongtrul Lodrö Tayé (Kong sprul Blo gros mtha' yas)
Elucidation of the Philosophy of Rangjung Dorjé
Rang 'byung dgongs gsal

Elucidation of the Profound Meaning
rNal 'byor bla med pa'i rgyud sde rgya mtsho'i snying po bsdus pa zab mo gi don nyung ngu'i tshig gi rnam par 'grol ba zab don snang byed

Mikyö Dorjé (Mi bskyod rDo rje)
Ocean of the Mind
Yid mtsho

Rangjung Dorjé (Rang byung rDo rje)
Profound Inner Meaning
Zab mo nang gi don

Showing the Essence of the Joyful Ones
bDe gshegs snying po bstan pa'i bstan bcos

Reference Bibliography

Batchelor, Stephen, trans. *A Guide to the Bodhisattva's Way of Life, by Shantideva.* Dharamsala: Library of Tibetan Works and Archives, 1987.

Bays, Gwendolyn , trans. *The Voice of Buddha: The Beauty of Compassion.* 2 vols. Berkeley: Dharma Publishing, 1983.

Bhatt, Govardhan P. *The Basic Ways of Knowing: An In-depth Study of Kumarila's Contribution to Indian Epistemology.* 2nd ed. Delhi: Motilal Banarsidass, 1989.

Cleary, Thomas, trans. *The Flower Ornament Scripture: The Avataṃsaka Sūtra.* 3 vols. Boulder and London: Shambhala, 1984, 1986, 1987.

Conze, Edward, trans. *The Large Sutra on Perfect Wisdom.* Berkeley: University of California, 1975.

Dhargyey, Geshe Ngawang. *A Commentary on the Kālacakra Tantra.* Translated by Gelong Jhampa Kelsang (Alan Wallace), edited by Ivana Vana Jakic. Dharamsala: Library of Tibetan Works and Archives, 1985.

Dudjom, Rinpoché. *The Nyingma School of Tibetan Buddhism, Its Fundamentals and History.* Translated by Gyurme Dorje with the collaboration of Matthew Kapstein. 2 vols. Boston: Wisdom, 1991.

Dutt, Sukumar. *Buddhist Monks and Monasteries of India: Their History and Their Contribution to Indian Culture.* 1962. Reprint, Delhi: Motilal Banarsidass, 1988.

Edgerton, Franklin. *Buddhist Hybrid Sanskrit Grammar and Dictionary.* 2 vols. New Haven, 1953. Reprint, Delhi: Motilal Banarsidass, 1985.

Gendun Drüb (dGe 'dun grub pa, Dalai Lama I). *Dam pa'i chos mngon pa'i mdzod kyi rnam par bshad pa thar lam gsal byed.* Sarnath, India: Elegant Sayings Press, 1973.

Grimes, John. *A Concise Dictionary of Indian Philosophy (Sanskrit-English).* Madras University Philosophical Series, No. 48. Madras: Radhakrishnan Institute for Advanced Study in Philosophy, University of Madras, 1988.

Guenther, H.V. *The Creative Vision: The Symbolic Recreation of the World According to the Tibetan Buddhist Tradition of Tantric Visualization Otherwise Known as the Developing Phase*. Novato, California: Lotsawa, 1987.

_________. *Meditation Differently*. Delhi: Motilal Banarsidass, 1992.

_________. *The Jewel Ornament of Liberation*, by sGam po pa. London: Rider, 1959. Reprint, Shambhala, 1971.

Gyatso, Geshé Kelsang. *Clear Light of Bliss*. London: Wisdom, 1982.

Gyatso, Tenzin (bsTan 'dzin rgya mtsho Dalai Lama XIV). *The Kalachakra Tantra: Rite of Initiation for the Stage of Generation*. Edited, translated, and introduced by Jeffrey Hopkins. London: Wisdom, 1985.

Hopkins, Jeffrey. *Meditation on Emptiness*. London: Wisdom, 1983.

Kalu Rinpoche. *The Chariot for Travelling the Path to Freedom: The Life Story of Kalu Rinpoche*. Translated by Kenneth I. McLeod. San Francisco: Kagyu Dharma, 1985.

Klein, Anne. *Knowledge and Liberation: Tibetan Buddhist Epistemology in Support of Transforming Religious Experience*. Ithaca, New York: Snow Lion, 1986.

Kloetzli, W. Randolph. *Buddhist Cosmology: Science and Theology in the Images of Motion and Light*. 2nd ed. Delhi: Motilal Banarsidass, 1989.

Kongtrul, Lodrö Tayé. *'Du shes gsum ldan spong ba pa'i gzugs brnyan padma gar gyi dbang phyug phrin las 'gro 'dul rtsal gyi rtogs pa brjod pa'i dum bu smrig rgyu'i bdud rtsi*. An account of the previous lives of the First Jamgon Kongtrul. Bir, Dist. Kangra, India: Kandro, Tibetan Khampa Industrial Society, 1973.

_________. *Phyogs med ris med kyi bstan pa la 'dun shing dge sbyong gi gzugs brnyan 'chang ba blo gros mtha' yas kyi sde'i byung ba brjod pa nor bu sna tshogs mdog can*. Autobiography completed after the author's death by his disciple gNas-gsar bKra-'phel. Bir, Dist. Kangra, India: Kandro, Tibetan Khampa Industrial Society, 1973.

Lati Rinbochay, Denma Lochö Rinbochay, and Pan-chen Sönam-drak-ba. *Meditative States in Tibetan Buddhism: The Concentrations and Formless Absorptions*. Translated by Leah Zahler and Jeffrey Hopkins; edited and annotated by Leah Zahler. London: Wisdom, 1983.

Lati Rinbochay and Jeffrey Hopkins. *Death, Intermediate State and Rebirth in Tibetan Buddhism*. 1979. Reprint, Ithaca, New York: Snow Lion, 1985.

Lati Rinpochay and Elizabeth Napper. *Mind in Tibetan Buddhism*. London: Rider and Co., 1980. Reprint, Ithaca, N.Y.: Snow Lion, 1986.

Lipman, Kennard and Merrill Peterson, trans. *You Are the Eyes of the World*. Novato, California: Lotsawa, 1987.

Longchenpa (Klong chen pa). *Chos dbyings rin po che'i mdzod*. Gangtok, Sikkim: Dodrup Chen Rinpoche.

__________. *Tshig don rin po che'i mdzod*. Gangtok, Sikkim: Dodrup Chen Rinpoche.

Maitreya. *Byams chos sde lnga'i rtsa ba phyogs bsdebs*. Sarnath, India: Kargyud Relief and Protection Committee, Central Institute of Higher Tibetan Studies, 1984.

Monier-Williams, Sir Monier. *A Sanskrit-English Dictionary*. New ed. Oxford: 1899. Reprint, New Delhi: Marwah Publications, 1986.

Nāropa, *Iniziazione Kālācakra*. Edited by Raniero Gnoli and Giacomella Orofino. Milan: Edition Adelphi, 1994.

Norbu, Namkhai and Kennard Lipman, trans. *Primordial Experience: An Introduction to rDzogs-chen Meditation* by Mañjuśrīmitra. Boston and London: Shambhala, 1987.

Obermiller, E., trans. *The History of Buddhism in India and Tibet* and *The Jewelry of Scripture*. 2nd ed. Bibliotheca Indo-Buddhica No. 26. Delhi: Sri Satguru, 1986.

Rabten, Geshé. *Echoes of Voidness*. Translated and edited by Stephen Batchelor. London: Wisdom, 1983.

Rabten, Geshé and Geshé Dargyey. *Advice from a Spiritual Friend*. Translated by B. Beresford et al. London: Wisdom, 1984.

Rahula, Walpola, trans. *Asaṅga's 'Le Compendium de la Super-Doctrine' (Philosophie) (Abhidharmasamuccaya)*. 2nd ed. Paris: École Française d'Extrême-Orient, 1980.

Roerich, George, N., trans. *The Blue Annals*. Calcutta, 1949; 2nd ed., Delhi: Motilal Banarsidass, 1976.

Sakaki, R., ed. *Mahāvyutpatti*. Tokyo: Suzuki Research Foundation, 1962.

Sherburne, Richard S. J., trans. *A Lamp for the Path and Commentary*, by Atisa. London: Allen and Unwin, 1983.

Snellgrove, David. *Indo-Tibetan Buddhism: Indian Buddhists and Their Tibetan Successors*. 2 vols. Boston: Shambhala, 1987.

__________, trans. *The Hevajra Tantra, A Critical Study*. Part I: Introduction and Translation. 1959. Reprint, London: Oxford University Press, 1964.

Snellgrove, David and Hugh Richardson. *A Cultural History of Tibet*. Boston and London: Shambhala, 1986.

Suzuki, Daisetz Teitaro, trans. *The Laṅkāvatāra Sūtra: A Mahāyāna Text*. 1932. Reprint, London: Routledge and Kegan Paul, 1978.

Tāranātha. *Dam pa'i chos rin po che 'phags pa'i yul du ji ltar dar ba'i tshul gsal bar ston ba dgos 'dod kun 'byung*. Sarnath, India: Elegant Saying Press, 1984.

Tāranātha's History of Buddhism in India. Translated by Lama Chimpa and Alaka Chattopadhyaya. Edited by Debiprasad Chattopadhyaya. Simla: Indian Institute of Advanced Study, 1970.

Tharchin, Geshé Lobsang and Engle, A.B., trans. *Nāgārjuna's Letter.* Nagarjuna's "Letter to a Friend" with a commentary by the Venerable Rendawa, Zhön-nu Lo-drö. Dharamsala: Library of Tibetan Works and Archives, 1979.

Thondup, Tulku Rinpoche, translated and annotated. *Buddha Mind: An Anthology of Longchen Rabjam's Writings on Dzogpa Chenpo.* Edited by Harold Talbott. Ithaca, New York: Snow Lion, 1989.

_________. *Hidden Teachings of Tibet: An Explanation of the Terma Tradition of the Nyingma School of Buddhism.* London: Wisdom, 1986.

Thurman, Robert, A. F., trans. *The Holy Teaching of Vimalakīrti: A Mahāyāna Scripture.* The Pennsylvania State University, 1976.

_________, trans. *The Speech of Gold: Reason and Enlightenment in the Tibetan Buddhism.* Princeton University Press, 1984.

Trungpa, Chogyam. *Glimpses of Abhidharma.* Boulder: Prajna Press, 1975.

Tsong-ka-pa. *Tantra in Tibet: The Great Exposition of Secret Mantra.* Translated by Jeffrey Hopkins. London: George Allen and Unwin, 1977.

Tsuda, Shinichi, trans. *The Samvarodaya-Tantra, Selected Chapters.* Tokyo: The Hokuseido Press, 1974.

Tucci, Giuseppe. *Stupa: Art, Architectonics and Symbolism.* Edited by Lokesh Chandra. English translation by Uma Marina Vesci. English version of Indo-Tibetica I, Śata-Piṭaka Series 347. New Delhi: Aditya Prakashan, 1988.

_________. *Minor Buddhist Texts, Parts I and II.* Rome: 1956. Reprint, Delhi: Motilal Banarsidass, 1986.

Ui, Hakuju et al., ed. *A Complete Catalogue of the Tibetan Buddhist Canons (Bkah-hgyur and Bstan-hgyur).* Sendai, Japan: Tohoku Imperial University, 1934.

Wayman, Alex and Hideko, trans. *The Lion's Roar of Queen Srimala.* New York: Columbia University Press, 1974.

Willson, Martin. *In Praise of Tara: Songs to the Saviouress.* London: Wisdom, 1986.

Index

Throughout the index, the Great Perfection system is abbreviated GP *and the Wheel of Time system is abbreviated* WT.

abhidharma. *See* phenomenology system.
abiding. *See* ages, the four: of abiding.
Acintyavimokṣa, 47
action. *See* evolutionary action.
age, cosmic, 144
Age, Fortunate, 43, 108-109
ages, the four: age of formation, 107-128; of abiding, 129-140; of destruction and vacuity, 140-145; duration of, 143-144; in other worlds, 145
aggregates, five: formation of, in GP, 217
Akṣobhya, Buddha, 222
Amitābha, Buddha, 222
Amoghasiddhi, Buddha, 222
animal(s): emptying world of, 140; habitat, 115; life as, 129; meaning of word, 115; mode of birth, 128; in WT, 154-155
articles, seven precious, of a wheel-monarch, 136-137
articles, seven semi-precious, of a wheel-monarch, 137-138
Asaṅga: *Facts of the Stages*, 130, 131; *Five Treatises on the Stages*, 119, 121, 127; *Synthesis of Phenomenology*, 190, 194
astrology, 19, 34, 45; in WT, 156-158
Avataṃsaka Scripture, 46, 47. See also *Flower Ornament Scripture*.
awakening mind (bodhicitta), 35, 86
awareness. *See* intrinsic awareness.
Bamten Trulku, 21
beings. *See* sentient beings.
Beyond the Limits of Sound Root Tantra, 221, 225
Blossomed Wisdom Scripture, 109
bodhisattvas, 23, 31, 44, 47-49, 263 n. 25; birthplace of, 119, 121; place of enlightenment, in WT, 153; path of, 262 n. 9; Mighty Lord of the World, 153; tenth stage, 105, 121; and vow to purify realms, 48, 97, 108, 145, 265 n. 3; and indestructible realms, 145.
body, human. *See* continents, the four: stature and lifespans of humans in.
body, human, in GP: development of, in womb, 216-217; formation of, in three realms, 215-216; and pervasive elements, 219-220; and superficial and ultimate elements, 217-219; three types of, 215-216
Bön, 15, 17, 18
Bountiful Cow, 110, 113, 141
Brāhmana Vyhāsa Scripture, 111
buddha(s): and their relationship to beings, 47-48, 96; and their presence in realms, 100
buddha families, five, 222, 223; and senses, 280 n. 36